Transforming Practice

TRANSFORMING PRACTICE

PASTORAL THEOLOGY IN AN AGE OF UNCERTAINTY

Elaine L. Graham

Wipf and Stock Publishers
150 West Broadway • Eugene OR 97401

Wipf and Stock Publishers
150 West Broadway
Eugene, Oregon 97401

Transforming Practice
Pastoral Theology in an Age of Uncertainty
By Graham, Elaine L.
©1996 Graham, Elaine L.
ISBN: 1-57910-922-5
Publication date: March, 2002
Previously published by Mowbray, 1996.

Contents

This book is dedicated to Martin Hall

Introduction

We live in an age of uncertainty. Contemporary Western society has been characterized as one in which there is no longer a consensus of values. The assumptions and criteria by which Western science, politics and philosophy have been guided for the past two hundred years, associated with the ideals of progress, humanism and reason have been discredited by critical voices which emphasize fragmentation, pluralism and scepticism. Some have diagnosed this as typical of the *postmodern condition*, which may be seen as destabilizing many of the nostrums of the Enlightenment by challenging prevailing concepts of truth, human nature, knowledge, power, selfhood and language that have informed Western thought for two hundred years.

The philosophical mood of postmodernism is one of scepticism towards any notion of an eternal, metaphysical human nature. The individual is always a cultural subject, inscribed in linguistic, historical and social contexts. Postmodernism also emphasizes the indeterminacy and fluidity of identity and knowledge and the rootedness of selfhood in social relations and language. The power of science to render a faithful account of reality – as the discipline which functions as a 'mirror of nature' – has been called into question by perspectives which emphasize the dependency of knowledge upon linguistic conventions and social context.

For some, postmodernity's mood is one of exhilaration. Its critical viewpoint debunks systems of thought which are believed to have excluded and objectified many social groups and perspectives: women, non-Western civilizations and non-conformist sexual and social lifestyles (Cornell, 1995). For others, postmodernism and its acolytes speak of a chaotic, amoral world, in which the thin fabric of representation has replaced the solid substance of truth and

1

reality. The only possible alternative to foundational grounds for knowledge and authority appears to be resignation and nihilism. Postmodernity erases humanist concepts of shared value and human nature and replaces them either with a ceaseless 'play' of differences or the 'iron cage' of deterministic and coercive regimes. No viewpoint exists independent of self-interest; there is no point from which humanity can gather to agree on the terms by which its affairs might be ordered. Such a vision appears to preclude any shared vision of ethics and politics, seems to fail to provide reliable and universally accessible accounts of human obligation in the face of suffering, and abrogates responsibility for social change or emancipation as we approach the millennium.

Whilst one of the features of postmodernity has been a resurgence of the sacred – especially in New Age and other new religious movements – the profound fragmentation of values has also afflicted Christian theology. Although the nature of Christian theological formation in a postmodern context has occupied some philosophical and systematic theologians, little interest has been shown from within the discipline of pastoral, or practical, theology.[1] Yet the strategic question of what sources and norms inform purposeful Christian practice – in church and world – is as problematic as the purely philosophical implications of postmodernity. In the face of the collapse of the 'grand narrative' of modernity, what values may now inform purposeful Christian action and vision? Do Christian truth-claims make any coherent sense amidst the multiple narratives of the public domain? Can Christian communities respond to changing values and competing world-views and construct a self-understanding that will sustain them through the challenges of the new millennium? These questions all concern the nature of Christian presence in the world, informed by traditions and conventions of faith, yet seeking anew to respond to the challenges of human need and ultimate value.

This book is an attempt to address some of these issues – and in particular, the relationship between the contemporary 'crisis' of Western culture and the future of Christian theology – from the vantage-point of pastoral/practical theology. In an age of uncertainty, the authority and status of the sources and norms of Christian pastoral care and social action can no longer be taken for granted. The traditional models of human nature, value and community drawn from Scripture and tradition appear anachronistic, especially in the light of postmodern insights into identity, power and knowledge. The purpose of this book is therefore to reconstruct the values by which Christian practice may be guided in a pluralist and fragmented society, and to identify a model of pastoral theology for a postmodern age. Can a reconstructed pastoral theology regulate the relationship between theory and practice and construct a relevant but authentic practical wisdom? Is it possible to maintain the *boundaries* of coherent community with binding truth-claims whilst remaining open to the *horizons* of diversity and provisionality?

The aims of this book are: first, to contribute to discussion of the relevance of contemporary cultural debates for Christian theology. It is my conviction that faithful Christian practice can only be effective and relevant if it takes seriously the challenges of the contemporary world. In so doing, I have already committed myself to a particular model of theological formulation and reflection by identifying cultural experience and social trends as valid and legitimate sources of Christian concern and Divine revelation. However, I am also concerned to reorientate the contemporary dimensions and tasks of the discipline of pastoral/practical theology; and in this respect, debates about postmodernity and the future of Western culture serve to illuminate the context within which such a reconstruction must take place.

Second, I wish to place such a re-evaluation in historical perspective. The disciplinary identity of pastoral theology can only be fully appreciated in the context of its development during the modern era. Despite its earlier dominance by clerical and therapeutic paradigms, pastoral theology has the potential to retrieve alternative strands from its tradition which enable it to give a critical account of the life of the Christian community as a whole. Such a perspective offers a renewed emphasis on the purposeful activities of the faith-community as the performative expressions of Christian truth-claims in a plural society. Theology is thus enacted and embodied in Christian practice.

Such a book as this is necessarily broad in scope. It is by no means exhaustive, and my hope is that others will develop and debate the insights contained here. In particular, although I have tested my model of pastoral theology as *critical theology of Christian practice* in relation to certain patterns of preaching, spiritual direction and liturgy, I anticipate that further, more detailed studies may be carried out. This book is therefore intended as an invitation for further debate and application. Whilst it is primarily aimed at students and teachers of pastoral studies and practical theology, I hope that all 'reflective practitioners' (Patton, 1990) within faith-communities, caring professions and ministerial training will also find it stimulating and instructive.

Summary of Chapters

In Chapter 1 I will outline the 'anatomy of uncertainty' which appears to beset late-twentieth-century Western culture. Western modernity, which gave birth to capitalism, liberal democracy and positivism, was founded upon particular economic, socio-political and intellectual conditions which shaped the cultural and philosophical contours of the age. Within these contours, certain models of human nature, identity, knowledge, action and ultimate value may be discerned which have definitively shaped our visions of selfhood and community.

However, such values may now be seen as fiercely contested by the perspectives of postmodernism and poststructuralism. One of the most powerful critiques emanates from twentieth-century feminist scholarship. Feminists have argued that dominant views of human nature, self, knowledge, action and value are constructed *androcentrically*: that is, they assume that maleness and masculinity is the norm for adequate accounts of what it means to be human, how I achieve a sense of self, what counts as verifiable and reliable knowledge, the relationship between thought, will and action, and the sources and norms of ultimate value, truth and beauty. Once we introduce the notion of these concepts as 'gendered', therefore, we gain a clearer sense of some of the ways in which Enlightenment views must necessarily be revised. Whilst feminism and post-modernism are by no means synonymous, many commentators would argue that feminism does expose the partiality and particularity of modernity, especially on matters of selfhood, ethics and community. The challenge of feminism illustrates the crisis of conventional values and the necessity of accommodating diverse and heterogenous experiences of personhood and community.

In Chapter 2, I will outline the contours of the postmodern crisis within Christian pastoral theology. As a practical and academic discipline, pastoral theology is an ideal prism through which to view the ferment in the churches of Britain and the USA as they debate how best to respond to contemporary social and intellectual trends. The challenge of feminism, other imperatives of social justice and the changing nature of authority within the churches are all factors contributing to a comprehensive re-evaluation of the fundamental aims and methods of Christian pastoral theology. In the process, the values informing strategies of ministry and personal care have come into question; but deeper issues also emerge. These concern the meaning of personhood, the very assumptions of Christian ministry and 'pastoral' intervention, the nature of church community, the relationship of church to world, and the relationship of sources and norms of theology to secular perspectives. Is it possible to reconstruct a discipline of pastoral theology that can reconceive these categories?

Since its emergence in the modern era in the mid-eighteenth century in the context of the German theological schools, pastoral/ practical theology has regarded itself as concerned with the practical dimensions of Christianity. Its traditional subject-matter and field of enquiry have been the activities of pastoral ministry: worship and ritual, preaching, social action, personal care, Christian education and formation, and community-building and organization. Historically, these have been regarded, with some exceptions, as the exclusive province of the ordained clergy. However, sociological changes have precipitated a greater demand for active participation in church life by the laity, and with it a more intensive scrutiny into the nature of the pastoral task itself. There has been a more open questioning of conventional wisdom concerning the identity and aims of the pastoral agent, as well as the self-understanding of the Christian community in a pluralist and secular society. In the process, pastoral/practical theology as a discipline has reviewed its own intellectual and epistemological status, seeking a new standing as a primary theological discipline, rather than an 'applied' or 'practical' offshoot of systematic and philosophical branches.

Chapter 3 develops this discussion to trace the historical self-understanding of pastoral/practical theology in relation to church, world and academy. If I have assessed the anatomy of our contemporary situation correctly, there can be no going back to former times of certainty and stability. For some, a retrieval of sources and norms entails a return to the traditional activities of premodern pastoral care; but for others, a more concerted engagement with contemporary experience (and especially the modern psychologies) is imperative. Christian pastoral practice must necessarily draw on a variety of sources, both sacred and secular; but it is less easy in an age of pluralism to reach agreement on the most authoritative sources and how they are to be used.

The contribution of Don Browning has been invaluable in focusing attention on the necessity for rooting pastoral activity in a discourse of theological ethics situated in a congregational context. However, his favoured model of 'practical moral reasoning' still takes place within a homogenous social and philosophical culture (see Chapter 4). Furthermore, attention to these values as the products of rational moral discourse alone is an inadequate reflection of the breadth of purposeful human action. A commitment to practical and enacted perspectives – such as those encountered in theories of gender – maintains a sense of the embodied, corporate, affective and symbolic dimensions of human practice. Moves to reorientate pastoral theology away from individual care towards embracing the diversity of all the pastoral activities of the Church are therefore consistent with an appreciation that human community, social and symbolic relations and definitive notions of value are generated by a diversity of practices. It is my contention that 'practice' as both the expression and creative locus of value is a sufficiently strong concept upon which to construct a renewed understanding of pastoral action.

Chapter 5 therefore returns to debates in social theory which echo the self-reflexive nature of action, knowledge and identity previously articulated in the anatomy of postmodernity. In the absence of 'foundational' or metaphysical principles by which ideals of hope and obligation may be realized, practice emerges as both constituting and reproducing the core values upon which human culture may be founded. I will identify themes which resist any notion of human value as derived from metaphysical foundations. Principles of truth and value are not to be conceived as transcendent eternal realities, but as provisional – yet binding – strategies of normative action and community within which shared commitments might be negotiated and put to work. Ethics and politics therefore become processes and practices, rather than applications of metaphysical ideals.

Strategies are beginning to emerge for bringing about a coherent ethical and political practice, without absolutizing those norms or elevating them beyond the context of their situation or agents. Such strategies draw upon an Aristotelian notion of practical wisdom (*phronēsis*) which locates truth in enacted or performative knowledge. Values are expressed not in abstract knowledge-claims but in the patterns and orderings of purposeful human activity. Practical wisdom attempts to establish criteria on which choices and moral values of purposeful practice may be validated.

Chapter 6 therefore assesses models of contemporary pastoral theology which offer a number of ways of articulating the resources by which Christian pastoral practice might be informed and directed. Some pastoral theologians regard the narrative of Scripture as the primary foundation for the formation of a community of faith and practice; others argue that there is a generic human story within which Christians find their identity. Feminist anthropology and liberation theology also make decisive contributions to the guiding principles of purposeful Christian action. They argue that Christian practice must be informed by struggles for justice and empowerment, and listening to voices from the faith-tradition which have often been marginalized.

I will argue that the proper focus of pastoral theology is not the pastoral agent, or theological ethics, or applied theology, but the pastoral *practice* of the faith-community itself. By focusing on the reality of practice, we are able to recognize that theory and practice do not exist independently. Metaphysical principles require concrete human agency. The arena of Christian *praxis* – value-directed and value-laden action – is understood as the medium through which the Christian community embodies and enacts its fundamental vision of the Gospel. Theology is properly conceived as a performative discipline, in which the criterion of authenticity is deemed to be *orthopraxis*, or authentic transformatory action, rather than *orthodoxy* (right belief) (Chung, 1990).

However, another problem remains: if no universal and overarching metaphysical guarantee is available for such principled living – if it has not been 'god-given' as it were – then on what terms is it constructed and contested? Values are no longer axiomatic and founded upon the grand narrative of historical certainty; rather, they are contingent and provisional. Who is thus to protect these values from becoming introspective and self-serving rather than generous and just? It is therefore important to think about the terms on which such binding values might be agreed, and whether a social and emancipatory project can emerge as a coherent under-taking.

In Chapter 7, therefore, I shall be taking insights from some contemporary commentators who are seeking the possibility of articulating and verifying questions of value for social theory, and developing critical studies of practice as a means of resolving the challenges of postmodernity. This is a search for ethical and political responsibility: a refusal to collapse into quietism in the face of dilemmas of suffering and injustice. In particular, I examine the contributions to this debate of Jürgen Habermas and Seyla Benhabib, two writers who locate themselves within the philo-sophical/political tradition of Critical Theory. They argue that the discursive practices of the community are the generators of normative principles for discerning and transformative practice, and thus for a 'communicative ethics' that informs liberative public policy. Habermas develops the notion of the 'ideal speech community' which will facilitate visions of political and moral responsibility; but Benhabib argues that it is a necessary tension between the 'generalized' and 'concrete' Other which ensures such a model is responsive to the dynamics of gender.

Such models of communitarian conversation present models of human practice and identity as neither the acting out of transcen-dent values transposed on to human subjects, nor the 'free-play' of human agency, where principles of value and truth are denied. They succeed in locating questions of ultimacy, purpose and value within a specific and enacted context; but Benhabib's feminist critique of Habermas – in particular on the locus of the utopian speech situation and the boundaries of the community – leads me to seek further elaboration of practical wisdom from other feminist sources.

Thus, I argue that a more adequate 'post-postmodern' practical knowledge would require a stronger notion of 'alterity' (Otherness) and its implications. The formation of communities of solidarity and communication creates 'Others' whose exclusion violates principles of difference and plurality. In the light of what I have already been arguing, it will be clear that I am particularly concerned to elaborate a gender-sensitive practical wisdom that will combat the binary divisions of public and private, of inclusion and exclusion, self and Other, which rest unchallenged in Habermas's ideal speech domain.

Therefore, in keeping with psychoanalytic, hermeneutic and feminist projects of recovering the unnamed, repressed 'Other', an adequate model of practical knowledge would exhibit a bias towards alterity, diversity and inclusivity. Whilst affirming the legitimacy of its own values and aims, it must seek patterns of knowing and acting that foster a self-critical generosity towards those communities, world-views and practices thereby denied and occluded.

The feminist writer Donna Haraway has advanced the notion of *situated knowledge* as the criterion by which the practical reasoning of a community might remain open and inclusive. Haraway insists upon the provisional nature of knowledge and identity; however, she also fosters an ethical and political vision by stressing embodiment, concretion and relationality. These are all characteristics of the postmodern understanding of personhood, community and knowledge, and thus emerge as appropriate qualities upon which to build a reconstructed practical wisdom. A 'situated' or 'positional' epistemology is able to acknowledge its own uniqueness and locatedness whilst still generating reliable political and ethical sensibilities. I will therefore propose that a critical and inclusive process of articulating and evaluating the sources and norms of purposeful practice would deploy the dialectic of *disclosure* and *foreclosure*. The former indicates those forms of practical reasoning which illuminate inclusive strategies and policies, enable the articulation of formerly hidden needs and experiences, but retain a responsible sense of their own provisionality. Foreclosive practices deny the association of knowledge with power and the violation of undifferentiated meaning wrought by the imposition of unitary identity. In their insistence upon universalist and essentialist models of human nature they refuse to acknowledge the partiality of experience and the existence of diverse ways of knowing, being and acting. In their absolutization of the specific, foreclosive practices draw tight and impermeable boundaries around their agents, refusing to acknowledge the interrelatedness of 'self' and 'Other'.

However, although the various perspectives of Critical Theory and feminist 'situated knowledges' offer valuable insights, it is important not to elevate them to the status of prescriptive or deterministic theories, formulating their critical criteria in abstraction from the activities and values in question. Critical evaluations of purposeful practices – such as pastoral theology – will therefore seek to discern and articulate interim principles for the practical knowledge of any particular community, and will cultivate a self-reflexive mood. In practical terms, such a perspective would pursue strategies which encourage empathy and solidarity with others, open up enlarged horizons of understanding and commitment and foster pastoral encounters which disclose new realities and perspectives on human experience and Divine reality.

Chapter 8 develops these suggestions towards a critical study of Christian pastoral practice. It examines three selected areas of feminist pastoral *praxis* in order to identify their prescriptive sources and norms and to evaluate the implicit models of human nature, knowledge, agency, selfhood and ultimacy which are embodied in their purposeful practices.

I will conclude by arguing that critical theories of gender offer significant challenges both to feminist theologies and to critical studies of pastoral practice. I will maintain that categories of human nature, experience, knowledge and truth do not rely on metaphysical foundations but emerge from the contingency of human practice. Thus, the terms on which feminist theologians rely for their critical and reconstructive tasks – such as that of 'women's experience' – are rendered problematic and uncertain. In turn, an emphasis on the performative and enacted realm of human practice – in Christian terms, the value-directed activities of pastoral action – offers pastoral theology a new role as the primary expression and generator of theological disclosure.

Another of my conclusions will concern the nature of theological and transcendent reality. The situated and contingent nature of value and meaning implies that any Divine, ultimate and transcendent dimension to human experience will only be authentically and reliably apprehended in the midst of human practice. The value-directed practices of the Christian community thus constitute the primary realm of human-Divine encounter; theological disclosure is therefore material, incarnational and sacramental.

My hope in this book is to put forward a model by which pastoral theology may offer the resources and methods which enable communities of faith (and their critics) to give an account of themselves in a fragmented and uncertain world. Recognizing that its truth-claims have currency in the lived, embodied realization of practice, theological discourse articulates the stories and accounts of the fundamental values informing and directing purposeful practice. However, this is also a public language, providing an accessible and accountable *apologia* by which the prescriptive ideals of faith may be expressed. Pastoral theology will also expose the social relations and enacted goals of a faith-community to scrutiny, testing how its contemporary practices seek to validate and revise historic ideals. In short, pastoral theology enables the community of faith to practise what it preaches.

Notes

1 The various usages of the terms 'pastoral theology' and 'practical theology' require some explanation. In North America, especially in Protestant traditions, the convention has been to distinguish 'pastoral theology' as the discipline of individual pastoral care and counselling, from 'practical theology' as the study of all functions of ministry – preaching, liturgy, church organization and administration and Christian education (Lapsley, 1969:31–4). However, it is notable that in many Roman Catholic works 'pastoral theology' denotes the discipline concerned with the life of the entire Christian community (Rahner, 1969; Imbelli and Groome, 1992). As I will argue in Chapter 3, this latter usage is related historically to the discipline of moral theology, and retains a sense of ministry as the establishment and maintenance of the boundaries of the faith-community.

Pattison (1994a) argues against the term 'practical theology' as too utilitarian, believing that the discipline must withstand the trends of instrumentalism. 'I think of pastoral theology not as the art of teaching clergy how to baptize babies, but as the place where religious belief, tradition and practice meets contemporary experience, questions and actions to engage in a transforming dialogue which has substantial practical implications' (1994a:1). For Pattison, the discipline is necessarily playful, apophatic and allusive, because ultimately it deals with the imprecisions of the human condition.

The two terms 'pastoral' and 'practical' therefore have specific historical and normative values. The usage of 'practical' theology is problematic given its associations with a division between practical and systematic theology since Schleiermacher, and an implicit separation of theoretical and applied knowledge. However, 'pastoral' carries implications of individually based pastoral care or counselling, with a similar neglect of the theological dimensions of Christian action. It also represents an unfortunate narrowing of focus into ameliorative ministry at the expense of wider functions of education and formation amongst the community of faith and the Church's mission (in its widest sense) in the world at large.

Whilst the terms are often used interchangeably (or often in conjunction, as in 'practical theology and pastoral studies') it is important to recognize the differences of tradition and emphasis behind them. Whilst I argue in this book for a reorientation of pastoral/practical theology which transcends the old emphasis on an 'applied' and clerically-dominated discipline, I am aware that inherited conventions governing terminology cannot simply be discounted or abandoned at will. Readers will note that my own preference is for 'pastoral' theology, although in discussing the work of other writers in this field I shall try to use their own preferred terminology.

CHAPTER 1

Anatomy of Uncertainty

Something has happened, is happening, to Western societies. The beginning of this transition can be dated somewhat arbitrarily from after the First World War in Europe and after the Second World War in the United States. Western culture is in the middle of a fundamental transformation; a 'shape of life' is growing old. The demise of the old is being hastened by the end of colonialism, the uprising of women, the revolt of other cultures against white Western hegemony, shifts in the balance of economic and political power within the world economy; and a growing awareness of the costs as well as the benefits of scientific and technological 'progress'.

(Flax, 1990:5)

My aim in this chapter is to explore the so-called 'crisis' in contemporary Western culture. The related – but separate – movements of postmodernism and poststructuralism have delineated our contemporary condition as variously one of moral and philosophical fragmentation, political cynicism, superficiality and collapse of legitimation. Ubiquitous as it may seem, however, postmodernism is complex and disparate; and the relationship of postmodernity to modernity is itself contested. I shall try to indicate how I regard modernity and postmodernity as the products of particular historical and social circumstances, in which economic, technological, political and intellectual currents converge.

I wish to insist on the importance of locating both epochs in material and social context: I believe that postmodernity, and the crisis of values it delineates and represents, is more than just a set of ideas. It concerns visions of ideal communities and human relationships in concrete terms. I shall refer to 'postmodernity' as the contemporary stylization of society as reflecting certain economic, cultural, political and intellectual trends. In particular, I shall be examining some of the ways in which postmodernity renders the axioms of modernity problematic. Contemporary

13

commentators have argued that the gathering pace of social, cultural and economic change has 'decentred' former values and allegiances which now appear fluid and fragmented.

I am also concerned to look at the connection between the stories circulating within contemporary Western culture and the self-understanding of Christian communities as embodied in their practices of care and moral arbitration. I want to trace the implications of the postmodern condition for the values and visions that inform Christian preferences for community, self-actualization and justice in Church and society. Some would say that these terms can no longer (if indeed they ever did) claim universal consensus, and that the ideals by which we choose to live have no metaphysical grounding independent of the very processes of representation themselves (Doherty, 1994).

The implications of the postmodern condition for our ethical and political ideals and practices are clearly exemplified in the troubled relationship between postmodernism and feminism. Feminism would not exist, at least in its present form, if it were not for many of the claims of modernity: emancipation, equality, social justice. Yet many feminists would argue that their analysis of the exclusion and objectification of women within Western society exposes the limitations of modernity. They argue for a decisive break from modernity's prevailing models of human nature, value and community. Feminism exposes the degree to which the fundamental organizing categories of modernity are *androcentric*: maleness as normative of generic humanity. Feminism's problematization of *gender* as a category of human experience and culture therefore serves to illustrate the limits of modernity, and exemplifies how postmodern perspectives have destabilized former notions of selfhood, knowledge and ethics (Flax, 1990).

However, this does not necessarily mean that feminism and postmodernism are untroubled allies. One major tension between the two movements rests upon postmodernism's supposed abandonment of – or at best agnosticism towards – the foundational ethical and political projects of human rights, equality and justice upon which so many of the moral and strategic demands of the second-wave women's movement were founded (as well as other civil rights movements such as racial justice and gay and lesbian liberation campaigns). Does the collapse of the 'grand narrative' of modernity and the 'death of the subject' of reason and self-actualization represent the beginning or the end of feminism? What wider crises of truth and value, what chances for retaining a vision of what I shall call 'hope and obligation', does such a debate indicate?

The Contours of Modernity

It is important to emphasize the complex and multi-dimensional nature of the historical passage to modernity. It is best regarded as the outcome of several related processes: political, economic, social and cultural. Essentially, the story of modernity is one of transition from one social and economic order to another; but also of the birth of a new way of thinking, at the heart of which was itself a curiosity about the very origins and dynamics of that same new society (Bocock, 1992). Certainly, it is clear that a revolution was effected in Europe and North America between the years 1750 to 1848 which radically transformed human society and human self-understanding in the West, with lasting implications for the entire world. I can give only a brief summary of events and figures described in greater detail elsewhere (Gay, 1973; Outram, 1995). Nevertheless, several significant characteristics may be identified as typical of 'modernity'.

Science

First, we can trace the emergence of a new intellectual and epistemological world, associated with the Scientific Revolution of the seventeenth century. Like other features of modernity, however, there were precursors in the form of such works as Copernicus' *On the Revolution of the Celestial Orbs* (1543), Galileo's *Dialogue on the Two Principal Systems of the Universe* (1614) and Newton's *Principia Mathematica* (1687). What distinguished the particularly modern understanding and practice of science was first a commitment to empiricism. It was believed that all knowledge about the natural and social world can be grounded in observable and verifiable facts. The experimental method was the foundation of all science. Second, scientific knowledge was believed to hold the key to all subsequent growth in human knowledge, founded not on superstition or dogma, but upon systematic methods and applications conditioned by the exercise of reason in relation to all human affairs. The activity of rational thought and discernment thus provided access to the universal laws that governed the entire cosmos.

The Enlightenment

A second dimension of modernity was the period of European intellectual history spanning the first to the last quarter of the eighteenth century, centred on France but extending across Europe and North America. 'The Enlightenment' was the sum total of an explosion of intellectual energy which gave philosophical definition and direction to 'modernity'. It prompted a new approach to the study of society founded on the idea of 'the social' as a distinct sphere of life, available to be analysed in human and material terms alone, and requiring no recourse to religious frameworks. Just as the laws of nature were discernible via rational observation and analysis, it was held that human society and behaviour could also be subjected to enquiry; hence the work of Montesquieu, Comte and Saint-Simon to establish the 'scientific' study of society (Hamilton, 1992).

The Enlightenment, like modernity itself, was a complex and heterogeneous phenomenon; but at its heart was a network of what Roy Porter has termed a 'secular intelligentsia' (Porter, 1990:73) – scholars, philosophers and social critics known as *les philosophes*, communicating and debating via pamphlets, newspapers and letters. Their work was characterized by a critique of traditional forms of authority and the promotion of alternative ideals by which human affairs might be governed. Once more, the notion of rationality as the key to progress lay at the heart of the thinking of *les philosophes*. The exercise of these qualities would, it was believed, bring about the abolition of corrupt religion, facilitate the flowering of human knowledge and consciousness and set humanity on the path to unprecedented prosperity and justice (Gay, 1973).

Industrial Capitalism

The birth of the modern is also associated with the massive economic and technological developments which contributed to the emergence of industrial capitalism in Europe and North

America. Production and consumption were organized on the basis of a market economy, involving large-scale monetary exchange and the accumulation of capital. The massive demographic shifts associated with the intensification of factory production and accompanying urbanization effected the decline of a social order founded on fixed and unchanging hierarchies and allegiances, and replaced it with a system characterized by social and sexual division of labour (respectively, the categories of social class and patri-archy). Modern society was dependent on constant innovation and new development in order to maintain the requisite levels of technological and economic growth (Bocock, 1992).

Secular Democracy

Finally, modernity may be characterized as an era of the dominance of secular forms of power and influence, especially notions of government, authority and the nation-state (Held, 1992). The 'Democratic Revolutions' of the late eighteenth century were self-consciously founded on the principles of reason and equality, eschewing authoritarian and traditional forms of rule by King or Church. The French constitution of 1790 instigated civil marriage, reflecting a conviction that matrimony was to be considered a legal contract between persons, free of intervention by religious authorities. Similarly, the separation of Church and State in the United States' constitution expresses the belief that the social realm should be governed by freedom of speech and conscience, immune from impositions of religious or philosophical world-views which might hamper the individual's right to choose. Another product of modernity was the nation-state, with institutions governed by principles of free association, rationality and bureaucratic, not traditional, rule (Held, 1992).

So, whilst we have to be aware of referring too glibly to 'modernity' or 'the modern era' without understanding its historical roots and its complexities, it is certainly possible to trace the development of scientific practices, economic trends, institutions, ideas and social movements which all displayed a concerted commitment to critical enquiry and the exercise of reason. By the last quarter of the eighteenth century certain major precepts had consolidated into an intellectual orthodoxy, although Romanticism was also emerging as a counter-trend, emphasizing sentiment, feeling, rural order, simplicity and conservatism (Hamilton, 1992; Gay, 1973). However, there are still questions to be asked about how secure and axiomatic the central principles of modernity actually ever were.

Whose Enlightenment? Whose Modernity?

The advocates of the Enlightenment advanced a powerful critique of models of organic, traditional society within which the powers of monarchy, church and landed aristocracy held sway. Their ideas offered alternative models of authority more genuinely representing the aspirations of a nascent technocratic class founded on individualism, rational and free enquiry, the onward march of history, the possibility of human amelioration and autonomous human destiny. As technological and scientific change struggled to come to birth, Enlightenment philosophers affirmed the necessity of human autonomy from the strictures of tradition and deference, seeking to release human society from captivity to the past in the name of the possibilities of the future. This in turn fuelled new social and political forms – such as the democratic revolutions of the United States and France – which legitimated the appeals to human reason, emancipation and progress.

The promise of the Enlightenment and modernity was not insubstantial. It rested on the possibility that authority could be exercised fairly, equitably and without undue favour or sectional interference, and that the world of politics, trade and civic life could be a harmonious equilibrium between all competing interests, resolved by the natural outworkings of rational forces. Yet these claims about truth, progress and human nature were actually the outcome of particular sectional interests and perspectives masquerading as 'universal' axioms.

One method of exposing the particularity of modernity has come from feminist scholars, and it is simply to ask how the social and intellectual movements characterized gender relations and gender divisions. Attention to the relations between, and the respective representations of, women and men within the principles of modernity begins to suggest that the tenets of modernity represent not the claims of universal human aspiration, but the interests and concerns of a small group of eighteenth-century educated men. 'Gender' as a category of analysis thus serves as a powerful critical filter, and we can begin to ask: did modernity and its aspirations really reflect universal interests? Has it achieved its goals of universal enlightenment and emancipation?

One of the earliest critics of the Enlightenment was particularly concerned to expose the contradictions between its claims to universal rationality and its denial of those qualities to women. Mary Wollstonecraft argued that the ideals of 'reason' and 'virtue' were held to be innate to all human beings; but virtue for women was defined as deriving not from their ability to participate in culture and the public domain, but from their greater proximity to nature and their essential capacity for domesticity. Either women were to be included in the Enlightenment project by virtue of their human faculty of reason shared with men, she argued, or else the claim to the common humanity of women and men must be abandoned altogether (Outram, 1995).

Contemporary feminists have also begun to ask whose interests the discourse of enlightenment and modernity actually serves. They have argued that not only were the precepts of modernity historically rooted, they also reflected particular renderings of the gendered division of labour of the time. Jane Flax has analysed Immanuel Kant's 'What is Enlightenment?' in terms of its implicit gender dualism (Flax, 1993:75ff). For Kant, true enlightenment involves necessarily passing from private to public, from familial to social realms, from the world of the child to that of the adult. Thus will rationality be fostered, and the self-directed individual take his (sic) place in civic society. One of the features of modernization was a greater separation of public and private, and a greater gendered differentiation within economic and political activity between the female domestic sphere and the male world of rational bureaucratized work and the State. The bourgeois concept of the public sphere rested on a particular emergence of the market economy and division of public and private interests. But this necessarily required a number of exclusions: gender being one. 'We can no longer assume that the bourgeois conception of the public sphere was simply an unrealised utopian ideal; it was also a masculinist ideological notion that functioned to legitimate an emergent form of class rule' (Flax, 1993:204).

Thus, Kant's analysis is implicitly gendered and echoes the dualistic patterns of Western culture: of maleness (and full humanity) as resting in reason, knowledge, adulthood and civilization; and femaleness with the non-rational, the private, childhood, dependence and nature (Graham, 1995:11–16). The claims of the Enlightenment may be read as the manifesto for the self-actualization of the male subject, growing to maturity only via a severance from the maternal and domestic.

So without rejecting the aspirations behind the claims of the Enlightenment, it is important to trace their 'genealogy', as does Flax, in particular and concrete understandings, and to retain the option to challenge the self-evidence and universal applicability of these beliefs to all places, times, and classes of person. This is not to question entirely the authenticity of such claims, nor to see them as merely the ideological superstrata of technological or economic determinism. It is merely to assert that modernity was a complex social and philosophical process, which interwove political and intellectual revolutions with technological innovation and massive social change. As such, the transformation of the West had its roots in specific social and economic experiences – of how simultaneously to generate, and respond to, the transition from low-population agrarian and mercantile communities to industrialized and urban societies – and thus is a process which was historically and culturally contingent. Its spirit of optimism and inevitability may therefore need to be regarded with circumspection.

Modernity and Postmodernity

Although 'the postmodern condition' is an interplay of various factors, a number of figures exemplify the mood of these times. By way of introduction to some of the major themes of postmodernity, therefore, I shall summarize the work of some of its leading prophets and proponents.

Jean-François Lyotard coined the phrase *postmodern condition* as one which exposes the tenuousness of the *grand narratives* of modernity and enlightenment:

> I will use the term *modern* to designate any science that legitimates itself with reference to a metadiscourse of this kind making an explicit appeal to some grand narrative, such as the dialectics of Spirit, the hermeneutics of meaning, the emancipation of the rational or working subject, of the creation of wealth . . . Simplifying to the extreme, I define *postmodern* as incredulity toward metanarratives.
>
> (Lyotard, 1984:xxiii–xxiv)

For Lyotard, the grand narrative of progress, optimism and rationalization which once claimed the hearts and minds of Western civilization cannot encompass the diversity and specificity of local interests. In fact, metanarrative is an abuse of difference, absorbing and smothering variety and pluralism into a global universal homogeneity. So an appeal to the abstract march of 'History' with all-embracing ideals and objectives, has collapsed in favour of a series of local narratives which do better justice to the proliferation of diverse experiences and communities (Lyotard, 1984).

Whilst the work of Jacques Derrida may be termed *postmodern*, it is more appropriate to regard it as symptomatic of *poststructuralist* thinking. Drawing upon the structuralist linguistics of Ferdinand de Saussure, who argued that meaning only arose as part of a system of similarity and difference, Derrida maintains that speech and writing have no ultimate authors. A text is never unitary or stable, because in the margins and between the lines lie the echoes of the meanings which were repressed and negated in the process of establishing closure, as well as the related associations to which the surface text is constantly alluding. This mixture of difference and deferral, which fundamentally destabilizes fixed meaning, Derrida terms *différance*. The implication of this is that words do not represent objects or concepts in a reality beyond language. Language is a self-referential system; the speaker or writer can never succeed in pinning down exact meaning. Meaning and authorship are never fixed, because they always carry the traces of other words and intentions (Critchley and Mooney, 1994; Weedon, 1987). The surface meaning is constantly being disrupted by the reappearances of the repressed or marginal 'differends' (Lyotard, 1984).

Michel Foucault's studies of the dynamics of modernity have served to concentrate scepticism on the innocence of reason and knowledge. The development of scientific reason never existed, he argues, independent of an associated project to objectify and dominate. His historical *genealogies* of the conjunction of power and knowledge acquire a foreboding irony: social inquiry into a particular human ailment or affliction – be it crime, mental illness or sexual disorder – appears superficially to be developed out of a desire to cure and ameliorate; but it is a necessary prerequisite to legislation and coercion. Foucault's historical studies were much informed by the confessional practices of the medieval Church, and led him to argue that, especially at times of social upheaval, the ruling classes will develop an interest in a particular human condition in order to contain and control it. The emergence of sexology in the early twentieth century was superficially permissive; but the medicalization of sexuality, especially male homosexuality, took place in order the better to pathologize and discipline (Foucault, 1979, 1980; Rabinow, 1984).

Richard Rorty displays much of the iconoclasm of French deconstruction, although his own intellectual background is that of North American pragmatism. However, he does reflect a post-modern consciousness in his eschewal of the viability of any final commitment to universal or consensual standards of rationality and value. In *Philosophy and the Mirror of Nature* (1980) Rorty advances his version of the *anti-foundationalist* attacks on realist philosophies of science. Realism venerates scientific knowledge as holding an empirical 'mirror' to Nature, and scientific rationality is accordingly deemed accurate and exemplary by virtue of its ability to record and reflect a determinate and external reality. However, Rorty argues that science cannot rest on such *foundational* assumptions. He dispenses with notions of objectivity and the distinction between 'hard' (natural) and 'soft' (social) science, fact and value, knowledge and opinion. This acknowledges the origins of all discourse in human activity, and fosters human conversation as the arbiter and end of knowledge. All human discourse, judgement and communication therefore has the right to qualify as 'truth', insofar as it fulfils conditions of tolerance, respect and willingness to honour the conversational paradigm. The project to construct an infallible and definitive epistemology must be abandoned.

Rorty therefore speaks of the 'end of Philosophy', insofar as the task of philosophy may be seen as setting the standards by which ultimate knowledge of the truth might be attained, and as arbitrating between competing epistemological accounts. On the contrary, values are not ultimate or transcendent, but merely 'temporary resting places constructed for specific utilitarian ends . . .' (Rorty, 1980: xli). Ideas and theories are tested and verified not in relation to their degree of congruence to some external and transcendent reality, but in relation to their effectiveness in enabling us to manage and manipulate the world. The lasting value of any form of human knowledge is therefore defined in terms of its historical success in solving problems, pursuing practical projects and settling disagreements (Rorty, 1989).

Postmodernity has therefore challenged the viability and supremacy of the Enlightenment project and in the process many of its central presuppositions concerning history, the self, knowledge and community. It, too, has emerged out of specific intellectual, economic and historical circumstances; and it makes claims for its own reading of human nature, history and truth.

Postmodern Science

Contemporary voices are heralding the redundancy of positivist and mechanistic views of reality. Scientists speak about the degree of interaction between the observers and the objects under experimentation; of hypothesis and probability characterizing the gathering and verification of data; of intuition and concretion replacing abstract thought as the mood of theoretical discourse. The quasi-mystic 'holistic' science of Fritjof Capra and the radical social constructionism of science advanced by Paul Feyerabend and Thomas Kuhn speak of the contextuality and contingency of scientific knowledge (Bhaskar, 1989). Scientific practice is not the objective, innocent pursuit of experimentation and empiricism; rather, that which counts as authentic knowledge is always already governed by 'paradigms' or conventions of truth. Arguably, however, Kantian epistemology always proceeded on the presupposition that our accounts of the world are constructed 'phenomena' which are the product of human cognition and consciousness, rather than an exact reflection of 'noumenal' reality.

Equivocation over the benevolence of scientific enquiry – coupled with disquiet at the effects of unrestrained economic growth – has also emerged to challenge the modern precepts of progress and rationality. The development of the environmental movement and ecological concern reflects both a loss of confidence in the fruits of Western technology and a scepticism towards conventional political strategies and solutions (Yearley, 1992). Whilst the success of the Green Party in West Germany in the 1980s represented a significant impact on parliamentary politics on the part of the environmental lobby, its success and attraction seems due as much to its emphasis on alternative, often locally-based, forms of political activism.

Reason and Totalitarianism

One major source of the critique of modernity comes from a tradition of social theory concerned with the 'rationalization' of human society. The German sociologist Max Weber characterized the development of modern society as one in which the progressive forces of reason would displace the powers of affectivity, tradition and religion. Yet he also warned that enlightenment might spawn the 'iron cage' of bureaucracy, in which modern culture, increasingly dominated by instrumental, secular and materialist reason, would itself experience a crisis of meaning due to the very loss of ultimate and spiritual values (Bocock, 1992; Weber, 1978).

The experiences of the twentieth century of genocide and totalitarianism have further shaken the Enlightenment faith in the self-evident benevolence of human reason. The Frankfurt School, a neo-Marxist group which emerged in inter-war Germany, established a critique of Enlightenment reason which argued that modernity's emancipation of humanity from superstition, tradition and autocracy had itself become totalitarian. Progressive and critical reason had been supplanted by instrumental and ideological reason (Rasmussen, 1994). Thus, as Zigmunt Bauman argues, echoing Walter Benjamin's aphorism that 'There is no document of civilization which is not at the same time a document of barbarism', the persistence and ubiquity of evil is not necessarily eradicated by emancipatory enlightenment. Civilization is no guarantee of justice and altruism; on the contrary, it may merely provide humanity with greater instruments of oppression:

> The unspoken terror permeating our collective memory of the Holocaust . . . is the growing suspicion that the Holocaust could be more than an aberration, more than a deviation from an otherwise straight path of progress, more than a cancerous growth on the otherwise healthy body of the civilized society; that, in short, the Holocaust was not an antithesis of modern civilization and everything (or so we like to think) it stands for. We suspect (even if we refuse to admit it) that the Holocaust could merely have uncovered another face of the same modern society whose other, so familiar, face we so admire. And that the two faces are perfectly comfortably attached to the same body.   (Bauman, 1989:7)

Logistics of Late Capitalism

Whilst commentators differ on its exact trajectory, it is clear that the global economy of late twentieth-century capitalism is in metamorphosis (Allen, 1992). The nineteenth-century capitalist economy involved a predominantly factory-based production founded on the import of raw materials and the construction of finished products by a regular (and organized) workforce. In the last quarter of the twentieth century this has shifted to a knowledge-based economy, with workforces of 'core' and 'peripheral' employees, reflecting a rapid turnover of skills and geographical flexibility. Centres of production no longer depend on the proximity of raw materials, labour and infrastructure; the medium of production, exchange and consumption is now transacted in electronic hyper-space.

With this comes a greater global flexibility: investment and production can be moved at whim around the world. There is less emphasis on mass standardized production founded on rationalization and more on flexibility of design, production and marketing, and deregulation of patterns of employment:

> In today's workplace, manipulating information is a primary business activity. Some industries, such as communications and entertainment, have found traditional jobs simply too inflexible to cope with the constantly changing work . . . The result is a workforce made up of so-called 'vendor workers' who sell their services to a variety of clients and work for them on projects on a short-term basis.
>
> (Kent, 1995)

The very future of work is therefore at stake: as a basic organizing feature of society and as a source of personal identity and status.

The End of History

In keeping with Lyotard's rejection of the grand narrative, Sabina Lovibond has characterized the prevailing mood of postmodernism as rejection of universalism. She singles out the demise of the universal rational subject and the totalizing narratives of progress (Lovibond, 1989). Any common discourse of a homogenous, universal human nature is attacked as effectively muting and silencing the experiences of those whom the Enlightenment subject as male, white, rational renders 'Other': not only women, but people of colour, dominated by neo-colonialism and racism (Hall, 1992).

Part of this awareness of 'difference' may be due to a greater sensitivity to the diversity of global cultures; a result of the growing accessibility and immediacy of the 'Global Village'. But here, it seems that the postmodern condition nurses a fundamental paradox; we are conscious of the diversities of race, class, gender and culture, and especially the extent to which Western modernity's vision of universal history cloaks cultural diversity. Yet global communications and consumerism contributes to an ever-greater homogenization of culture (Hall, 1992). This perhaps identifies another feature of postmodernity, epitomized by the work of Jean Baudrillard: that genuine cultural diversity and creative expression is commodified or objectified by the capitalist economy into an image or product to be consumed. Nothing has any significance, aesthetic status or value beyond the degree to which it can be appropriated to the interests of the market (Doherty, 1994).

Some commentators would attribute this trend to economic forces and assert that this is the appropriate cultural expression of late capitalism in which consumerism – and the passive, privatized mode it both engenders and requires – has replaced production and social class as the primary mode of participation in society. The past, too, becomes merely a set of images and representations to be plundered: the spirit of history and the witness of past generations to a seamless tradition of progress, become simply branches of the heritage industry (Allen, 1992).

This same mood, that nothing has intrinsic or eternal value beyond its market or commodity value, is reminiscent of another strand of postmodernism. The postmodern critique of Western modernity has been to identify how dominant structures are rendered stable by the occlusion of the marginal, eccentric, Other. No identity can be constituted without also delineating difference, non-being. Foucault's work rests on the realization that Western civilization is drawn around the 'fault-lines' which distinguish health from illness, sanity from madness, transgression from conformity; but these distinctions are enforced by material and ideological practices. 'The logic of binary oppositions is also a logic of subordination and domination' (Benhabib, 1992:15). Thus, the release of difference from the unifying grip of a totalizing grand narrative allows alternative accounts of human nature, progress and history to flourish. But at the same time, the 'end of history' deprives postmodernity of any clear foundation upon which such perspectives might ground their ethical and political legitimacy.

Post/modernity in Perspective

Whilst many would question the easy delineation of contemporary society into two clearly distinguished eras of modernity and post-modernity, their respective philosophical, economic, political and cultural trends are also the bearers of implicit world-views. At the heart of post/modernity are particular understandings of human nature (ontology); authoritative knowledge (epistemology); the trajectory of history and the good (teleology); personal identity (subjectivity) and the individual's inhabitation of the social and natural world (agency). They reflect certain ways of talking about selfhood, knowledge, history and community which continue to shape contemporary society and which offer decisive pictures of goodness, truth and value. They guide our understandings of the nature of private and public virtue; of the possibilities for justice; and the principles on which an ordered and democratic society may be conducted. In short, these fundamental visions of humanity, identity, knowledge, value and action mould our political and ethical horizons and offer vocabularies of hope and obligation for the future.

Ontology

The Enlightenment vision of human nature was optimistic and all-embracing. All persons were possessed of the unique potential for rational thought and enquiry (a principle enshrined in the thought of Descartes and Pascal). Modernity posits the uniformity and universality of human nature as axiomatic. All people (men) are deemed to share the same conditions and characteristics; all are united and equal by virtue of the possession and exercise of reason.

Postmodernism emphasizes the diversity and contingency of human nature. It is constructed via the play of factors such as class, race, sexuality, region, and there is no essential or abstract 'human nature'. Derridean 'Being' is never fixed, but always endlessly displaced, always potentially absent. Theories of gender have made significant inroads into the dissolution of the concept of a universal, fixed human nature. A feature of contemporary feminism is the 'politics of difference': that no universal human nature (which was always a male human nature, as Mary Wollstonecraft made clear) can be posited outside the moderating categories of culture, race and class.

Subjectivity

Modernity regarded selfhood as the product of uncomplicated consciousness characterized by the capacity for rational thought and decision. True identity disregards bodily or physical dimensions; reason is juxtaposed against desire, affectivity and the unconscious. Transcendent reason determines identity, unassailed by contradictory forces of embodiment, desire or specificity.

The most abiding motif of postmodernism is the *death of the subject*. Many scholars of postmodernity – including feminists – regard the idea of reason as self-evidently leading to self-knowledge, truth and emancipation to be fundamentally destabilized by postmodern models of the self, the most powerful of which is offered by Freudian psychoanalysis. It denies the possibility of an unambiguous rational unitary Ego not in some way subtended and fragmented by the desires and drives of the instincts. Thus, the boundary between rational and non-rational is not certain; nor is the subject a fixed self, but contingent upon repressed memories, fears or distresses which may displace the self-controlled conscious Ego. The existence of the repressed world of fantasy, memory and desire which exerts tangible influence upon conscious subjectivity undermines the Enlightenment model of selfhood as resting upon the autonomy of reason and the equation of consciousness, reason and mind with the stability of self-identity (Flax, 1990; Graham, 1995).

This is a reflection of the postmodern contention that the self is finite, contingent and embodied, and not a 'disembodied cogito' or a collection of qualities existing independent of context. Theories of gender similarly undermine models of the self which rest upon the unitary, rational subject, and emphasize instead the 'self-reflexivity' of gender. Selfhood is only realized in interaction with others, culture and language:

> The Enlightenment conception of the disembedded cogito no less than the empiricist illusion of a substance-like self cannot do justice

to those contingent processes of socialization through which an infant becomes a person, acquires language and reason, develops a sense of justice and autonomy, and becomes capable of projecting a narrative into the world of which she is not only the author but the actor as well. (Benhabib, 1992:5)

Epistemology

Positivism, a central element of the epistemology of modernity, claims that the 'real world' is available and accessible to rational enquiry – the 'metaphysics of presence'. A neutral yet self-evidently emancipatory reason is exercised via free and open enquiry, and the application of a scientific method offers disclosure of the world as it really is, undistorted by superstition or speculation.

Postmodern epistemology regards truth as a web of discourse, with rules and assumptions shaped by context and self-interest. Knowledge is socially constructed and non-representational; but no one story is any more authoritative, foundational or truthful than another. No pure observation or understanding is available to us outside language. Language therefore constitutes reality, rather than reality being communicated through the neutral vehicle of language. Meaning is dependent on 'discourse' which replaces foundational truth; but discourses are highly context-dependent. Major contributions have been made in this area by feminists, especially in the philosophy of science, to reveal how scientific knowledge and practices also reflect social structures of power and gender (Harding, 1986, 1989; Graham, 1995:192–213). Postmodern epistemology challenges the capacity of philosophy to provide an all-encompassing system of thought which is unitary, foreclosive, transparent (Flax, 1990:33).

Agency

The view of the enlightened agent stresses the primacy of individual rational action. The authorial 'I' is the bearer of specific positions and initiates rationally-directed action in pursuit of calculated ends. Society is the sum or product of the thought and reason of individuals, and is a human creation, not divinely ordained. There is thus an ineradicable link between will, reason and action; and language is held to be 'referential', the transparent expression of objective, external reality. 'Speech acts' similarly, are not the autonomous individual's expression of independent reasoning or experiences, but are constructed within the conventions of discourse (Flax, 1990:204–10).

For postmodernism, non-teleological criteria guide human purposeful activity. All is practice: legitimation, values, community; but none of these rest on metaphysical categories. Similarly, human identity is constituted via the primacy of human agency. Person-hood is not a set of metaphysical or ontological qualities but the discursive result of our inhabiting a culture. The 'death of the subject' has implications for understandings of agency: the self is a reactor rather than self-actualizing actor, constituted by discourses of power, rather than creator of her own social world. For Foucault, agency is not the effect of the autonomous actor but constructed through mechanisms of social control.

This gives rise to an understanding of human agency as historically situated, embodied and contingent. The feminist and 'queer theorist' Judith Butler exemplifies this position when she speaks of the 'performative' nature of identity. There is no core self – all is discursive; no prediscursive identity who acts. 'There is no gender identity behind the expressions of gender; that identity is performatively constituted by the very "expressions" that are said to be its results' (Butler, 1990:25).

Teleology

The grand narrative of the Enlightenment heralded the inevitability and supremacy of progress. The human condition could be improved by the application of rationality to all matters, thus ensuring a limitless and ever-increasing level of happiness and prosperity. History unfolded in a progressively more benign fashion and bore witness to human control over its own destiny. *Les philosophes* of the eighteenth century believed themselves to be the bearers of a sacred project, to liberate humanity from the shackles of tradition, autocracy and superstition towards a bright future of universal enlightenment. This entailed respect and toleration for all individuals regardless of religious or moral convictions and freedom of speech and expression. Modernity's watchwords were liberty from traditional authority or constraint, be it in trade, political expression and government, religion or ownership of property. Modernist teleology thus presupposes a single transcendent position – that of progress – from which the whole of history can be authenticated.

Postmodern teleology may have two versions: one is scepticism towards the overarching and absolutized tendency of grand narratives – no one group or account can represent universal human consensus. The second, stronger, version would argue that any theoretical or historical narrative is redundant: no one can make claims that apply to more than the local, specific and provisional. Thus, no group struggling for justice can lay claim to historical or moral principles that might apply across cultures and experiences.

For theorists of gender, teleology is not a 'truth' of history and progress but a product of patriarchy. History has been forced into a narrative unity and direction that ignores cultural diversity or the voices of the underside. Visions of the end of history therefore reflect a partial version of human nature, truth and value against which all others are rendered 'fictions':

> [A]ll history is told from the point of view of the victor, who as a 'master narrator' . . . simply subsumes other competing narratives within a totalized framework, and assigns the competing narratives to a marginalized position. Those margins have, in modernism, been occupied by various figures such as dissidents, intellectuals, communists, women, lesbian and gay people, 'foreigners', and so on. (Kearney, 1994:493)

Postmodern Ambiguities

A rejection of 'foundationalist' accounts of subjectivity, of scientific knowledge and moral discourse therefore militates against a return to metaphysical or transcendent criteria for truth and value. The reflexive nature of human understanding renders *a priori* principles of justice, human rights or equality vulnerable to charges of sectionalism, partiality and self-interest masquerading as universal truths. No grand narrative is available to legitimate or motivate the search for knowledge, driven by an ideal of human emancipation through greater mastery of the world via the application of human rationality. Poststructuralism has succeeded in its dethronement of 'pure reason'; prescriptive knowledge has been corrupted by its (Foucauldian) identification with oppressive mastery; and notions of human progress and enlightenment have been exposed as the narratives of self-interest rather than universal axioms. Postmodernity reveals the paradox of its own self-defeating claims to truth:

> The problem, therefore, becomes a problem of the internal coherence of a position which would defend 'progressive' values while so systematically undermining the discourse of 'progress' itself. How can a postmodernist perspective consistently present itself as 'liberating' while conducting such an unyielding critique of the metaphysics which have grounded all talk of liberation? . . . It is precisely at this point, then, that we can demand that the 'postmodernists' show their hand, and admit either that they are not really advocates of any form of political change or programme whatsoever . . . or else that they can only consistently present themselves as defenders of non-conservative political values by surreptitiously invoking the foundationalist positions in social theory they have explicitly rejected.
>
> (Soper, 1990:100–1)

This requires us to ask questions about how to locate modernity and postmodernity in relation to one another. Is postmodernity a successor phase to modernity; a collapse and negation of the project of modernity; or a critique and revision of modernism, drawing out ambivalences and contradictions present at the heart of Enlightenment thinking?

It is easy to assume that the metanarratives of human nature, knowledge, history, selfhood and agency of modernity were homogenous, stable and absolute. But as the protests of Mary Wollstonecraft, the counter-revolution of Romanticism and the disquiet of Weber and the Frankfurt School indicate, modernity itself was always contested from its very beginnings (Thompson, 1992).

Frederick Jameson (1991) argues that postmodernity is 'high modernity' and reflects the aesthetics and power structures of late capitalism. It is literally that which chronologically follows the modern era. Others, such as Jean Baudrillard and Michel Foucault, regard postmodernity as the negation of modernity. They deny any coherent grounds for the establishment of reason and emancipation, and argue that only superficiality, simulation, pastiche and irony remain.

Others characterize postmodernity as a critical standpoint in relation to modernity; not so much an epoch as a perspective (Critchley and Mooney, 1994; Doherty, 1994). For Lyotard, the postmodern condition exposes the contradictions at the heart of modernity, but is essentially a 're-reading' of modernity that retrieves the concerns of the 'Others' of history and reason who were silenced in the name of a grand narrative. For the Frankfurt School, repression and ambivalence were always present at the heart of modernity; the task is now to reconstruct the terms on which renewed communities may be established (Habermas, 1984, 1989).

Postmodernism and the Question of Value

What, therefore, is to remain of the project of enlightenment, progress and freedom? Is it to be abandoned as itself cloaking tendencies to domination and totalitarianism beneath a veneer of impartial, universal emancipation; or can its aspirations to justice and equality be redeemed? Voices are beginning to emerge which ask whether questions of value can actually be expunged from contemporary social theory and philosophy (Dews, 1987:xi–xvii; Soper, 1991). Whilst theorists of postmodernity endorse the deconstruction of fixed essences and naturalized values inherent in Enlightenment rationality, they are also disturbed by poststructuralism's dystopian vision of the ubiquity and inevitability of domination and illusion (Flax, 1990; Lovibond, 1989; Soper, 1990).

Concerned that the collapse of metanarratives means the impossibility of a postmodern politics and ethics, such critics seek the conditions in which a vocabulary of what I shall term *hope and obligation* might be retained as the context for the continuation, albeit on rather different terms, of the Enlightenment project of progress and human flourishing:

> We may no longer be able to legislate comfortably between opposing or competing political systems, for we can no more subscribe to such totalizing forms; but we can address the instance, the event, of judging and of justice in its singularities. Here lies the basis of the ethical demand in the postmodern . . . We must judge: there is no escape from the necessity of judging in each particular case. Yet we have no grounds upon which to base our judgment.
>
> (Kearney, 1994:497)

This represents a return to questions about the prescriptive nature of social theory, and whether it is possible to articulate models of human nature and knowledge which are neither foundationalist or relativist. Further, whether it is possible to derive normative principles by which to guide purposeful, critical and transformatory engagement with the postmodern condition.

Postmodernism, Gender and Feminism

> Postmodernism is an ally with whom feminism cannot claim identity
> but only partial and strategic solidarity.   (Benhabib, 1992:15)

The end of the 'grand narrative' may be the foregrounding of formerly silenced marginalities, a proliferation of truths, all of whom can appeal to principles of emancipation and autonomy. Alternatively, it represents the death of 'Truth', the fragmentation of meaning and the loss of any political or ethical foundation – a vocabulary of hope and obligation – for a postmodern world. As the troubled relationship between feminism and postmodernism indicates, a dilemma faces all those who wish to maintain a commitment to the progressive and emancipatory project of modernity whilst acknowledging its shortcomings.

The dynamics of post/modernity are acutely illustrated in the claims of critical studies of gender. 'Gender' has become one of the most powerful categories out of which the hypothesis of the universal rational subject is challenged. Theories of gender – especially in feminist scholarship – challenge modern images of human nature, identity, knowledge, action and ethics; but does that make feminism postmodern? Feminism owes a great deal to the fruits of modernity: the grand narratives of liberalism and socialism generated the theory and practice of 'the rights of women', and advances in science and technology have freed women from the perils of childbirth and the burdens of housework.

However, many feminist theorists would insist that women were never fully at home in the grand narratives of liberalism and Marxism (Evans, 1995). Feminism exposes the extent to which such universal claims for human emancipation were always grounded in selective accounts of liberation and political agency. For some, the postmodern fragmentation of the unitary – and essentialist – category of 'Women' duly celebrates the pluralisms of race, class, sexuality, culture and religion. Far from undermining feminist commitments, poststructuralist views of subject, agency, identity promote its causes. Critical consciousness and action arises not from ontologically given priorities but out of shifting identities and actions (Cornell, 1995a). Drucilla Cornell argues that the heterogeneity of multiple identities and narratives is the way by which feminism can escape from the totalizing discourses of modernity within which they had no stake in the first place. That includes any kind of stereotyping or objectification of women. 'But it is precisely because there is no firm ground for the identity of Woman that allows us to endlessly challenge any interpretation of us as our ultimate truth' (Cornell, 1995a:98).

Yet there are still problems with the demise of any clear historical project that carries within itself an implicit commitment to progress and social justice. Many feminist theorists are suspicious of the political and ethical implications of adopting a poststructuralist evocation of 'difference'. Chiefly, it risks depriving feminism of a clear moral and political identity:

> [I]f women cannot be characterized in any general way, if all there is to femininity is socially produced, then how can feminism be taken seriously? . . . If we are not justified in taking women as a category, then what political grounding does feminism have? Are these the only choices available to feminist theory – an adherence to essentialist doctrines, or the dissolution of feminist struggles into localized, regional, specific struggles, representing the interest of particular women or groups of women?   (Grosz, 1990:341–2)

This is to admit that modernist utopianism has sanctioned terrible excesses of instrumentalism and authoritarianism in the name of the means justifying the ends, but that feminists must still insist on the 'ethical impulse of utopia' (Benhabib, 1992:229). Women's lives have so often been determined on their behalf by others; all the more reason for asserting a clear sense of identity and selfhood. Hence the dangers of postmodernism's erasure of definitive norms of identity, justice and self. 'There is the refrain that, just now, when women are beginning to assume the place of subjects, post-modern positions come along to announce that the subject is dead . . .' (Butler, 1995a:48).

The African-American writer bell hooks argues something similar. Whilst postmodernist thinkers celebrate heterogeneity and plurality, their evocation of 'Otherness and difference' seldom allows space for formerly silenced groups to speak for themselves.

At the same time, hooks experiences a refusal on the part of black women and men to countenance postmodernism because they find little in the way of a 'strong' discourse of identity and teleology within which black struggles can occupy a privileged 'critical location'. However, hooks argues for a circumspect adoption of postmodernist discourse which repudiates the essentialism both of racist master narratives and of simplistic identity politics:

> The critique of essentialism encouraged by postmodernist thought is useful for African-Americans concerned with reformulating outmoded notions of identity. We have too long had imposed upon us from both the outside and the inside a narrow, constricting notion of blackness . . . Abandoning essentialist notions would be a serious challenge to racism . . .
>
> When black folks critique essentialism, we are empowered to recognize multiple experiences of black identity that are the lived conditions which make diverse cultural productions possible . . . Coming to terms with the impact of postmodernism for black experience, particularly as it changes our sense of identity, means that we must and can rearticulate the basis for collective bonding.
>
> (hooks, 1991:28–9)

So in the midst of pluralism and the absence of foundational grounds for hope and obligation, how do we judge anew? Can a suitable consensus be created? Under conditions of postmodernity there may be no single over-arching notion of the common good; but some social theorists still insist that principles may – must – be indicated and delineated. Some feminists argue that whilst wishing to rule out essentialist, monolithic metanarrative, it is possible to enshrine a commitment to transformation and emancipatory change:

> I regard neither the plurality and variety of goodnesses with which we have to live in a disenchanted universe nor the loss of certainty in moral theory to be a cause of distress. Under conditions of value differentiation, we have to conceive of the unity of reason not in the image of a homogenous, transparent glass sphere into which we can fit all our cognitive and value commitments, but more as bits and pieces of dispersed crystals whose contours shine out from under the rubble.
>
> (Benhabib, 1992:75–6)

It may not be possible to derive principles of hope and obligation from some transcendent power or force which automatically guarantees their authenticity and success. However, it may yet be feasible to develop strategies by which such values can be reconstructed out of the fragments of pluralism and difference.

❧

CHAPTER 2

Pastoral Theology in an Age of Uncertainty

> What is it today that demands the revisioning of Christian theology? . . . It seems that it is . . . that of the 'passage' of history – the passing of Western bourgeois culture, with its ideals of individuality, patriarchy, private rights, technical rationality, historical progress, capitalist economy, the absoluteness of Christianity, and so on. It *feels* as though we are reaching the end of an historical era since we find ourselves in the midst of cognitive, historical, political, socioeconomic, environmental, sexual/gender, and religious changes of vast importance, comparable perhaps to the great Enlightenment that inaugurated the modern age. Can we speak, then, of a second Enlightenment, a new watershed, a new paradigm in theology?
>
> (Hodgson, 1994:53)

What does the transition from modernity to postmodernity represent for religion, theology and Christian practice? One of the principles of modernity was its conscious secularism: the replacement of religious authority and theological speculation by humanism, reason and empiricism (Gay, 1973). However, one of the implications of the postmodern return of the repressed 'Other' of modernity involves a resurrection of the spiritual and the numinous. Whereas 'religion' as an institutional form may be regarded as an invention of modernity – corresponding to bureaucratic logic and shaping its beliefs according to scientific reason – the emergence of postmodernity promises the radical transformation of modern religion into postmodern spiritualities (Tracy, 1994). Hodgson (1994) speaks of the transition to postmodernity as a *kairos* or defining moment for Christian theology: a shift of 'paradigms' from one period to another. Certainly, many theologians have begun to address the implications of the *postmodern* paradigm for the nature, tasks and status of their discipline.

38

A British theologian well known for his examination of the philosophical and ethical tenets of postmodernism and post-structuralism, and their ramifications for Christian faith, is Don Cupitt. He places himself in the intellectual tradition of Kierkegaard and Nietzsche: religious sceptics for whom faith cannot rest in metaphysics but in radical humanism. Cupitt argues that the transcendent God of Christian myth and dogma must diminish before individuals' spiritual journeys can really begin. A post-modern world in which all is revealed to be of human construction requires that we sever the ties of metaphysics and theological realism in order to embrace the void of nothingness (1994:92–116). Our religious quest becomes a self-created (and self-creating) phenomenon, yet still essentially religious: 'the maintenance of God-talk with a denial of the reality of its referent' (Hart, 1994:8).

Ethically, Cupitt's vision promises the end of the 'sexual subjugation' and tyranny of religious totalitarianism. It proclaims liberation from all the certainties – and thus abuses of power – associated with dogma, hierarchy, conformity and patriarchy. However, some kind of church is still envisaged: 'as a community, a vocabulary, a starting-point, something that we are proposing eventually to transform' (1989:102). Cupitt models his 'future church' on Latin American basic ecclesial communities, but as a self-consciously minimalist institution, maintaining little in the way of officials, plant or tradition. It is a sacramental and quasi-(post-?) Eucharistic community, meeting also for study, training, art and social action (1989:168–73).

However, it is not clear whether such groupings exist as *choices* or *givens*. Cupitt's work is heavily devoted to the problems of belief in the postmodern world; and there is a sense in which his model believer is one who grapples with her faith and then finds a congenial community and practice (of 'scepticism, minimalism, emptiness, the discipline of the Void') which most suits that stance (Cupitt, 1989:172). I wonder then, about the balance between 'believing and belonging' (Davie, 1995) in Cupitt's scheme: are we to struggle existentially with the void and hope our solutions fit those of others? I would argue that such a quest is always necessarily corporate and social, in that personal belief and commitment is preceded by our inhabitation of a multiplicity of faith-communities (some of them religious) in which the telling and retelling of narrative and meaning is already taking place.

Cupitt's point may well be that the Church's claim to pre-exist human discourse is part of its repressive strategy; but however contingent and non-realist our social and theological worlds may be, they do endure as material and ideological realities which are more than the sum of individual actions. Cupitt gestures in the direction of communities of faith and practice, but I suspect that he does ultimately privilege believing over belonging as the foundation of theological discourse. Such communities are collectives of individual choice rather than historical realities into which individuals are incorporated.

John Milbank's *Theology and Social Theory: Beyond Secular Reason* has attracted much debate in relation to the future of theology after postmodernity. Like many secular social theorists, Milbank emphasizes the violence done by technical rationality to the realms of spirituality, affectivity and tradition. The rise of modern social theory – especially sociology – rested upon the expulsion of religion from the dominant values of selfhood, truth, knowledge and history. However, Milbank argues that secular theory has simply colonized theological terms whilst cloaking them in a spurious value-freedom that represses their true origins (1993:105–6).

After an exhaustive critique of secular philosophy and social science, Milbank concludes that the retrieval of a renewed Christian discourse after modernity lies in the 'renarration of practice': namely the rooting of Christian truth in the life and work of the Church. This is evidently a recovery of a *metanarrative,* because Milbank clearly regards the Church as the 'exemplary form of human community' (1993:388) in which all can settle into a harmonious whole.

Unfortunately, Milbank does not elaborate on the precise workings of these communities of practice: how, in detailed terms, the actual activities of community-building, liturgy, discipleship and mission might actually express the truth of the Christian Gospel. We are left with a tantalizing vision of a Church about whose internal dynamics we can only speculate. What are these renarrated practices, who are their agents, and to what end are they directed? Critics of Milbank have surmised that the blissful homogeneity of such a reiteration of Christendom represents a denial of pluralism and heterodoxy. This is not a Church that tolerates dissent or indeed adequately reflects postmodernity's recovery of 'difference'. Nor is it open to critical scrutiny; the actual practices of Milbank's community are never elaborated. Apart from anything else, the diversity of Christian practice throughout history would invalidate Milbank's portrayal of harmonious continuity. Milbank's solution has a distinctly premodern, rather than postmodern, tenor; and it seems he is less interested in constructing a public theology in the midst of shifting values than espousing 'a highly structured and settled ecclesial order' (Lakeland, 1993:69): an enclave for the like-minded.

For others, the option for a postmodern theology is not to attempt to return to a premodern theological era, either in the form of fundamentalist, precritical religion, or in the form of a narrational community of belief and practice. Instead, a reconstructive theology is proposed, to embrace both the ambivalences of modernity and the dilemmas of postmodernity. Mark C. Taylor has developed an *a/theology* which adapts the traditions of *negative theology*. He refashions apophatic spirituality – which emphasizes human contemplation of the essential mystery of God – to argue that the Divine symbolizes the void beyond human constructions of reality. Taylor invokes the Derridean notion of *différance* to depict a mysterious 'non-absent absence' at the margins of meaning and representation. The realm of transcendence is equated with this 'Other' of language, silenced by the assertion of definitive meaning, and resembles the ultimate signified which can never absolutely be encapsulated in speech. It remains as an absent presence, only ever glimpsed in the allusive interplay of texts or speech acts:

> The sense of the unpresentable that haunts all presence and every presentation is sublime. The postmodern sublime, however, is not an extension of either Kant's dynamic or mathematical sublime. It results from neither the erasure nor the multiplication of form, image and representation. The sublime that is neither the fullness of the signified nor the plenitude of signifiers lies – always lies – between, in the differential strife of images . . . It is to this deserted space that we are called by an Other we can never name.
>
> (Taylor, 1992:26–7)

A similar mood is reflected in many of the essays in *Shadow of Spirit*, published in 1992. The illusion of fixed identities and meanings, and the death of metaphysics, has opened up new sacred spaces beyond human contingency in which it is possible to discern signs of transcendence, mystery and numinence. Many poststructuralist thinkers are redeploying traditional theological language to exemplify the transgressive sphere of what Kristeva has termed 'madness, holiness and poetry'. Its very existence beyond the technical-instrumental world of rationality, empiricism and foundational thinking renders it suggestive of new forms of consciousness and being which will shatter logocentric and phallogocentric reason (Berry, 1992a:5). However, criticism of such celebration of the playful, non-rational and spiritual expresses dissatisfaction at its indifference to ethical and political engagement. Whilst such work is philosophically exciting, it locates religion in a presocial, prediscursive Void of undifferentiated otherness and silence without adequately addressing issues of transformative practice (Williams, 1992).

All these postmodern theologies share a number of features. They reject God as an absolute 'Being' in place of a transcendent 'Other' equated with the realm beyond human agency and rational consciousness. They also emphasize the 'self-making' qualities of religion (Cupitt's metaphor is one of theologians and believers as 'artists' and creators of their own reality), whether that is through narrative or other forms of Christian practice. The nature of communities of faith after postmodernity also emerges as a priority, whether that is of Milbank's neo-Augustinian Church reasserting the normative vision for humanity, or the 'gathered and dispersed' groupings of Cupitt, dedicated to the '*continuous* reinvention and renewal of humanity' (1989:172, my emphasis).

I am intrigued by this recurrent theme in postmodern philosophical theology, that in the absence of metaphysical truth-claims independent of language, culture and context the only ultimate reality to which anyone of faith can attest is that made incarnate in, and proclaimed by, the life of intentional communities of Christian practice:

> [T]he permanent self-identity of the Christian faith cannot be presupposed . . . There is no purely theoretical centre of reference which can serve in an abstract, speculative way as a norm of identity. Truth does not yet exist; it cannot be reached by interpretation, but it has to be produced by change.   (Davis, 1994:90–1)

It is perhaps surprising, therefore, to find that such themes of Christian belief and practice after postmodernity find relatively little resonance within pastoral and practical theology.[1] Yet the emphasis in the work of Milbank, Cupitt and others on the domain of Christian practice, community and ecclesiology as the resolution of Christian truth-claims would seem to offer a clear opportunity for practical and pastoral theologians to contribute their own particular disciplinary resources and insights. It is possible to discern such work emerging, albeit gradually, within Christian pastoral theology. In the changing priorities and self-understanding of contemporary pastoral care there are some signs of a transition from modernity to postmodernity: a passing of particular notions of selfhood, truth and community and the identification of new points of departure.

Shifting Paradigms in Pastoral Theology

I shall be drawing on a number of recent publications in the field of Christian pastoral theology from Britain and North America in the course of this discussion. A volume of essays, *Pastoral Care and Social Conflict,* from the North American pastoral care movement represents a particularly clear diagnosis of many of the uncertainties currently afflicting Christian pastoral/practical theology (Couture and Hunter, 1995). They include a questioning of the individualism of contemporary Western pastoral care and a greater emphasis on social justice dimensions of Christian ministry; a move to reconnect the pastoral counselling movement (as a specific arm of pastoral care) with the life of local Christian congregations; a similar quest for a more distinctive theologically-based foundation for pastoral care as a reaction to the dominance of psychologically-derived models; and a tension between the personalist, therapeutic tradition of pastoral care and counselling and the symbolic, liturgical and sacramental modes of wider pastoral activity.

Another recent collection, *Life-Cycles: Women and Pastoral Care,* attempts to articulate a feminist pastoral theology from the British context (Graham and Halsey, 1993). Similar shifts in the traditional contours of pastoral care may be evinced: a critique of the dominant patterns of giving and receiving care as simultaneously ignoring women's distinctive experiences as clients and as active agents of care within and beyond the Christian community. The retrieval of women's pastoral needs – conditioned by their passage through the life-cycle and socio-political factors – must take place by naming these experiences and challenging the taboos that surround them. Yet the challenge of gender issues to pastoral care does not simply involve the inclusion of women into traditions and models of ministry which otherwise remain unchanged. Instead, it is a programme for reconstituting the very values and assumptions which underpin Christian practice (Graham, 1993).

A Critique of Pastoral Care seeks an overview of the discipline of pastoral/practical theology in Britain and the United States (Pattison, 1993). Pattison's second edition contains a critique of his earlier perceptions in the first volume. He identifies the issue of gender, and feminist critiques of conventional patterns of pastoral care, as the most significant development in the interval between the two editions. He also discusses some other questions: the search for an adequate definition of pastoral care; its defining sources and norms (the authoritative bodies of knowledge for the practice of care, particularly use of the Bible, and the role of ethics); and the relationship between the activity of pastoral care and the life of the gathered Church. Implicit within this is a theme shared with the other volumes: that of the problematic relationship between the practices of human or pastoral care and the traditions and teachings of Christian theology.

David Lyall, a Scottish practical theologian, is writing for a secular audience about the religious dimensions of pastoral counselling. It is therefore not surprising that the contemporary pluralism of world-views preoccupies him. He is concerned to trace the resurgence of theological questions implicit within the counselling relationship, something he identifies as constituting a significant shift of emphasis. He draws an analogy between the changing nature of pastoral counselling in a spiritual and religious context and the life of the contemplative and activist Thomas Merton:

> An early liberalism accommodating itself to the dominant secularity of the age is followed by a conservative reaction which in turn gives way to the search for a different kind of spirituality, one which encounters God not in religion as such, but in the suffering and striving of the world. (Lyall, 1995:106)

I cannot say whether David Lyall intends to identify this third phase of pastoral counselling as specifically postmodern, although

I detect some parallels. The waning of a modern perspective on religion which assumed its ultimate decline (or reduction to privatized, individual concerns) has been superceded either by a return to premodern religious certainties or a search for more eclectic, informal spiritualities. Lyall's discussion suggests to me a movement beyond a modern and secular pastoral care (defined largely by the modern psychologies) towards one that seeks not the homogeneity and security of unreconstructed Christian identity, but one which embraces the contradictions and complexities of pluralism:

> Set free from the compulsion to talk about God, there is a new and deeper freedom to talk about God and *not* to talk about God . . . In its engagement with the secular psychotherapies, neither does pastoral counselling need to lose its Christian identity as care offered in the context of the community of faith. Set free from the compulsion to be 'religious', it has a genuine freedom to point beyond the secular to the One who is the source of all healing.
>
> (Lyall, 1995:107)

Thus, Lyall's book contains a useful awareness of the necessity of working across the boundaries of secular and religious. Indeed, in an age of the resurgence of spirituality – but also in its greater diversity and reworking – many of these old boundaries may themselves be open to revision.

Pastoral Theology and Post/Modernity

Within these selected volumes, therefore, it is possible to see many shifting priorities as to the nature and identity of contemporary Christian pastoral care. How do the contested areas of epistemology, ontology, agency, teleology and subjectivity, already outlined, reflect some of these changing visions?

Privileged Knowledge

This aspect centres around debates in pastoral/practical theology about the most authoritative sources of expertise for the practice of care. Whilst the paradigm of pastoral counselling, with its explicit links to the values (and professional career structures) of humanistic psychologies and psychotherapy has predominated, there are signs of reorientation. This is particularly manifest in the tension expressed between sacred and secular sources of pastoral care and counselling (Hunter, 1995:17–23). It is suggested that there has been too uncritical an acceptance of secular theories and therapies at the expense of theological models of selfhood, health and healing, sin, guilt and forgiveness in pastoral care (Pattison, 1993:194ff).

Writing at the interface of secular and religious counselling, David Lyall is well-placed to review the differences of opinion over what now constitutes definitive knowledge for the practice of care. Specifically, this is a question of how psychological and theological perspectives are to be integrated in the practice of the Christian counsellor. The adoption of secular therapies in pastoral care is a clear sign of modernity; but religious world-views persist, even revive (Lyall, 1995:134–5). Lyall emphasizes the power of stories to shape and guide identity – individual and corporate – through which effective values may be articulated. Lyall's instinct that counselling may be more open to the expression of religious value – albeit within an overtly pluralist context – suggests that matters of faith are no longer regarded as privatized and personal, necessitating their 'bracketing out' of the non-directive therapeutic encounter, but may actually form a crucial resource for locating our own story in relation to broader human stories (1995:97).

Human Nature

Within the literature surveyed here it is clear that the implicit assumptions of human personhood as encapsulated in prevailing models of pastoral care are subject to fundamental revision. In this respect, pastoral/practical theology is experiencing a shift of paradigms from modernity to postmodernity. Much of the twentieth-century pastoral care movement reflects modernist commitments to a shared and universal human nature defined by a common core of reason and self-actualizing agency; a sense that rational knowledge will provide the grounding for empirically viable therapeutic techniques; and an optimistic teleology concerning the promise of human fulfilment via the attainment and application of such rational laws of personality and salvation (Hunter, 1995; Hunter and Patton, 1995). This is epitomized by the separation of pastoral counselling from the worshipping community and its absorption into a medical model of curative, clinical care.

However, the notion of a universal human nature defined according to the norm of the self-actualized rational individual is undergoing revision in the face of a recovery of race, class and gender as 'sites of difference'. The emergence of feminist pastoral theologies suggests that traditional models of ministry and care presuppose androcentric criteria of pastoral need, norms which silence the specific experiences of women and objectify them via patriarchal constructions of appropriately feminine roles (Miller-McLemore and Anderson, 1995; Graham and Halsey, 1993). Feminist perspectives call for a greater attention to the particularity and diversity of (gendered) human nature. By sustaining a notion of a universal or single definition of experience and need practitioners may actually perpetuate the interests of a patriarchal social order. Pastoral care conducted according to unexamined axioms of personhood, may effectively reproduce oppressive norms: *see Redlie*

> The question is not whether men and women are different, but rather what value we shall place on these differences and how we shall live with them. At stake is not just the question of gender but the question of the human capacity to live with difference among persons in a planet that continues to shrink. For that reason, we regard gender studies as a necessary endeavor in pastoral theology, because the celebration of diversity and respect for human uniqueness is at stake. (Miller-McLemore and Anderson, 1995:105)

The implications of ethnic, cultural and racial diversity are underdeveloped in contemporary pastoral literature, although emergent contributions suggest similar themes to those of feminist writing: attention to the diversity of human need, recognition of a variety of models of pastoral care and the importance of integrating theological understandings generated by cross-cultural differences (Ma Mpolo, 1990; Harris, 1991; Lartey, 1993).

Pastoral Agency

One of the most contested areas in contemporary pastoral literature concerns those *persons* deemed fit to dispense care; the *methods* by which such care is administered; and the *locus* of purposeful care. Since its foundation as a discrete theological discipline in the eighteenth century, pastoral theology – in academic and popular literature – has tended to concentrate on the qualities that characterize the good pastor. Pastoral *theology* has therefore been synonymous with writings on the activity and qualities of the pastoral *agent*. For most of the modern period, until very recently, this has also meant that pastoral theology so understood has necessarily restricted itself to the study of the activities of male, ordained and professionally accredited persons.

Therefore, the needs of the *client*, or the dynamics and relationships within the Christian community as a whole, have been marginal. Alternative models of pastoral agency to that of the ordained minister – and in particular, forms of care exercised by lay women – were ignored. The supposedly normative pattern of the practice of Christian care therefore reflected the powerful and privileged status of the clergy; the contributions and gifts of women as pastoral agents were undervalued and unacknowledged. Women's unequal position in society has thus gone unchallenged by the churches because pastoral theology has been caught in a paradigm of 'sexism and clericalism' which implicitly disavows the expertise of lay people, and especially women (Graham, 1990).

In this respect the question of gender, and specifically the historical invisibility of women, exposes the limitations of old definitions of pastoral care and points towards new horizons. For example, Pattison asserts that feminism completely transforms the parameters of pastoral care such that its normative agent must now be considered the 'non-trained woman' (1993:194) rather than the ordained and professionally-accredited male.[2] Feminist insights thus shift both the agent and the locus of care away from the ordained minister in ecclesiastical institutions towards secular contexts or informal settings, such as parallel or alternative communities of faith, women-centred liturgies or care groups (Graham and Halsey, 1993; Ruether, 1985).

An emphasis on pastoral counselling within the modern pastoral care movement also privileges scientific and medical models of care in preference to models of practice which deploy sacrament, prayer, sermon or symbol (Hunter, 1995). However, as the feminist reconstruction of pastoral theology indicates, the tradition is being revised to provide new sources and norms for person-hood, healing and community. This restores a broader definition of pastoral activity as encompassing not only individual care and counselling, but a diverse set of pastoral *practices*:

The care of the church is constituted by the whole variety of ways the life of the church seeks to promote the flourishing of God's creation in enactment of the gospel: through worship, prayer, Bible study, fellowship, social ministry, music, preaching, and so forth.

(Lyon, 1995:97)

Clearly, there are complex ethical and political dimensions to the caring relationship, and it cannot be assumed that the counselling or helping encounter is immune from the values and power structures of society at large. The potential for the abuse of power in the therapeutic relationship has become a matter for concern in recent years, and is emerging into pastoral theology as well (Graham, 1993; Poling, 1991, 1995). Contemporary writers thus seek a greater equality in the pastoral encounter, arguing that the dynamics of power and difference (of gender, race, class, sexuality and professionalism) need to be addressed honestly and openly. The emphasis is on the mutuality of care in contrast to the formality and hierarchy of old. It is held to be a more authentic expression of Divine *kenosis* and vulnerability and stresses a model of pastoral care as shared companionship on life's journey rather than the imbalance of client/expert or sheep/shepherd (Campbell, 1981; Pattison, 1993).

Teleology – or the Aims and Ends of Care

However, such a model of companionable care raises for many commentators the problematic issue of moral judgement and discipline in Christian pastoral care. Whilst the unquestioned hierarchy of status and expertise of older models of pastoral relationship seem inappropriate for the post/modern era, there are also questions to be asked about the degree of moral authority a pastor (however chosen and accredited) may be called upon to exercise. The twentieth-century tradition of non-directive or *eductive* counselling advocates a non-judgemental stance on the part of the pastor. In part, this may reflect the extent to which the contemporary pastoral care movement is embedded in a modern grand narrative of progress and amelioration. It is implicitly committed to a humanist tradition of faith in the powers of reason, optimism and scientific method and practice to effect human healing and growth:

> In the therapeutic perspective the distortions of human life are believed to be largely of contingent historical and social origin, accessible to human effort and intelligence; thus human beings are capable of participating in significant ways with God in saving and restoring human life at its deepest ('spiritual') levels of struggle and distortion. Such commitments are cautiously optimistic concerning human powers and possibilities, compared with the exclusive emphasis on sin, the bondage of the will, and dependency on divine grace that has characterized much of the Western religious tradition.
>
> (Hunter, 1995:18–19)

Thus, the ultimate goal of the modern pastoral care movement has been one of personal wholeness and well-being; but the individual is seen as possessing an innate orientation towards such self-actualization. Certainly, there is some concession to moral judgement in the form of confrontation in the counselling relationship; but this seems orientated more towards encouragement of ethical autonomy than obedience to external moral codes. Such a bracketing of pastoral *discipline* (traditionally an emphasis of pastoral ministry) may have been a welcome antidote to the more severe forms of judgementalism, and allowed alternative models to flourish which emphasized unconditional forgiveness and the importance of self-esteem (as in, for example, Paul Tillich's stress on 'acceptance'). Arguably, however, contemporary pastoral care finds itself with an impoverished vocabulary of moral discernment – in relation to the individual *and* the collective – as a result (see chapters 3 and 4).

Another sign of change is a growing concern for the social and political dimensions of care. The personalist tradition of pastoral care, with its focus on the immediate feelings and responses of the client, may obscure the extent to which social and economic factors enhance or impede our growth to full personhood. It also neglects the sense in which we are always already relational selves, formed by communal and social contexts (L. K. Graham, 1995; Marshall, 1995). James Poling argues that the modern pastoral care movement was concerned to listen to the voices of suffering and dispossession from its earliest inception. He argues that the contemporary postmodern challenges of racial and gender justice (and, we might add, the economic dispossession of the poor, locally, nationally and globally) demand a similar response of compassion which goes beyond individual amelioration. It will require the reform and revision of the dominant models of pastoral care:

> The pastoral care movement has two choices. Either it is still a reform movement to change church and society, or it is a profession within the established patriarchal church and society concerned mainly with its own financial future, accreditation, and making sure it has a secure place for its members . . . If our pastoral care movement decides to return to its earlier reformist goals, it must respond to the present crisis in the area of sexuality by focusing on issues of the liberation of women, African Americans, and gays and lesbians from the traditional sexual ethics that support male dominance.
>
> (Poling, 1995:122)

The feminist maxim that 'the personal is political' is nowhere more true than when applied to Christian pastoral care. As the examples of women-centred care are making clear, women's personal circumstances and pastoral needs are not simply individual problems but occur within a social context of health and illness, reflect the influence of cultural norms and the dynamics of family life on dominant expectations of the giving and receiving of care, and reveal the impact of structural and institutional trends in public policy and socio-economic change (Graham and Halsey, 1993; Marshall, 1995). Changing understandings of the pastoral responses most appropriate to the needs of women therefore serve as a prime example of pastoral/practical theology's revision of its priorities away from models of amelioration or crisis management towards the promotion of more proactive strategies of social change and political intervention (Graham, 1990).

The Subject of Care

Postmodern perspectives portray the self as a subject-in-relation, whose identity is forged within the complex interplay of economic, cultural and political factors. Contemporary pastoral/practical theology is gradually revising its own implicit ideals of the person to encompass such contexts. The subject of care is shifting from that of a self-actualized individual for whom care functions primarily at times of crisis towards one of a person in need of nurture and support as she or he negotiates a complexity of moral and theological challenges in a rapidly-changing economic and social context (Pattison, 1993).

The task of care is thus to equip individuals and communities with the resources by which they might respond to such complexity – be it in the form of changing conditions of work, citizenship, relationships or gender roles. In this respect, Lyall's emphasis on counselling as facilitating the stories by which we learn to locate ourselves and make sense of our world emerges as one strategy for nourishing a sense of personal identity within a wider complex of cultural, religious and political factors. However, such a model may be as much about disturbing as establishing a sense of security and locatedness, given the complexity of human experience and identity:

> The important notion is not to do away with the conflict but to utilize it to create opportunities for communities to engage in theological reflection about what it means to be an inclusive and meaningful faith community in a complex world. Congregations fractured by the issues of class, race, sexual orientation, or gender need opportunities to enter into moral discourse and not merely to dismiss those with whom they disagree.   (Marshall, 1995:175–6)

Conclusion

The preceding issues reflect signs of restlessness and dissatisfaction with conventional wisdom within pastoral/practical theology, and a search for new, more inclusive paradigms. The practice of pastoral care has been central to the disciplinary identity of pastoral/practical theology; but a central concern in much of the contemporary literature is a search for an adequate *definition*. The dominance of therapeutically-derived models of care is being displaced by a re-discovery of wider horizons: pastoral activity as entailing liturgy, preaching, Christian nurture, social action, community formation, spiritual direction as well as crisis counselling. Such a shift from *pastoral care* to *pastoral practice* will be a recurrent theme of this book.

A greater diversity of pastoral practice also broadens prevailing notions of the *methods* of pastoral ministry. The use of secular therapies founded on methods and objectives of humanist self-actualization is supplemented by more symbolic and sacramental models. Whilst the pastoral conversation in the form of one-to-one interview may appropriately be considered a legitimate form of pastoral encounter (confession, spiritual direction or pastoral counselling), other forms of corporate practice – most especially in liturgical and ritual forms – may also be seen as the occasion of healing, reconciliation, support and induction.

The emphasis on a diversity of practices also challenges the primacy of such activities as the exclusive domain of the ordained (male) pastor. The gathered community may also be the *agent* of Christian practice, either in its enactment of ritual functions, or by its emphasis on the shared ministry of the laity. However, there may still be proper scope for specialist ministries, and this raises questions of how pastors, lay and ordained, might be selected and trained, and what might constitute definitive bodies of *knowledge* by which their actions and values are guided.

I have also identified considerable equivocation concerning the proper *locus* of Christian pastoral activity. There is concern that pastoral care became privatized under modernity, both in the over-individualistic emphasis of humanistic psychotherapies and in the bracketing of religious and theological values out of secular care. Accordingly, there are calls to relocate the focus of care back into the communal context of the regular gathered Christian congregation. However, this also raises the question of the responsibility of the Christian Church for the wider world; is pastoral ministry merely about building up the faithful, or is there, as many contemporary writers suggest, also a wider agenda of social justice? It may also be important to note that 'lay ministry' can be interpreted either as inducting church members into ecclesial roles and offices, or as facilitating Christians to exercise faithful vocation in their 'secular' life and work.

Finally, the *aims and objectives* of pastoral care have been fundamentally questioned. Is the aim of care the amelioration of existential and personal distress and trouble, or the pursuit of proactive projects to establish social justice? Such a dichotomy may in fact be establishing a false distinction between broadly 'pastoral' or 'prophetic' ministries; but a number of writers are seeking to challenge the dominance of a broadly curative model of 'crisis-management' in favour of perspectives which seek to ground the functions of ministry in wider understandings of Christian formation (Pattison, 1993:199). For such models, the aim of care is to build up the believer to exercise an effective ministry in the world, or to define and nurture an image of 'Christian perfection' by which moral and social responsibility can be guided. However, if the Church is to perceive its pastoral role in terms of programmes of social intervention, in whatever form, the question remains as to the normative values by which such campaigns for justice and change are guided. Will such pastoral/prophetic action reflect humanistic models of universal reason and progress; or more distinctive visions of Christian hope and obligation?

My survey of the shifting paradigms of pastoral/practical theology has highlighted a move towards a diversification of practices to include sacramental as well as therapeutic and clinical models, a reclamation of the moral and normative nature of care and a shift towards Christian formation within the community of faith as well as amelioration of individual distress. In Chapter 3, I will examine the proposition, current amongst many pastoral/ practical theologians, that the changing priorities of postmodern pastoral care actually represent not a break with past tradition, but a recovery and reaffirmation of Christian roots. But such perennial pastoral functions may still require reinterpretation for a postmodern age. Current tensions in the literature reveal shifting paradigms in which old certainties surrounding appropriate knowledge, authoritative agency, normative personhood and ultimate ends are undergoing transformation and may require not a return to premodern axioms but a forging of new programmes out of the old. However, there is still a major problem concerning the role of the historic narratives of the Christian faith in informing purposeful action, and the relationship of the inherited tradition to the changing context that confronts every new generation.

In a lecture to the Clinical Theology Association on the future of Christian pastoral counselling, Gordon Oliver contrasted the metaphors of 'boundary' and 'horizon' and suggested that the latter is a more appropriate, inclusive and liberating perspective by which Christians may orientate their visions of mission and ministry (Oliver, 1991). For Oliver, 'boundaries' circumscribe the possible and the acceptable, suggesting security, the known and the achievable. 'Horizons', by contrast, indicate, and invite 'mystery, discovery, exploration, and the possibility of further encounters' (1991:9). The authentic practice of the Church necessarily occupies the tension between the two: 'the limitations of the present and the possibilities of transcendence' which are suggestive of a vision of ministry and pastoral care 'that relates to boundaries as if they were horizons' (1991:9).

I find the twin images of boundaries and horizons very evocative in relation to a new vision for pastoral theology. The cultural, economic and intellectual shifts of contemporary society present Christian theology with new *horizons* of pluralism and diversity. However, there is still a concern to uphold questions of value and to retain a clear identity for Christian ministry in the midst of such a changing and complex culture. The distinctiveness of a theological identity informing pastoral practice, the nature of the communities within which pastoral care is exercised and the principles on which human flourishing and social justice are to be founded, all suggest a concern for the *boundaries* by which purposeful and authentic Christian activity might be evaluated. However, my overview of contemporary pastoral theology in this chapter suggests that many of the old boundaries no longer seem adequate; in fact, they are perceived as exclusive, constraining and inappropriate. It remains to be seen whether a reiteration of historical tradition in pastoral theology will provide contemporary Christians with adequate sources and norms for the challenges of the postmodern world. In the context of radical shifts in Western culture in which consensus surrounding a likely vision of hope and obligation is fragmenting into many competing horizons, and the norms and values of Christian care are themselves under duress, the reconstructive task is complex.

Notes

1 There are some honourable exceptions. I shall discuss the work of Don Browning, and his response to the dilemmas of ethical pluralism, in Chapter 4, although I find him remaining within a largely modernist and rationalist framework. Edward Farley's most recent work also embraces postmodern themes of epistemological, political and ethical uncertainty. He uses the writings of the philosopher Emmanuel Levinas on *alterity* to resolve some of these issues (Farley, 1990).

2 However, this should not be used as an argument against offering training to such women as a means of enhancing their expertise, simply a reminder that such education and accreditation should be appropriate to the needs of women ministers, lay *and* ordained! See Parsons, 1993.

CHAPTER 3

Pastoral Theology in Historical Perspective

> Pastoral theology is a place where religious belief, tradition and practice meets contemporary experiences, questions and actions and conducts a dialogue which is mutually enriching, intellectually critical and practically transforming . . .
> Pastoral theology is more like living water than a tablet of stone. It is something that moves and changes shape, content and appearance, like a lake, over time. (Pattison, 1994a:9–10)

The disciplinary status of pastoral theology is problematic, in both historical and contemporary perspective. Some would deny it the privilege of 'discipline' at all, given that it appears to have little unity or coherence. Historically, pastoral theology has been portrayed as merely the practical and applied aspects of the more systematic (and therefore more intellectually weighty) fields of philosophical, biblical and doctrinal theology. Contemporary pastoral theologians have inherited a curriculum held together more by contingency than epistemological congruence, reflecting in its disparate sub-disciplines the pragmatic and essentially reactive tasks of pastoral ministry. Pastoral theology, especially in theological education, is therefore regarded as the study of the work of the professional (invariably ordained) pastor, as he or she dispenses care – shaped by a paradigm of individual counselling – to a passive and unreflective congregation.

In this chapter, I shall argue that although the emergence of modern pastoral theology in the academy is associated with the professionalization of clergy training, the emphasis on pastoral studies for the preparation of the ordained ministry represents a task-orientated approach which has specialized and circumscribed the discipline to its detriment. This narrowing of focus represents a surrender to an 'applied' model of activity which stresses technical and pragmatic skills at the expense of questions of ultimate value and objectives. However, a changing social and ecclesial context of moral and religious pluralism, the empowerment of the laity and the emancipation of women has prompted a reappraisal of the disciplinary status and operational scope of pastoral theology over the past twenty years. As a result, a simplistic rendering of the development of pastoral theology as 'applied theology' must be replaced by a more sophisticated attention to the changing identity, methods and foundations of the discipline over successive generations.

One central theme emerges from the following historical survey: that although pastoral theology has been cast in the role of the applied, the phenomenological and the practical, and has often been portrayed as abandoning theological rigour for the 'cheap grace' of secular psychotherapies, it never abandoned its search for a distinctive disciplinary identity, aware that the relationship between the *theory* of Christian tradition and theology could not be severed from the *practice* of enacted ministry and care. However, as I shall argue later, it proves more difficult to articulate an interpretative basis by which a satisfactory unity of theory and practice might be achieved, especially in the face of postmodern uncertainty.

Pastoral Theology in the Modern Era

Literature concerned with the nature and exercise of Christian pastoral ministry is as old as the activity itself. Since Gregory the Great's systematic account, *The Book of Pastoral Rule* (c. 590 CE), there has been an enduring tradition of pastoral 'manuals', identifying those tasks appropriate to the pastoral office and the personal qualities necessary to cultivate such responsibilities. Many of these works remained classics of clergy formation until relatively recently (Oden, 1984). The terrain of pastoral practice reflects those activities nominated by canon law or church rules: preaching, administering the sacraments, personal visiting, works of charity, teaching the faith and church government. There is evidence at particular historical periods of some of these tasks being exercised by lay people, and of personal prayer, reading of the Bible, acts of charity and mutual support in the faith being encouraged within a context of the priesthood of all believers. However, it is perhaps the unification of the pastor's various offices into the function of the ordained clergy that characterizes their persistent and enduring nature (McNeill, 1951; Clebsch and Jaekle, 1964; Oden, 1984).

Moral theology was traditionally the discipline which ordered all ministerial activities, especially within a Roman Catholic tradition which linked matters of individual cure of souls and church discipline to the right and proper administration of the sacraments. The priestly functions of hearing confession and administering absolution prepared the laity for receiving communion; but admission to the sacraments also defined the boundaries of the Body of Christ by only including those in good moral standing with the Church. However, the establishment of pastoral or practical theology and the codification of Christian ministry effected the divorce of pastoral and moral theology (Mahoney, 1987).

The beginnings of 'practical theology' (*praktische Theologie*) lie in the establishment of ministerial training in the German universities in the mid-eighteenth century. A rationalization of theological education took place by which a recognized syllabus with coherent elements emerged. This occurred primarily through the publication of the theological encyclopedia which sought to categorize theological texts according to their major emphasis, pertaining either to matters of dogma and belief or to practice and conduct. The boundary between theoretical and applied knowledge in theology was thus established, with the study of Scripture, doctrine and church history in one category, and the practical disciplines of ministry in the other (Farley, 1983:56–84).

Within the single discipline of practical theology were grouped the following sub-disciplines: homiletics (preaching); poimenics (pastoral care or the 'cure of souls' (Browning, 1983:10)); liturgics (public worship); jurisprudence (church government and discipline); and catechetics (education, usually of children). In principle it was understood that these various activities were indicative not just of the clerical or priestly office, but characteristic of the life and work of the whole Church. However, in practice, as Farley argues, these areas of church practice became narrowed into disciplines of clergy pedagogy (Farley, 1987:4). By the first quarter of the nineteenth century, the term 'practical theology' was coming to denote the various functions of ministry, whilst 'pastoral theology' indicated the more specific tasks of, in the classic definition, 'four pastoral functions of healing, sustaining, guiding, and reconciling' (Clebsch and Jaekle, 1964:79).

Schleiermacher

Friedrich Schleiermacher (1768–1834) is responsible for what many regard as the definitive categorization of theological studies in the academy, and is the theologian from whom several significant trends in modern pastoral and practical theology can be traced. Schleiermacher set about providing a coherent rationale with the publication in 1811 of his theological encyclopedia, *A Brief Outline on the Study of Theology* (Schleiermacher, 1966). This was essentially an attempt to re-establish the scientific status of theology and its epistemological claims by locating the study of theology in the service of the Christian Church. The community of faith was primary for Schleiermacher, serving as the critical point of reference for the truth-claims and relevance of the scholarly study of theology.

Schleiermacher argued that theology could be systematized into different constituent disciplines according to their intellectual and philosophical status and their role in serving all forms of Christian ministry. He therefore categorized theological studies into three sub-disciplines: philosophical, historical and practical theology (see Figure 1).

Figure 1 *Schleiermacher's Theological Schema*

Branch of Theology		Sub-disciplines	Function
PHILOSOPHICAL	'Root'	Apologetics, polemics	Normative
HISTORICAL	'Body'	Exegesis, dogmatics Church history	Descriptive
PRACTICAL	'Crown'	'Techniques for maintaining and perfecting the Church'	Prescriptive

This characterization reflects a classical hierarchy of knowledge, the pinnacle being 'pure' or philosophical enquiry, out of which 'applied' and practical understanding could emerge. However, by uniting the various sub-categories of theology under the general rubric of ecclesial practice, Schleiermacher represented a departure from previous models. He argued for the essential unity of theory and practice, by stating that the practical should be given preferential status in assessing the authenticity and validity of the truth-claims of theological discourse. Thus it is the congregational reality that serves as the validating norm for Christian theology, and not simply abstract or ideal philosophical principles.

It is in this insistence upon practice as the outworking and enactment of the claims of the Christian tradition that we can see Schleiermacher struggling to articulate a model for the relationship of theory to practice, history to modernity, general to specific, and reflection to action. Ultimately, there can be no qualitative difference between these dualisms (beyond, perhaps, a heuristic one), because they are all simply forms of Christian faith and action at specific times and places of history. Theology as a discipline is the reflection on various records of Christian faith throughout history, be they enshrined and encoded in historical texts or available in contemporary actions and behaviours.

However, although Schleiermacher emphasized the integrated nature of theological studies, and the serious contribution of practical theology to the academy, it is clear that he regarded it as of itself intellectually inert. In Schleiermacher's terms, the exercise of Christian leadership and ministry is an important field in which the truths of philosophical and historical enquiry must prove their bearing and relevance. The practical situation has neither autonomy nor power to define or determine the nature of philo-sophical or historical enquiry, which are understood as givens. Although in theory Schleiermacher's system offers practice an equal partnership, in reality its status is ultimately subordinate to the fixed truths and established modes of enquiry and verification of the other two sub-disciplines in his theological schema:

> He recognizes fully, as had Augustine and Anselm and others before him, that there is no true understanding apart from believing. *Credo ut intelligam.* Believing affects thinking, not to constrict or shackle it . . . but to enlighten and empower it. Faith gives reason reasons for being. Nevertheless, what Schleiermacher fails to notice or understand in any effective way is that if believing affects thinking, practice influences theory . . . although Schleiermacher knows, and knows thoroughly, that thought itself can be transformative, he nevertheless does not come to realize that life itself can be illuminative. In a word, his own life and thought

did not bring him to a̶ ystematic understanding of the inter-
pretive dimension̶   (Burkhart, 1983:52–3)

The n̶   stian pastoral ministry are perceived
by̶   ̶al, derived from abstract philo-
                    ̶ugh history. The immediate context
                    ̶is deemed irrelevant to the formation and
                    ̶ogy. It might therefore be designated as *applied*
            ̶, whereby pastoral ministry is the outworking, rather than
       ̶e source, of theological understanding. Furthermore, if the
purpose of theology is to 'service' the congregation, Schleiermacher
fails to articulate any critical criterion, or independent standard
of truth, by which the nature and mission of the Church itself may
be assessed. Thus there is no potential for the Church or practical
theology to learn from secular or non-theological repositories of
information.

Notwithstanding, there is an essential unity to Schleiermacher's
vision of theology, because he regards the validity of the philosophical and historical dimensions of the discipline as only effective
and authenticated in historical contexts of practice. Schleiermacher's contribution must be placed in the context of his claim that
faith must be rooted in, and therefore ultimately integrated with,
human history.[1] Theology is not a separate category of experience
or knowledge, but a resource for faithful living, carrying its
own particular perspectives and practical values. Practice is thus
afforded a central position in Schleiermacher's theological schema,
but as the application, rather than the generating source, of theological norms and truth-claims. The extent to which the pastoral
encounter might be of itself theologically disclosive remained a
persistent undercurrent within the discipline until the present day.
However, for 150 years after Schleiermacher, his legacy dominated:
as the discipline in the service of Christian ministry, the focus of
practical theology was more or less exclusively upon the activities
of the ordained pastor.

Pastoral Theology as a Science of Ministry

Throughout the nineteenth and early twentieth centuries, therefore, in Europe and North America, pastoral theology came
to mean a body of literature pertaining to the office and function
of the pastor. The tradition of the pastor's manual thus continued

to dominate pastoral literature into the middle of the twentieth century. The discipline had a recognized place within the seminary or university, but its intellectual standing was regarded as derivative, secondary and applied in relation to the 'fundamentals' of systematics, philosophy and doctrine. By the end of the nineteenth century, the emphasis had turned to practical advice to young clergy from experienced pastors on church procedures, pastoral conduct and other handy tips. The plethora of 'hints and helps' literature[2] effectively severed the connection between systematic and doctrinal theology, and the practical conduct of Christian ministry in the world. Furthermore, it bolstered the clericalism of Christian churches by excluding the exercise of lay vocation and the self-understanding of the whole Church from its definition of pastoral agency.

This phenomenon was not unconnected to the sociological position of the churches. From the middle of the nineteenth century, the clergy were experiencing an erosion of their status in the community, owing partly to the rise of rival professionals in medicine, government and business, and partly to the beginnings of a (middle-class) decline in church attendance. Some of the trends within pastoral ministry in the early twentieth century, such as the foundations of clearer patterns of training and accreditation, the systematization of parish work and the search for the 'scientific' status of pastoral ministry, were attempts to bolster the professional standing of the clergy at a time of significant social change.

As a result, pastoral theology at this time regarded its task as the induction of the ordained ministry, especially in the Protestant churches, into a kind of pragmatic expertise, where the axioms of ministry were elevated to scientific and specialist status. Washington Gladden offered a typical definition of pastoral theology in the Preface to his book, *The Christian Pastor and the Working Church*, published in 1898. Gladden, an exponent of the Social Gospel movement, is recognized as valuing the 'priesthood of all believers' and regarding pastoral ministry as the work of the whole Church, within which the pastor serves as a democratic leader and educator. However, he was sceptical of terminology which designates as theological an activity which he clearly believed is simply to do with the application of Christian truths to human situations:

> This book is intended to cover the field of what is known as Pastoral Theology. The technical phrase is not well chosen: theology, by any

proper sense of the word is not connoted by it. It deals with the work of the Christian pastor and the Christian church. Its subject is applied Christianity. It is concerned with the ways and means by which the truth of the Gospel of Christ is brought to bear upon the lives of men, in the administration of the local congregation. It seeks to show the pastor how he may order his own life and the life of his flock so that their joint service may be most effective in extending the Kingdom of God on earth. It is not wholly a matter of methods and machinery, for the spirit in which the work is done is the main concern; but it is a study of the life of the church as it is manifested in the community where it is planted.   (Gladden, 1898:v)

In Britain, Clement Rogers, Professor of Pastoral Theology at King's College, London in the years prior to the First World War, effected a notion of his chosen discipline that seems to owe much to an English tradition of social empiricism. The contents of his book, published in 1912, emphasize the scientific skill and precision with which the office of pastor must be conducted. The focus is firmly on the work of the clergy, enlightened by the principles of empiricism and rationalism, proceeding via ordered observation and criticism towards the aim of 'searching out by what spiritual laws the healing of souls may be furthered' (Rogers, 1912:34). However, despite claims for pastoral theology to be guided by such scientific norms, there was never any intention that these should be related to systematic, philosophical or historical theology, which were assumed to be completely separate disciplines.

Pastoral theology at the turn of the century was therefore aware of the value of 'secular' sources of knowledge and of the need for Christian pastors to respond in relevant and appropriate fashion to the society around them. In particular, a search for scientific and empirical resources to serve as practical and prescriptive tools in the furtherance of the pastoral task led many into an engagement with the new psychologies, psychiatry and psychoanalytic theory. The status of such new therapies in guiding the aims and ends of pastoral practice, and their compatibility with the traditional insights of Christian theology, thus became a major matter of contention.

Pastoral Theology and the Modern Psychologies

During the early years of the twentieth century in Europe and North America, a variety of new psychologies and psychotherapies began to come to prominence, amongst them Freudian psychoanalysis, the psychology of religion and medical psychiatry (Holifield, 1983; Fuller, 1986). The work of William James in the psychology of religion and John Dewey in religious education contributed to the growing interest in the modern psychologies in the United States and Britain. Popular accounts of Freud's work were beginning to appear in the United States during the early 1900s. The enthusiasm for these new disciplines was widespread, and the Christian churches were no exception to this trend. Many working pastors became interested in these new sciences of personality, and observed their potential benefits in the service of Christian ministry. A cluster of networks and associations were established during the first decade of the twentieth century, devoted to the greater deployment and synthesis of Christian ministry and the modern psychologies.

An early example was founded in 1906 by Elwood Worcester, the minister of Emmanuel Episcopal Church in Boston, Massachusetts. Like Gladden, Worcester was an exponent of the Social Gospel, but a growing conviction that the churches should seek to promote mental health as well as social justice led him to initiate lectures and surgeries on the cure of nervous and psychological illness. The *Emmanuel Movement* established a precedent in its use of new psychologies and therapeutic techniques and in its alliance between religious and medical professionals.

The various subsequent configurations of pastoral and therapeutic practitioners in dialogue came to be known as the *religion and health movement*, which has exerted considerable influence upon pastoral theology in the United States, and to a lesser degree Britain, to the present day. However, the relationship between religious ministry (chiefly Christian, but involving Jewish participants as well) and psychotherapeutic perspectives was neither a straightforward nor a singular phenomenon. Nor was it a case of ministers abandoning theological value-commitments in favour of embracing secular theories of human development and healing, as some later commentators were to claim. The story of the relationship between religion and health is one of constant debate concerning the respective truth-claims of pastoral and therapeutic practices, and the significance and relevance of the traditional formulations of Christian theology in the pursuit of human healing.

Clinical Pastoral Education

As well as advancing dialogue between religion and medicine for the working parish clergy, the new psychologies also established themselves within the field of pastoral training and clergy formation. Several schemes emerged during the early 1920s, most notably a scheme which began at Worcester State Hospital, Massachusetts, in the summer of 1925. The two figures behind this were Anton Boisen, a Congregational minister and hospital chaplain, and Richard Cabot, a psychiatrist and a Unitarian. Cabot had recently published a paper advocating the exposure of theological students to a period of clinical placement in hospital; Boisen's own experience of mental breakdown had convinced him of the efficacy of psychiatric medicine in the service of the 'cure of souls'. Together they formed an alliance, founding the Council for the Clinical Training of Theological Students in 1930, through which the Clinical Pastoral Education (CPE) movement came into being.

Clinical Pastoral Education was from its inception a divided movement. Cabot was part of a faction which believed that mental illness was physical and somatic in origin; this contrasted with Boisen's identification with proto-psychoanalytic concepts like guilt, repression and the dynamics of the unconscious. As a result, Boisen had split with the Council for Clinical Training by 1938, eventually basing himself in New York and collaborating with Helen Flanders Dunbar, a Viennese-trained psychoanalyst (Holifield, 1983:231–49; Stokes, 1985: Chapter 3).[3] Boisen argued that pastoral ministry had a crucial role to play in the treatment of mental illness, as psychopathology was often the expression of spiritual malaise. In this respect, he underlined the non-physical nature of mental illness, establishing the autonomy of the psychological realm and the importance of non-physical factors – familial, psychodynamic and cultural – in the development of psychiatric distress and disorder. Boisen's emphasis on what he termed the 'living human document' (Nouwen, 1969; Holifield, 1983:244–7) at the heart of the pastoral encounter expressed his conviction that events and situations could be regarded as akin to 'texts' in their potential for interpretation, revelation and disclosure. This was further developed via a model of educational supervision using 'verbatim' accounts, whereby the student would carefully record the details of a visit or pastoral conversation and reflect on it within the context of a session with a tutor.

Another tension within the movement concerned the role of CPE within pastoral education and training. Cabot regarded the clinical placement as instrumental for the development of the ordinand's professional competence, rather like medical training. In contrast, Boisen and Dunbar advocated what would be regarded today as a 'client-centred' perspective, allowing students to understand the experience and causes of mental illness in all its immediacy and concretion by directly exposing them to human pastoral need. It was believed that this would elicit deeper understanding of the existential meaning and significance of psychopathology.

Clinical Pastoral Education remains influential, and seminaries and colleges throughout the world offer programmes of hospital and other clinical settings in which theological students can prepare for pastoral ministry. As can be seen in the differences between Boisen and Cabot, its clinical emphasis offered the potential for prompting a renewed perspective of the pastoral and clinical as primary material for a theological hermeneutics, but this tended to be lost in favour of its value as a tool in ministerial training. The loss may be partly attributed to the continued hegemony of the clergy and of the dominance of clergy formation within theological education. So long as the latter was understood as a process of theological apprenticeship, of inducting and socializing clergy into the time-honoured and established principles and habits of their elders and betters, pastoral experience was unable to become a sphere of disclosure of human and theological truths and remained a field for the testing and application of competence in prescribed patterns and offices.

The crucible of psychiatric healing forged a debate within pastoral theology concerning the significance of the emerging relationship between religion and health, and in particular the implications of the increasingly widespread adoption of psycho-therapeutic principles and methods by Christian pastors. Debates turned upon the relative status of theological values expressed in traditional practices, texts and doctrinal formulations of the churches, and whether these were distinct from the models of human growth and healing portrayed by the newer therapies. Although many Christian pastors turned to the modern psychologies in the middle years of the twentieth century merely as a means of enhancing clergy efficiency, with little examination of the underlying world-views of such therapeutic models, there is plenty of evidence that in other quarters a critical dialogue took place that was vigorous and sophisticated (Holifield, 1983; Stokes, 1985).

The Consolidation of Pastoral Counselling

The period 1930–1960 can be said to have been the heyday of psychological influence upon pastoral theology, especially in the popularity of pastoral counselling which drew upon a variety of psychotherapeutic perspectives, both analytic and humanistic.

During the 1940s the work of Carl Rogers (1902–86) became increasingly influential. Rogers advocated a model of *eductive* counselling, in which moral exhortation and explicit guidance were eschewed in favour of a humanistic psychotherapy which emphasized the integrity of the client in determining the nature of the counselling relationship. The role of the counsellor was seen as providing a supportive and non-judgemental environment of 'unconditional positive regard' and 'empathy' (Rogers 1942, 1951, 1961). Rogers had been brought up in a Presbyterian home, but rejected what he regarded as the legalism of Protestant theology, whilst retaining a view of human nature as inherently virtuous and capable of 'self-actualization'. Echoing existentialist and psychoanalytic perspectives, Rogers argued that society imposed repressive norms on the individual, who could only be liberated to ultimate growth through self-acceptance.

Rogerian therapy was received by many Christian ministers as an attractive antidote to theological traditions which over-stressed human sinfulness, self-abnegation and Divine judgement. The power of unconditional love, and the absolute freedom of the client to find paths of growth and forgiveness via the therapeutic relationship, all appeared to resonate with Christian values, yet to articulate them in terms accessible to modern culture. Despite its popularity, however, writers were already subjecting the claims of such non-directive counselling to criticism. The insistence of many pastoral theologians on not abandoning theological insights and on interrogating the underlying truth-claims of the pastoral counselling movement reflects an enduring wish to affirm the religious, or spiritual, dimensions of health and healing. Thus, the popularity of eductive counselling never completely eclipsed other models of pastoral care, often originating in traditions of pastoral discipline, or resting upon the corporate life of the faith community. Much writing of the time sought a critical and considered synthesis between theology and psychology (Dicks, 1944; Day Williams, 1961; Oglesby, 1969) and explored the nature of the ultimate values embodied in pastoral care (Halmos, 1965; Wise, 1966).

A prominent figure in the religion and health movement in Britain was Leslie Dixon Weatherhead (1893–1976), who worked to evaluate the significance for Christian pastoral ministry of the work of Sigmund Freud, Carl Gustav Jung and Alfred Adler. He introduced their work to a wide audience, and was responsible for the integration of an element of psychological training into theological education for Methodist ministers. His work was characterized by a thorough and extensive knowledge of many psychological schools, combined with a willingness to entertain psychological critiques of religion (Weatherhead, 1929, 1951). He argued that 'neurotic' expressions of religious faith were a distortion of the Gospel, and that practices such as confession, liturgy and prayer could be harnessed in the service of psychological healing. His emphasis was therefore upon achieving a critical synthesis of religious concepts and practices with newer therapies. He argued that the existential insights and cures of the modern psychologies could be integrated with theological themes of sin, forgiveness and salvation.

Weatherhead's approach may be distinguished from other British writers on religion and psychology during this period, in that he seemed concerned with the critical interpretation of the significance of the modern psychologies for the human condition, rather than their appropriation in the service of more effective pastoral ministry.[4] This perhaps reflected the more 'popular' emphasis of his work, aiming to make therapeutic theories and practices more accessible to the ordinary Christian.

To understand the adoption of the new psychologies by pastoral counsellors as total surrender to the hegemony of secular therapies is to misrepresent the intentions and faith of many of the protagonists, and to ignore the theological tradition and context within which the relationship between the modern psychologies and pastoral theology was conducted. There were undoubtedly factors of sociological and theological influence at work: the secularization of society meant that many clergy felt lost for a clear role, and believed that the adoption of the new psychologies would win them respectability and relevance.

However, there were also pastors and theologians concerned that the Christian Church should live obediently and authentically in the contemporary world, and they regarded the insights and contributions of the new psychologies and psychotherapies as nothing short of providential in providing a relevant and accessible language by which human wholeness and salvation could be effected.[5] This was entirely consistent with a liberal Protestant tradition characterized by its willingness to entertain the insights and trends of modernity, by its sense of God at work in everyday and immanent events and by a belief in human progress and the powers of reason. Theologians and pastoral counsellors therefore entered into dialogue with psychiatrists and physicians in the belief that, through such therapeutic practices and theories, God was revealing new truths about human suffering and its amelioration to the present generation.

> Religion and Health pioneers gave first allegiance to the gospel of Christ; they adapted the findings of Freud and his followers *in the service of ministry*. Grounded firmly in evangelical, liberal faith, they were not persons to flit from one passing theological or psychological fad to another in search of an elusive identity or security. Rather, with Christian purpose sure, they quickly identified and freely explored the significance for the Christian faith of the work of one of the most outstanding thinkers of the twentieth century.   (Stokes, 1985:149)

Tillich and the Correlation of Theology and Psychology

Paul Tillich (1886–1965) was of considerable influence through his work on the theology of pastoral care. He was an enthusiastic advocate of Freudian psychoanalysis, and directed his attention to the means by which the insights of depth psychology into the human condition might be reconciled with the traditional perspectives of the Christian faith (Tillich, 1948, 1951, 1952, 1957, 1963). Tillich pursued a fairly orthodox academic career whilst in Germany, but achieved immense popular celebrity status through the publication of *The Shaking of the Foundations* (1948), following his flight to the United States in 1933. Tillich pursued his interest in religion and psychology under the auspices of the New York Psychology Group, a symposium of psychoanalysts, psychiatrists, theologians, pastoral educators and clergy who assembled regularly between 1941 and 1945 to debate the inter-face between their various disciplines (Stokes, 1985). Tillich also contributed to the journal *Pastoral Psychology* after 1950, in which he pursued his examination of the congruence of psychology and Protestant theology (Holifield, 1985:328–33).

In his model of 'critical correlation' Tillich sought to establish a model whereby theology could address the changing circumstances of human history. He argued that the existential and cultural ques-tions of each new generation formed the subject-matter to which Christian theology must address itself.

> Being human means asking the question of one's own being and living under the impact of the answers given to this question. And conversely, being human means receiving answers to the question of one's own being and asking questions under the impact of the answers. In using the method of correlation, systematic theology proceeds in the following way: it makes an analysis of the human situation out of which the existential questions arise, and it demon-strates that the symbols used in the Christian message are the answers to these questions.   (Tillich, 1951:70)

Tillich argued that theological doctrines could be integrated with psychological insights, thus rendering the Christian message accessible to a secular world. He characterized God as 'Ground of Being'; reinterpreted the Protestant doctrine of justification in terms of a 'power of acceptance'; and articulated notions of courage, freedom, anxiety and guilt as psychological realities with transcendent and theological dimensions (Tillich, 1959, quoted in Stokes, 1985:136–41).

Pastoral counsellors saw Tillich's work as an affirmation that their everyday encounters with human struggles for healing and personal growth could reveal the greater themes of salvation, grace and 'ultimate concern'. Tillich always regarded theological revelation as a 'given' truth, and pastoral practice as the outworking of Divine solutions to existential and psychological troubles. However, his model assumes that the values of theology and psychology point to one single convergent, and ultimately Christian, Truth. Although consistent with a providential view of revelation mediated by the highest achievements of human reason, the risk is of refusing any distinction between Christian truth-claims and the faith community, and secular culture.

The claims of theology, and the conversation with psychology, are also singularly disembodied and abstracted from actual pastoral care. Tillich correlated psychological theory with systematic and dogmatic theology, once again divorcing theological formulation from the living human situation. It is therefore significant that one of the chief critics of Tillich within pastoral theology was Seward Hiltner, who acknowledged his indebtedness to Tillich, but also endeavoured to return to the emphasis of Boisen and the pastoral educationalists upon the concrete and immediate 'human document', and to reinstate the field of pastoral activity as the proper focus of critical study.

Hiltner and the Theology of Pastoral Care

Seward Hiltner (1909–84) spent most of his long career at the forefront of pastoral theology, working in an academic context and on the boundaries between pastoral counselling and psychotherapy. Hiltner developed some of the earliest courses in pastoral counselling at Union Seminary, New York, became the first executive secretary of the Federal Commission on Religion and Health in 1937, and was a member of the New York Psychology Group. Under the influence of Tillich's model of critical correlation, Hiltner endeavoured to articulate the theological nature of pastoral ministry as a process of dialogue between the revealed tradition and the questions and insights emerging from any given pastoral encounter. He thus moved beyond Tillich's position towards one which anticipates the 'revised critical correlation' of David Tracy and others. Hiltner maintained that Christian truth is never complete in itself, but remains to be informed by the revelation of God within the immanence of the present situation:

> Not everything is yet clear about Tillich's use of the key term 'correlation' to describe his theological method. Plainly he intends by it to establish theological relevance; theology does not talk in a corner by itself but speaks to the vital questions men ask. Thus he says to the theologian that culture and life cannot be neglected, and to the ordinary man that faith has a message for him. But to what extent is correlation a two-way method? . . . We believe that a full

two-way street is necessary in order to describe theological method. If we hold that theology is always assimilation of the faith, not just the abstract idea of the faith apart from its reception, then it becomes necessary to say that culture may find answers to questions raised by faith as well as to assert that faith has answers to questions raised by culture.   (Hiltner, 1958:223)

Theology is therefore perceived by Hiltner as not a final or absolute *kerygma*, but always open to new insights from contemporary experience:

In the process of helping and the never-ending self-reflection that is a vital part of the helping and the inquiry the shepherd is aware that the theology – as the reception and assimilation of faith – is always in the making and never finished. (Hiltner, 1958:222 n. 7)

In *Preface to Pastoral Theology*, published in 1958, Hiltner attempted to delineate the scope and nature of pastoral theology. It is possible to discern the following themes: the accommodation of pastoral theology to secular theories, especially psychodynamic theories of the self; the relationship of theology to pastoral practice; and the scope of the field of activities identified as 'pastoral'. Hiltner stressed the potential of the pastoral encounter as a place of disclosure for the 'ultimate dimensions' of meaning: instead of theological tradition determining the normative principles for pastoral care, the pastoral sphere would provide the raw material out of which theological formulations can develop.

In *Preface to Pastoral Theology* Hiltner insisted upon the primary status of pastoral theology, and therefore challenged the notion that the practical situation has no bearing upon the content of the theological reflection. He argued that pastoral theology was a legitimate branch of theology, but qualitatively and methodologically different from biblical, systematic or historical disciplines, which he defined as 'logic-centred' rather than 'operational' disciplines (Hiltner, 1958:28). All information proceeding from the 'operational' work of shepherding, communicating or organizing constituted its subject matter, just as a text of Scripture or a doctrine of the Church would be of concern to biblical or systematic scholars:

Within the whole body of divinity what is distinctive about the operation-centred inquiries such as pastoral theology is that their theological conclusions, or theory or basic principles, emerge from

reflection primarily upon acts or events or functions from a particular
perspective.   (Hiltner, 1958:20)

Hiltner thereby effected one important shift in pastoral theology by
transferring attention onto the activity of shepherding (or caring),
rather than the individual exercising the pastoral office. The effect
of the 'hints and helps' literature had been to fuse the *activity* with
the *agent*, so that pastoral theology was synonymous with the work
of the ordained minister. Hiltner broke this connection by emphasizing not just the functions of shepherding, communicating and
organizing, but also the normative quality of pastoral activity,
which he terms 'tender and solicitous concern' (1958:18). Thus
pastoral ministry was defined in terms of particular 'perspectives'
or aims and ends: ministry as directed towards a Church that cares,
communicates and is embodied.

However, this is still an inadequate system of categorization,
owing to Hiltner's failure to develop his remarks about the *theological*
status of shepherding, communicating and organizing. Hiltner's
focus never transcended the phenomenology of the 'operations' of
ministry, and although he glimpsed the theological implications
of practice, he never made them explicit. In his concern to render
the practical, shepherding sphere the primary datum of pastoral
theology, Hiltner failed to develop any system of critical engagement
with more theoretical resources or questions of theological values
and formulations. He neglected to question the aims and ends of
shepherding; the relationship of contemporary to historic practice;
and how norms of practice were integrated with models of the
Church's own self-understanding or theological apprehensions of
the nature of God. Hiltner's pastoral theology promised to enquire
into Christians' exercise of solicitous concern for one another and
the world; but did not extend to theological interpretations and
manifestations of the revelation of God's purposes for the world.

Therefore, although Hiltner articulated the potential of pastoral
practices to disclose theological meaning, his system remained
undeveloped. He took for granted the fundamental objectives of the
Christian ministry, and so failed to interrogate the values by which
the historical offices of caring, communicating and organizing are
guided. He thus inevitably circumscribed the immediate, practical
and the interpretative response into a task-oriented empiricism.

Reactions to Liberalism

Dissatisfaction with the 'eductive' tradition was growing through-out the 1960s, fuelled by writers from the Protestant Evangelical tradition, such as Wayne Oates and Jay Adams. They were concerned, albeit with different emphases, to explore the bearing of classical biblical themes and perspectives upon psychotherapeutic notions of healing, human potential and growth.[6]

Another reaction to the liberal tradition in pastoral theology, and one which sought theological norms for pastoral practice in the 'neo-orthodox' legacy of Karl Barth, was represented by the work of Eduard Thurneysen (1888–1974). Neo-orthodoxy sought to return to the theology of the Bible and the Protestant Reformers which emphasized the absolute authority of a transcendent God who could only be apprehended through the vehicle of God's own self-revelation and not the exercise of human reason. Humanity was subject to the judgement of God and dependent on grace to achieve enlightenment and salvation (Thurneysen, 1962).

Although Thurneysen had considerable knowledge of Freudian psychoanalysis, he eschewed secular models of healing and therapy, preferring to regard authentic pastoral care as emanating from the Christian community. Pastoral care relies upon the Word of God, which is God's self-revelation in Jesus Christ, as witnessed to in Scripture. Pastoral care is effectively *kerygma*, or proclamation, by word or deed; the pastor can listen in a pastoral relationship, but only insofar as such listening clarifies and informs the subsequent and necessary act of exhortation. The exposition of scriptural truths as the guiding norms of pastoral practice and human fulfilment, understood as relationship with God, is the chief end of pastoral ministry.

Thurneysen emphasized the authority and primacy of the grace of God in effecting healing; but in so doing, he denied the possibility of God's revelation occurring through secular insights, or beyond the boundaries of church membership. Only the exercise of preaching the Word could constitute disclosive or revelatory theological truth; Christian faith was restricted to receipt of a narrowly *kerygmatic* communication, to the exclusion of practical discipleship in the world. Such a perspective is effectively therefore another form of applied theology, in which the homiletic function of pastoral practice is elevated above all other models, as is the authority and function of the pastor as privileged interpreter of the Word.

A similar reaction to the perceived evacuation of theological norms from pastoral counselling emerged in Britain through the work of Frank Lake (1914–82), the founder of the Clinical Theology Association (Lake, 1966, 1978; Peters, 1986). Lake had received a medical education and later studied psychiatry and psychotherapy, and grounded his ideas in various versions of object-relations psychoanalysis. He placed great emphasis on the existential convergence of psychodynamic catharsis and spiritual healing. He was responsible for initiating Clinical Theology workshops and programmes within ministerial pastoral studies training in British theological colleges. However, Lake has been criticized for his uncritical use of Scripture and the reliance of the psychic and spiritual healing process upon the supernatural intervention of a mystical healing Christ-figure. In this respect, therefore, Clinical Theology did not exhibit the mutual, revisionist and critical integration of psychology and theology sought by more liberal traditions (Peters, 1986).

Thomas C. Oden's *Kerygma and Counselling* (1966) adopted a neo-orthodox position in arguing that the revealed truths of the Word of God in Jesus Christ and Scripture constituted the substance of such values. His concern was to recapture the distinctively Christian identity of pastoral ministry, through a restatement of enduring patterns of care – administration of the sacraments, preaching, confession and penitence – which he believed had been devalued by the preference for counselling and secular therapeutic techniques. Furthermore, he challenged what he perceived to be the value-neutrality of pastoral care, by arguing that authentic pastoral relationships must contain an encounter with the demands of the Gospel, a *kerygma* which confronts pastor and client with the distinctive truth-claims of God's revelation in Jesus.

Oden cast his call for the re-establishment of pastoral identity in terms of his own disillusionment with contemporary pastoral care, which had allowed the modern secular psychotherapies and psychologies to eclipse older classic traditions of Christian pastoral care. He accused pastoral theology as follows: 'Pastoral theology has become in many cases little more than an accommodation to the most current psychological trends (often . . . a pop expression of a bad psychology to begin with), with only the slenderest accountability to the classical pastoral tradition' (Oden, 1980:13). Although Oden claimed to seek a synthesis between history and modernity, he was more concerned to reintroduce the classical orthodoxy as authoritative and normative rather than exemplary and indicative. In 'Recovering Lost Identity', Oden records his own intellectual odyssey: from the neo-orthodox roots of *Kerygma and Counselling* he pursued a number of different therapeutic models and philosophies before becoming disillusioned with what he regarded as the antinomian tendencies of secular psychologies. His later work therefore rejected the possibility of a correlative model, and in recent years his attentions have turned to the recovery and publication of classic texts of Christian pastoral care (Oden, 1984, 1987, 1989a, 1989b). He might therefore more appropriately be identified as offering a *premodern* rather than a *postmodern* solution: 'Oden has shown that Origen or Tertullian or Ambrose had some very valuable and interesting things to say about pastoral care; he has not shown how it would be valuable for the practice of a contemporary pastor to read Origen or Tertullian or Ambrose' (Mitchell, 1990:290). Oden's historicism fails to incarnate theology in the uniqueness of each historical era, which for the present day is to deny the transformation effected in our understanding of the human condition by the Reformation, the Enlightenment, the Industrial Revolution and the Holocaust; and the profound influences on human self-understanding of Marx, Darwin, Freud and Nietzsche. Oden's disavowal of the integrity of such an enterprise betrays his own value-commitments to a model of theological revelation that refuses to regard 'secular' knowledge as providential or disclosive.

The Changing Context for Pastoral Theology

By the 1970s, pastoral theologians were addressing the values and objectives at the heart of Christian ministry with greater intensity. A number of significant sociological and ecclesiastical trends compounded the complexity of the pastoral task, challenging predominant models of the pastoral agent as ordained and male, and of pastoral care as necessarily and exclusively effected within a church-related context. The self-identity of pastoral theology, its relationship to changing social and cultural trends, to its own tradition and to the nostrums of the modern psychologies, were therefore thrown even more sharply into relief. It was no longer possible to claim that any consensus existed about the nature of pastoral care, how it should be exercised, by whom, within what sort of church, its proper sphere, its relation to mission and social action, and the truth-claims upon which it rested. This led to a renewed search for an authoritative source of norms or prescriptive values that could guide Christian pastoral ministry in a pluralistic and changing society, and the guiding truth-claims which would give pastoral theology its distinctive character and purpose.

Sociological factors after 1945 decisively contributed to a changing climate in church and society. In Britain and the United States, the expansion of educational opportunities contributed to the emergence of a more articulate laity, many of whom were qualified in theology or the social sciences. The rise in popularity of the latter, and their establishment in higher education (from the 1940s in the United States and 1960s in Britain) contributed to a greater popular interest in social issues and in all aspects of therapy and psychology. This was the 'second wave' of adoption into North American society for psychoanalysis, and other branches of psychotherapy, such as the self-help and human potential movements and child psychology, also attained a more widespread popularity and currency (Holifield, 1985; Evans, 1961). More recent appraisals have affirmed the significance of social and ecclesial change, including the greater appropriation of psychotherapeutic perspectives in the churches, for shifts in the identity of pastoral theology (Dyson, 1983; Howe, 1984).

The development of welfare economies in Europe, as in the legislation to consolidate and universalize socialized health care, education and social security in Britain after 1945, may also have contributed to a cultural environment more aware and sympathetic to aspects of health and healing, in terms of both curative and preventative medicine. Treatment for forms of mental illness, depression and psychological disorders became more accessible and less stigmatized, probably also increasing public receptivity to psychotherapy and psychiatry.

Another hugely significant social trend of the late 1960s was the emergence of second wave feminism. Building upon earlier political achievements, most notably the enfranchisement campaigns of fifty years previously, feminism was advanced by economic and technological changes after 1945 that gave women greater freedom from domestic and child-bearing responsibilities, whilst offering wider opportunities in the labour market. The movement for greater political, legal, sexual and medical freedoms for women was fuelled by the articulation of the theoretical ambitions of feminism in the political and academic spheres. Although the movement encountered considerable resistance, and was never a unified univocal organization in any sense, some advances had been made by the mid-1970s, particularly in securing some equal rights and sex discrimination legislation, and enshrining the principles of women's equality into some areas of the legal and welfare systems (Evans, 1995).

A contentious aspect of the development of Western society after 1945, much discussed by sociologists, historians and theologians, is that of secularization. Any analysis of this phenomenon must proceed with caution, especially in interpreting the available information on declining church attendance and waning institutional influence, as well as advancing theoretical frameworks which are themselves redolent with value-judgements (Davie, 1994). Notwithstanding, this was clearly a period of readjustment in religious affiliation, with sharp changes occurring in patterns of formal observance, most particularly in Britain, but also in the United States. The established churches found themselves in competition with secular institutions as rival sources of social networks, belief systems, welfare and healing centres and even as places of entertainment.

Thus a number of social changes were contributing to a changing climate within the churches, beginning in the early 1960s and gathering pace by the late 1970s. Many of the patterns of leadership and authority were called into question by a more articulate and assertive laity, who were seeking new models of Christian vocation in keeping with the changing times (Gibbs and Morton, 1964). The Charismatic Movement of the early 1970s inspired many lay people to assume leadership within the evangelical churches (Bebbington, 1989). Theological developments during this period also reflected some of this ferment. Incarnational theologies which emphasized the importance of human history and the secular for the foundation of the Kingdom of God in a 'world come of age' reflected the popularity of theologians such as Dietrich Bonhoeffer, Reinhold Niebuhr, John Robinson, Gibson Winter and Harvey Cox. Other specific areas of Christian practice, such as industrial and urban mission and the theologies of work, also exemplified the celebration and affirmation of the world of technology, economic activity and social change as the rightful locus of lay vocation and Christian mission (Wickham, 1957, 1964; Davies, 1991).

Greater participation by the laity in church government and formal ministry had been occurring gradually throughout the twentieth century. In the early years of the century, the Protestant churches had experienced a remarkable upsurge of enthusiasm for programmes of lay ministry, especially amongst young people. They began to found their own organizations, devoted to overseas volunteer missions schemes, settlements and other lay charitable and social concerns. It is widely acknowledged that the influence of such an educated, articulate and international group was responsible for many subsequent developments in the churches, most particularly the formation of the ecumenical movement. Such lay organizations also furnished the world Church with a network of lay leadership, at the highest levels, and this trend continued after 1948 with the founding of the World Council of Churches, which inherited an emphasis on the participation of the laity (Rouse and Neill, 1967).

The mood in the Roman Catholic Church in the 1960s was also one of change. The Second Vatican Council (1962–5) issued statements on a wide range of issues, especially those concerning the primacy of the vocation of the Church in the world, and the centrality of lay Christian discipleship to that mission (Abbott, 1966; Imbelli and Groome, 1992; Brennan, 1967; Sunderland 1990). *Gaudium et Spes* in particular provided the impetus for a renewed pastoral practice, affirming the calling of the whole 'People of God' in working for peace and justice in the world. The role of the laity within the priesthood of all believers in the exercise of Christian discipleship in their secular vocation therefore achieved prominence, and reflected a sacramental theology and ecclesiology which emphasized the reality of the concrete and the everyday as the proper arena of mission and ministry.

The affirmation of a corporate and structural dimension to pastoral ministry also came through Papal Encyclicals such as *Mater et Magistra* (1961) and *Pacem in Terris* (1963). These called for economic and social justice, especially in areas like work and employment, human rights and education. *Populorum Progressio* (1967) concentrated on the relationship between rich and poor nations, condemning a legacy of colonialism and an unhealthy balance of trade that left developing countries dependent on fluctuating world commodity prices, pushing their economies into debt and perpetuating massive internal inequalities of wealth and income (McGovern, 1989; McCarthy, 1990). These developments encouraged groups of church members, religious, pastoral workers and academic theologians in Latin America to pioneer new models of theological education and formation.

At the same time, innovations were taking place in clergy education and training, especially during the 1960s. Many of these attempted to respond to developing models of 'the priesthood of all believers' by encouraging clergy to see themselves as managers and facilitators of the community, rather than leaders and authority-figures. There was also a noted expansion of lay professional ministry, although this may in many circumstances have created a 'clericized laity' and reflected a greater institutionalization and professionalization of church ministry and administration, rather than greater democracy and lay participation (Weber and Neill, 1963).

All this represented a fundamental challenge to traditional models of pastoral ministry, and in particular to the values and preconceptions upon which they were founded. The empowerment of the laity, and consequent re-evaluation of the authority of the clergy, served to undermine the automatic equation of pastoral ministry with ordination or the religious life, and relocated pastoral practice in the faithful witness of the whole Church in the world and not purely in the enactment of the functions and offices of the ordained ministry. The norms of pastoral practice which rested implicitly upon the centrality of the clerical agent could no longer be upheld.

Similarly, the greater assimilation of humanistic and secular therapies and anthropologies undermined models of practice which drew upon theological assumptions of revelation as a closed and absolute phenomenon. Pastoral theologians such as Hiltner had already glimpsed the possibilities of an alternative, but by the late 1970s the question of the relationship of theological norms for Christian practice to insights derived from the new psychologies, social and human sciences and even of other world faiths, had re-emerged with a new urgency fuelled by the realization that pastoral ministry was to be exercised in a truly pluralist society.

Therefore, the challenges of the late twentieth century have represented a new context for Christian pastoral practice, in terms of changing economic, political, technological and ethical realities. It was to this changing context that Don Browning addressed his attention, arguing not for a recovery of anachronistic models, but for a reconstruction and revision of an enduring tradition which engaged critically with contemporary values and experience.

Notes

1 The sense of 'history' and 'tradition' is carried by two terms in German: *Historie*, the documented and recorded past, and *Geschichte*, the movement of time within which human destiny unfolds. It was the latter, as the arena in which each generation faces new challenges, forging and articulating new understandings from the resources of tradition, that Schleiermacher regarded as the context for all theology. Theology is thus the discipline that discerns the task of the Christian community in any given age (Burkhart, 1983; Farley, 1983).

2 So called after William S. Plumer's *Hints and Helps in Pastoral Theology*, published in 1874; see Hiltner, 1958. Other examples of pastoral theology as the study of the ordained ministry from this period are Vinet, 1855 and van Oosterzee, 1878.

3 The psychoanalytic faction based in New York gravitated towards theological seminaries and formed the Institute for Pastoral Care, operating clinical placements in a wide variety of ministerial contexts, especially sector ministries. The Boston group, under Cabot and Russell Dicks, remained in the psychiatric and mental health field, as the Council for Clinical Training. Eventually the two associations reunited in 1967 to form the Association for Clinical Pastoral Education.

4 For British writers on pastoral ministry at this time besides Weatherhead, see Balmforth, Dewar, Hudson and Sara, 1937; Dewar and Hudson, 1932; Waterhouse, 1939. An alternative tradition within Anglicanism emphasized ascetic practices, especially confession, penance and spiritual direction, eschewing the modern psychologies. An early and much-read example was F. G. Belton, *A Manual for Confessors* (1916); and a popular latter-day exponent was Martin Thornton (1958) who envisaged pastoral care as the cultivation of a sacramentally-based community or 'remnant'.

5 There has always been an interest in the use of psychology in pastoral ministry. Holifield (1990), whilst not immune to the view that a distinctive shift did take place toward a 'secular' psychotherapeutic emphasis in North American tradition, insists that this tendency was

present in Puritan spiritualities through writers such as Jonathan Edwards.

6 Oates came from an evangelical background, but adopted a sophisticated correlation approach to the theological and psychological foundations of pastoral counselling (Stokes, 1985: 175–8; Oates, 1953, 1962, 1974). Jay E. Adams adopts a more fundamentalist reading of Scripture, in which the counsellor turns to biblical texts for a solution to pastoral predicaments (Adams, 1976). For a critical account of Adams' methods see Pattison, 1993, Chapter 6.

CHAPTER 4

Pastoral Care in a Moral Context

Pastoral care of congregations is a moral activity, and the call to participate in justice will create tension and conflict within congregations. The important notion is not to do away with the conflict but to utilize it to create opportunities for communities to engage in theological reflection about what it means to be an inclusive and meaningful faith community in a complex world. Congregations fractured by the issues of class, race, sexual orientation, or gender need opportunities to enter into moral discourse and not merely to dismiss those with whom they disagree.

(Marshall, 1995:175–6)

So far, I have argued that attempts to establish the disciplinary identity and terrain of pastoral theology have necessarily rekindled attention to the normative nature of the principles which guide and define pastoral practice. Don Browning's proposals to ground pastoral activity in theological ethics reconnect patterns of care and the governance of the Christian community with ideas of the good, the true and the normative. However, I am concerned in this chapter to examine whether Browning's model of 'practical moral reasoning' will prove an adequate basis for a pastoral theology sensitive to the critical perspectives of postmodernity.

Don Browning's first book, *Atonement and Psychotherapy*, published in 1966, argued that all therapies embody implicit value-commitments which are ultimately only articulated as religious ideals. He pursued a Tillichian model whereby the themes of Christian revelation in critical dialogue with secular knowledge supplied the religio-ethical root metaphors of human flourishing. By the late 1970s he returned to these concerns to develop claims about the central prescriptive norms on which pastoral theology could found its methodological and epistemological identity. In emphasizing that all pastoral care presupposes value-commitments,

Browning acknowledges a debt to the work of David Tracy, who argued that religious practices possess a 'limit-language' which assumes a coherent and ultimately theological commitment (Browning, 1983:187–202).

In *The Moral Context of Pastoral Care*, published in 1976, Browning offered a diagnosis of the contemporary context within which pastoral care and moral discourse takes place. He argued that the features of modernity have conspired to sever the connections between the 'disciplines of care' and the religio-ethical belief systems that used to underpin them. In such an age, Western society finds itself experiencing 'moral pluralism, moral confusion and moral relativism' (Browning, 1990:365).

Browning's portrayal of the dynamics of history is Weberian in nature, influencing his account of the chief characteristics of modernity, as well as his understanding of the role of religion as the symbolic representation of the social order. Thus, modern society is characterized by a commitment to technical rationalization: the division of labour; an emphasis on instrumental modes of action prompting greater efficiency; rapid social change with the resultant speed of accommodation and adaptation; and religious and ethical pluralism. Matters of care, faith and ethical development have become privatized due to the sociological factors of secularization and industrialization, resulting in a split between private and public values, so that ethics is no longer sustainable as a public discourse.

Browning also identified the rise of Protestantism and its pursuit of ascetic rational individuality as contributing to the privatization of ethical guidance and its detachment from the corporate moral universe of the Church. Whereas the Roman Catholic tradition rooted pastoral guidance firmly in a tradition of moral theology which understood the ministerial task as that of incorporation of the individual into the sacramental corporate Body, Protestantism reduced such spiritual and ascetic matters to individual conscience. Thus the Church lost a crucial link with the normative tradition of moral theology, and the understanding that church discipline and individual salvation are grounded in ethical precepts.

At the time that secular society lost its public moral consensus, therefore, the churches lost their ability to ground their practice in a clear ethical framework. Pastoral counsellors, convinced by the value-neutral claims of psychotherapy to adopt non-directive counselling, failed to recognize the implicit norms inherent in all practices of care: '[C]are in a Christian context . . . should exhibit a kind of practical moral inquiry into the way life should be ordered' (Browning, 1976:15). Lacking theological or ethical norms, the pastor is guided only by egotism or unreflective pragmatism. Whilst Browning does not dismiss the value of non-directive counselling, recommending the 'bracketing' of ethical norms in acute circumstances, he does believe that the non-directive traditions – inherited from the 'unconditional positive regard' of Rogers, and the 'eductive' model of Hiltner – precluded the pastor from ever being guided by explicit notions of virtue, goodness and truth:

> At a time when moral clarification is most needed because normative cultural values are in a state of crisis, pastoral care and counseling have, for the most part, abandoned the task of moral guidance . . . Eductive counseling does not impose solutions on the person needing help; it tries to educe solutions, both emotional and moral, from the individual seeking counseling. Whatever the virtues of eductive counseling as a model for pastoral care (and there are many), its over emphasis signals a default on the part of the Protestant community. It is unwilling to tackle the hard problems of reconstructing the normative moral and cultural value symbols by which the church and its members should live. When the spirit of eductive counseling pervades the church, the tough value issues are left up to the individual's tastes and preferences.   (Browning, 1976:25)

Browning thus mirrors Clinebell, who pointed to similar flaws in the non-directive tradition, believing that certain new challenges demanded a more directive approach.[1] Browning has therefore sought a recovery of ethics as the guiding norms for a 'critical practical moral theology of care' (1983:16).

Another basic precept of Browning's project to reconstruct the ethical core of pastoral care is his belief in the fundamentally religious nature of ethics. This is not an attempt to impose an uncritical or fundamentalist Christianity upon a secular world – a return to premodern organic religion – because Browning remains firmly committed to secular pluralism. Instead, he argues that care in every culture has always been rooted in a moral vision, and centred in a community ethos which is ultimately religious. It is embodied in myths and narratives which articulate the deepest aspirations and values of any given culture (Browning, 1976: Chapters II, III and IV).

Browning adopts Weberian sociological theories of human action in insisting that all human behaviour carries meaning, and all activity is purposive and expressive of one type or another of rationality. Thus caring activity which claims to be free of all meaning ceases in any sense to be purposeful or caring: '[L]ove or communitas are meaningless and formless concepts without a context of moral norms, judgements and structures' (1976:77).

Practical moral rationality is therefore the creation of a coherent ethical world within which human behaviour can be understood and ordered. Religion consolidates and codifies these principles of organizing reality, but can also carry within it the seeds of evolutionary development necessary to respond to changing moral and social contexts. Pastoral care is thus understood as 'incorporation of persons into a given moral universe' (Browning, 1976:90).

Thus care should not be divorced from the purposive, communal and theological identity of the Church, which is what generates the ethical norms by which pastoral ministry is guided and directed. Practical theology takes its cue from the articulation of the themes of Christian doctrine as they find expression in the values that constitute moral meanings within the community of faith:

> In other words, pastoral counseling must be founded on a context of moral meanings that is, in fact, the province of practical theology. Practical theology is a branch of theology that attempts to state explicitly the ultimate grounds upon which we shall order the everyday moral meanings of our lives. It has a close relationship with theological ethics. It is different from fundamental theology, which attempts to explain the ultimate grounds and justifications for the basic symbols of a particular religious tradition . . . Practical theology goes beyond a theology of pastoral acts and sets forth a theology of practical living – a theology of work, business, sexuality, marriage, child-rearing, aging, youth, etc. Practical theology in this sense of the word is the most neglected of any of the specialties of theology.   (Browning, 1976:109)

Therefore, care cannot be exercised outside normative ethical understandings; but those understandings must be critical of the theological tradition, integrative of the insights of dynamic psychology into human behaviour and motivation; system-orientated, not individualistic or privatized. Nor is Browning concerned simply to root Christian pastoral care in theological ethics which only have credence and viability within the life of the community. Following the revised critical correlational model of David Tracy, Browning insists that the moral commitments inherent in Christian pastoral care must also be publically accessible and accountable. Much of the later development in pastoral/practical theology in the 1980s and 1990s has been within a revised critical correlationist framework, stressing as its field of study the critical interpretation of the lived experience of the whole Christian community (Browning, 1983: Chapter 5; 1987; Tracy, 1975, 1981, 1987; Day Williams, 1961; Whitehead and Whitehead, 1980).

Thus, in order to respond pastorally to its contemporary context, the Church must retrieve itself as a community of moral discourse, and build a practical method of moral reasoning. Again, the emphasis on 'practical moral rationality' is distinctive and derives from Browning's Weberian influences. Ultimately, his programme is rooted in an understanding of theological ethics as a technical rational discourse: '[F]or congregations to reconstitute their caring practices, they must become adept in the skills of practical thinking . . .' (Browning, 1983:16).

Browning devotes detailed attention to a method and process of practical moral reasoning. He considers there to be five levels of ethical discourse, which can be understood as shaping individual moral character and expressive of objective universal moral questions. The norms and values which underpin each level may differ, but a critical process of interrogation enables the five levels of moral principles as they are manifested in the Gospel witness, 'significant cultural options' and personal experience, to engage in a critical correlation (1983, 1987):

Metaphorical: What kind of world is this?

Obligational: What are we called to do?

Tendency-Need: What basic values and satisfactions do humans seek?

Context-Predictive: What constraints are imposed by culture and society?

Rule-Role: What patterns and processes must be followed to establish moral ends?

Browning roots his emphasis on the ethical nature of pastoral practice in a conviction that human moral action is characterized by a particular level or configuration of rationality. Ultimately, all human moral decisions and actions are expressions of rational calculations based on a hierarchy of needs and considerations. Moral discourse is the systemization of human rationality upon which all behaviour rests, and religion is the symbolic and mythical vehicle of such moral-rational debate. Yet ultimately, it has no autonomous use beyond rationality, and so the symbolic, ritualistic and mythical dimensions of religion tend to be discounted.

In constructing his methodology, Browning abandoned theological principles for a system of practical moral reasoning founded in developmental psychology. He also drew upon life-cycle theories from developmental psychology: 'Pastoral theology involves stating the appropriate relation between a moral theology of the human life cycle and psychodynamic, developmental, and other social science perspectives that describe or explain how human development comes about' (1983:187). This emphasis on human development sprang from Browning's understanding of pastoral theology as reflection on care; and he therefore chose to characterize the human context in terms of a psychodynamic model of personality. However, this choice mutes the theological by concentrating on the ethics of the human life-cycle. Browning thus betrays a preference for a model of human growth based upon technical-rational action over a system of norms grounded in theological discourse. As the debates surrounding the sufficiency of psychotherapeutic and psychodynamic theories illustrated, pastoral theology may in part be an enquiry into what it means to be human, but its traditions also insist upon a Divine or transcendent dimension to human affairs and Christian practice.

Furthermore, the emphasis on dynamic psychology represents only a partial analysis, precluding attention to the corporate and institutional dimensions of any given situation. This fails to do justice to Browning's own claims to be reintegrating Protestant ascetic-rational ethics back into a Roman Catholic moral theology which emphasizes the primacy of the Church as moral community and institution. The emergence of liberation theology with its emphasis on *orthopraxis* constitutes an eschewal of the Western (especially Protestant) model of theology and the Christian life as comprising correctness of belief and congruence to philosophical or propositional truth-claims, and therefore to a model of human knowledge as entirely cognitive and rational. It neglects the social and material dimension of *praxis*, of faith as doing or living the truth, rather than apprehending it intellectually.[2] The result of this is to adopt an individualistic and cognitive model of human nature and faith development, which falls into a dualistic understanding of logic and rationality as in some way superior to other forms of human expression. Browning does emphasize the community of faith, but the prevailing model of moral reasoning is still one of logic-centred rationality.

Fundamental Practical Theology

Browning's vision of pastoral/practical theology takes an important turn with the publication of *A Fundamental Practical Theology* (1991), where he moves further into the study of the sources and norms which inform the collective life and action of Christian congregations. In this respect, he sees himself as the inheritor of a tradition of congregational studies, but brings to bear his conviction that the congregation is essentially a community of *moral discourse* (Dudley, 1983; Hopewell, 1987). This represents a further shift in pastoral/practical theology away from a focus on the activities and identity of the minister towards an emphasis on the values and activities of Christian community in its entirety.

The central question for Browning in *A Fundamental Practical Theology* is: 'in what way do faith-communities exhibit practical theological and moral reasoning?'. He is concerned to trace the changing dynamic of three very different congregations: the Wiltshire Methodist, Centerville Presbyterian and Chicago Apostolic churches which serve as case-studies for his discussion. For Browning, practical theology is a critical engagement with the 'thickness' of values which inform congregational self-understanding and practice. However, Browning rejects Cartesian and Barthian notions of a hierarchy or dualism of theory and practice in which theological truth is imparted independent of human agency, opting instead for the Aristotelian model of *phronēsis*, or practical reasoning (pp. 5–6). Communities of faith are both communities of tradition and practical enactment, and their fundamental truth-claims are embodied in the practical reasoning of purposeful pastoral activities (pp. 34–47). 'I find it useful to think of funda-mental practical theology as critical reflection on the church's dialogue with Christian sources and other communities of experi-ence and interpretation with the aim of guiding its action toward social and individual transformation' (1991:36). Thus, his enquiry follows a movement from 'Practice to Theory to Practice' (p. 9) as a means of engaging with the practical reasoning of a congregation and thence interrogating the values which inform and direct congregational life. This process may best be thought of as one of *excavating* the many accumulated layers of tradition, material context, values and visions which constitute a congregation's common life. However, it is impossible to gain access to these values independent of the contexts in which they are put to work in forms of pastoral ministry. Ideally, says Browning, such a study is best illuminated by a community in crisis, facing some kind of change of direction or reappraisal of its common life. The process of reflecting on its fundamental commitments thus crystallizes the values, or theories, informing its practices, institutions and self-understanding (p. 6).

The 'thickness' of practical reasoning reflects the diverse sources which serve to shape and inform the moral commitments of a congregation. Browning thus adopts his earlier categories of moral reasoning as encompassing the metaphors of the common good, visions of obligation, the basic tendencies and needs of human existence, as influenced by social context and mindful of rules/roles, as a means of structuring the various dimensions and sources of Christian moral reasoning (pp. 105–9). These dimensions are necessarily forged from a synthesis of secular and theological sources, and much of *A Fundamental Practical Theology* is devoted to their elaboration and interrogation.

Browning's model adopts the notion of *phronēsis* as the solution to a dualism of theory and practice. Yet there is an unresolved dualism in his evocation of congregational life, in that a congregation's practical reasoning is essentially a body of theoretical (moral) principles wrapped up in practice. Thus in the place of theology he places a rationalist version of Christian ethics whose precepts can actually be distilled from their narrative, interpersonal or liturgical setting. This is not a true unity of theory and practice; he is, despite his emphasis on *phronēsis*, more interested in looking for metaphysical moral principles rather than in truly listening to the embodied, incarnational practical wisdom of the congregations. The primary language of his practical reasoning is thus a pre-existent system of theological ethics, rather than the 'living human documents' of liturgy, personal care and social witness of the congregation. Browning constitutes Christian pastoral practice as a form of moral conduct and the expression of value-commitments. However, such values are not, as Browning tends to assume, pre-existent. Instead, the visions of selfhood and virtue inherent in Christian practical moral reasoning have human authors, derive from specific social and cultural contexts, and reflect particular patterns of social relations.

Browning is, I believe, still firmly rooted in a modernist, Weberian rationalist tradition. His understanding of the human subject and pastoral agency illustrate this, in the primacy he affords to moral reasoning. However, the legacy of Freud extending to postmodernism speaks of the 'decentering' of human reason as the paramount model of human motivation and self-understanding. Feminist critiques of Western Cartesian philosophy have also pointed to the androcentricism implicit within such privileging of rationality as superior knowledge. Yet Browning fails to rid himself of the Protestant individualistic ascetic-rational tendencies in reconstructing his ethical system, which he had previously criticized as so corrosive of theological ethics in the modern world. Nor are processes of practical reasoning necessarily as logic-centred as Browning claimed, because the life of a faith-community involves more than moral decision-making. It is also concerned with worship, social action, teaching and learning, spirituality and public *apologia*, all of which are just as expressive of ultimate values and truth-claims, if not more so, than ethical discourse. This makes it more appropriate to place practical/pastoral theology in the sphere of practical wisdom, rather than within the model of moral reasoning expounded by Browning.

Browning is especially vulnerable to criticism on these grounds, in terms of his lack of any gender perspective; as I have already argued, notions of selfhood, virtue, knowledge and agency have all been constructed within a patriarchal culture. Thus Browning neglects to consider that the fundamental moral principles of Christian action will require critical revision in the light of feminist claims. However, since Browning portrays such values as axiomatic, he has no mechanism for their contestation and rearticulation. There is little attention to the internal power relations of the congregations, nor any commitment towards looking at exclusions of gender, race or class within them. The moral sensibilities of the congregations are understood to find their defining nature in relation to a 'canon' of liberal theology which does not sufficiently acknowledge the diversity or heterogeneity of contemporary theology. Browning might have come to very different conclusions if he had started with the kind of devotional and theological literature that the congregations themselves were reading, and the degree of correlation between the insights and world-views of such material and their self-professed practice and ministry.

Conclusion: Reconstructing Pastoral Theology

The prevailing definition of pastoral theology as the theory of individual care, current in Britain and North America for much of the twentieth century, represented a narrowing of its traditional focus. This specialist definition effectively divorced the cure of souls from the collective life and practices of the faith-community, and from normative questions of how such a community should be ordered. The cultivation of individual virtue and salvation became detached from questions of the nature of the Church, its mission and presence in any given context, and what all this proclaimed about the purposes of God.

The work of Schleiermacher highlighted the theological nature of Christian faithfulness in a changing world, but lacked the conceptual and hermeneutical processes by which experience might illuminate and transform the received tradition. Tillich introduced a model by which insights from culture might be integrated with the historic truth-claims of theology; but it remained a deductive and abstract tool, divorced from any phenomenological process by which persons actually come to new theological understandings. Hiltner struggled to articulate a model of pastoral theology which focused on the concrete practices of ministry; of theology as a body of practical wisdom, facilitating renewed action as well as intellectual correlation. However, he concentrated on the immediate tasks of the minister at the expense of a wider critique of the social and theological context by which the priorities of the pastoral office were determined.

As Chapter 3 argued, the separation of pastoral care from the truth-claims of Christian theology did not go unchallenged. Many pastoral theologians struggled to establish a methodology by which the two could be reintegrated. The relationship of pastoral practice to 'secular' theories and therapies highlighted the possibility of revelation about the human condition and the nature of salvation outside the specific claims of Christian tradition; but tended to intensify the notion of pastoral care as the application, rather than the primary source, of theological formulation.

Arguably, Browning has succeeded in refocusing critical attention upon the guiding norms of Christian pastoral care. In this respect he reunites pastoral theology – as the critical study of such sources and norms – with moral theology of the Roman Catholic tradition, which regards itself as the study of the pastoral ordering of the Church (Duffy, 1983: Chapter 2; Mahoney, 1987; Brennan, 1967). This fact begins to wrest pastoral activity from narrow definitions of individual care or therapy into the realm of all pursuits designed to maintain the common life of the Church. Browning's vision of a public theology in a pluralist, postmodern culture also shifts attention away from pastoral theology as the study of Christian ministry (implicit in Hiltner's work) towards that of critical enquiry concerned to question the fundamental vocation of the Church in the world. Thus, a focus on the norms guiding Christian practice, rather than the agent of predetermined functions, does promise a renewed attention to the activities – sacramental, symbolic and interpersonal – by which the boundaries and self-understanding of the faith-community are determined.

Yet although Browning reconnects pastoral theology to traditions of moral theology, grounding all forms of pastoral practice in the ordering of the Church, his authoritative source – theological ethics – tends to discount the problematic nature of such prescriptive norms. His scheme privileges rational-ethical action at the expense of other manifestations of Christian pastoral action of a more symbolic and affective nature. Browning's vision fails to take account of the plurality of human reasoning and agency; the social context of values and morality; and oppositional accounts of truth and virtue generated by marginalized and occluded groups. Nonetheless, it heralds a revival of interest in pastoral theology as a primary theological discipline, approaching Christian pastoral action as a form of moral or normative practice, and the life of the Christian community as expressive of fundamental truth-claims.

I have surveyed the development of pastoral theology since the mid-eighteenth century and its developing self-understanding as a discipline in relation to church, world and academy. A dominant model of pastoral theology identified its concerns as reflecting upon the clerically-dominated sphere of pastoral care and counselling, an emphasis characterized by Edward Farley as that of the 'clerical paradigm' (Farley, 1983). Such a vision is especially clear in the visions of practical theology propounded by Schleiermacher and Hiltner, in which the diverse activities of the Christian community have narrowed into a study of the ordained ministry. The epistemological focus of pastoral theology thus uncritically replicates the taken-for-granted functions of church leadership and offers no opportunity for scrutiny of the theological and sociological roots of ordained ministry, let alone a wider attention to the self-understanding of the entire Christian community:

> The ... public tasks and responsibilities of clergy (preaching, counseling, managing, organizing, teaching, evangelizing) represent altogether only a formal, sociological description of a minister or priest. They pertain to the social duration of the Christian community as it would be *sociologically* described. Passed over is the Christian community in its essential, defining, ecclesial aspect of being a redemptive community, with a leadership whose tasks center in the corporate and individual occurrence of redemption.
>
> (Farley, 1983:127)

For Farley, the fourfold division of theology into Bible, church history, doctrine and practical theology has effectively ruptured the essential unity of theological knowledge. It represents a narrowing of practical theology into a 'clericalization of practice' (1983:133) and a fragmentation of practical theology into the mundane functions of church leadership. It has resulted in the evacuation of any theological or value-laden notion to pastoral practice: a schism, therefore, between *theoria* and *praxis*.

Farley's project is to reconnect the clerical paradigm with a wider tradition of pastoral practice – and thus of critical theological enquiry and construction – which is collective, value-bearing and self-critical. This he identifies in the notion of practical theology as a form of *theologia* or practical wisdom which transcends clerical technique and circumscribes instead the qualities required of persons who occupy a *habitus* of faith. Farley characterizes this not as a body of technical knowledge, but a disposition or orientation devoted to the practical but critical living out of faith. Theology as *habitus* is thus portrayed as 'a cognitive disposition and orientation of the soul' (1983:35): a kind of 'indwelling' of a tradition of practical knowledge.

However, I wonder whether Farley's scheme is essentially the product of a premodern age of Christendom, in which it is appropriate to contemplate a unity of theological wisdom. Whilst Farley refers to a bygone age of a monastic *habitus* of faith, he does also appreciate that the disciplinary developments of the past two centuries cannot be unmade. *Theologia* cannot be 'raised from the dead' in an attempt to impose on a fragmented academy and secular society a confessionally-based pursuit of theological wisdom that arose in a different cultural context. Rather, Farley proposes that the study of theology can and should find its focus in the self-critical reflections on forms of Christian practice which transcend the limits of the clerical paradigm:

> To the degree that faith itself continues at all . . . a certain pre-reflective insightfulness will attend it. Further, human beings rarely if ever exist in the world without reflective responses of some sort. Accordingly, even in the modern, highly secularized and pragmatic religious community, faith's prereflective dispositions find ways to rise into understanding: in reflections of believers, in acts of ministry such as preaching, in church schools and educative processes, in Christian feminism and black theology, in technical and scholarly inquiries. Theological understanding occurs in these matrices even though it is itself rarely thematized and pursued as such . . . The task before us, then, is not so much to resuscitate the dead as to persuade the living to incorporate into their educational paradigms something which is in fact at work in their midst.
>
> (1983:160)

Farley is adamant that a recovery of *theologia* is viable in a postmodern pluralist age (1983:161); but any notion of *habitus* must be reconfigured out of postmodernity, not in spite of it. A simple retrieval of *habitus* runs the risk of imposing an anachronistic unity on postmodern Christian practice, and of regarding tradition as unchanging and monolithic. However, we need a model of practical wisdom which is both 'indwelt' *and* 'constructed': *habitus* as handed down and reinterpreted anew for every generation.

My next two chapters will therefore pursue this on two fronts. Chapter 6 will investigate three alternative paradigms of Christian practical wisdom: of *narrative* as constituting the authoritative resource by which purposeful practice may be guided; of *women's experience* as constituting an essential source and norm of Christian critique and reconstruction; and of *liberating praxis* as the criterion by which theological truth and authenticity may be judged.

However, it is to the notion of *practice* itself – as the embodiment of the self-understanding of the Christian community – that Chapter 5 will direct its attention. Although I wish to endorse Browning's claim of the inherently value-directed nature of Christian pastoral practice, I am also committed to seek a wider grounding for Christian practical wisdom than Browning's in theological ethics. Christian pastoral practice is more than rational moral discourse, just as it must encompass a greater diversity of activity than individual 'cure of souls'. Thus, it may be appropriate to speak not of pastoral care, nor ministry, nor moral reasoning as the normative core of pastoral theology: all these are too narrowly circumscribed. Perhaps a broader category of analysis would simply be to talk about 'Christian practice'. This restores, but also transcends, the various activities of 'practical theology' at the dawn of the modern era: preaching, liturgy, cure of souls, church management and Christian formation. Schleiermacher's scheme regarded Christian practice as central, but allowed it to be subsumed under the ministry of the Church. Our era is perhaps less ready to identify ministry with ordination, and to appreciate a vision of pastoral agency founded on 'the priesthood of all believers' and secular vocation and to develop a discipline that encompasses a diversity of activities on the part of the faith-community. So are we in a position of a *turn to practice* as the focus of contemporary pastoral theology? It is my contention that we are; but first we must explore what is meant by such a phrase.

Notes

1 Clinebell (1984) identifies a 'contemporary renaissance' in pastoral counselling which 're-visions' the discipline as concerned with healing and growth in a social and political context. The impact of feminism and civil rights movements impel the counselling movement to adopt proactive models of social as well as individual change.

2 A similar criticism is voiced by Rebecca Chopp (1987) against the liberal school of revised critical correlation, which she accuses of being too concerned with generating a theology which debates matters of cognitive and intellectual belief rather than a discipline that fuels a commitment to socio-political *praxis*. See also Chapter 6, in which I discuss a model of pastoral practice founded on the paradigm of *liberating praxis*.

CHAPTER 5

Practice and Human Value

Practice has a logic which is not that of the logician. (Bourdieu, 1992:86)

In this chapter, I shall examine perspectives within the social sciences which place the notion of 'practice' at the heart of the dynamics of the formation and maintenance of the social order, both material and symbolic. Such perspectives effectively mediate between theories of society which regard human relations as determined by the laws of history or forces of nature, and those which portray human culture as little more than agglomerations of the random activities and choices of individual actors (Dawe, 1979). Rather, practice emerges as something which mediates between structure and agency, seeing culture as a human creation which nonetheless persists over time; and of the norms of practice as in some sense rule-governed and institutional but still dependent on individual and collective agency for their maintenance. Such a focus avoids rooting the values of hope and obligation in a metaphysical extra-cultural realm, but rather allows us to plot the dynamics of the ways in which purposeful practices are the implicit bearers of ultimate truth-claims.

We might trace the beginnings of a critical attention to 'practice' in social science perspectives which stress social action. Perhaps the most important theorist of social action was Max Weber, whose interpretative methods drew attention to the influence of human interpretation and agency to the maintenance of social order and the creation of social relations (Weber, 1978). This was in contrast to structural-functionalist models which regarded the teleology of social systems as primary, and individual action or interpretation as mere epiphenomena to the dynamics of social order and social change. Since Weber, there has been a greater emphasis on the centrality of social practice – material and symbolic – as a key concept in understanding how human culture is produced and reproduced. Members of society contribute to the active construction of the social order; but they are simultaneously situated in a world of pre-existing structures, representations and conventions. The sociological school of social interactionism understands society not as impersonal structures but as a performative reality, constantly open to reinterpretation and regeneration. Social life is a constant accomplishment, a performance, bound by rules and roles, but reliant upon the tacit consent of the 'players' to stick to the script. Similarly, phenomenology is the study of how human meaning is rooted in human relations and activity. It studies 'the practice of consciousness', not as innate essence, but a construction, the point at which mind meets the social world (Kearney, 1994). Perception is thus not the passive internalization of pre-given information, but an active *practice* of apprehension.

Giddens' perspective of 'structuration' develops such a synthesis of structure and action. Social systems are enduring and historical in that they persist through established structures; yet they are dependent upon human agency to reproduce them via everyday practices. Giddens stresses the 'duality of structure': human agents act within certain social conventions to generate activity, but their very practices serve to reproduce and embody the values of that social system. 'Structure' implies a patterning of social relations enshrined formally over time, but this is not purely external, but also internalized, like a language. Practice is therefore structured behaviour which follows certain rules or patterns. However, social actors are not unthinkingly rehearsing social conventions, but purposefully reproducing them. Thus social structures are 'reproduced social practices' that endure to orientate 'the conduct of knowledgeable human agents' (Giddens, 1984:80). The rules of social life are 'procedures' applied in the reproduction of social structures; but these rules are themselves reinforced by the very practices that enact them: 'According to the notion of the duality of structure, the structural properties of social systems are both medium and outcome of the practices they recursively organize' (Giddens, 1984:87). Within this perspective of social theory, therefore, culture is constructed and maintained via human practices; and *practice* is also the medium by which moral values are articulated and enshrined. In the context of his discussion of virtue as practical accomplishment, involving the inhabitation of a cultural tradition and community, the philosopher Alasdair MacIntyre develops the concept of practice as the means by which human action is the bearer of a consistent and historically rooted system of values. Individual actions are not isolated, atomized events; they are part of a coherent scheme of 'enacted narratives' (1987:211). For MacIntyre, we are both the characters and the authors of this narrative, and it is sustained in and through human practice:

> By a 'practice' I am going to mean any coherent and complex form of socially established co-operative human activity through which goods internal to that form of activity are realized in the course of trying to achieve those standards of excellence which are appropriate to, and partially definitive of, that form of activity, with the result that human powers to achieve excellence, and human conceptions of the ends and goods involved, are systematically extended.   (1987:187)

However, practice is never merely a set of technical procedures, nor the exercise of instinctive action. It necessarily involves the inhabitation of communal conventions of speech, meaning and action. Even if one is acting in isolation, one's practice is governed by rules and systems of meaning which have been historically formed. Moral norms are thus built into practices; but equally, practice must be seen as the outworking and re-enactment of those values. The 'virtues' for MacIntyre are those values which enable us to give moral substance and direction to practice. That requires immersion in relationships of obligation and honesty with others; the practices that sustain and continue human culture are inconceivable without institutions or structures by which they are given tangible and external form.

However, I would suggest that practices are not simply moral entities; they have creative and epistemological status as well. Engagement in new practices gives rise to new knowledge. Some of this may be in the form of enhanced technical competence, as, for example, one might apply the adage 'practice makes perfect' in connection with learning to roller-skate or swim. But practice may also be intrinsically disclosive of new realms of understanding: reading a poem and making a connection with a deeper level of meaning or experience; or listening to the stories of others as in a pastoral encounter or therapeutic conversation. Practical knowledge involves the inhabitation of a moral or existential universe as much as it entails the exercise of pure technique. Practice has the capacity to engender new realities as well as develop greater skill; and in turn, practice informed by new insights may transform subsequent experience.

Bourdieu and the 'Logic of Practice'

Pierre Bourdieu's idea of practice is an attempt to transcend the dichotomy between what he terms 'objectivism' and 'subjectivism'. Objectivism sees the social world as external and pre-existent to the actor; practice is seen as acting out of roles and enactment of scripts. Objectivism treats realities as already structured outside of the processes of taxonomization and analysis. Subjectivism regards all action as the outworking of individual consciousness, failing to realize that experiential and phenomenological meaning is always already socially constructed.

We can discern the influence of Claude Lévi-Strauss' work in ethnography and anthropology on Bourdieu, in the form of the latter's early studies of ritual in Algeria. Structuralism emphasizes the necessity of regarding every element of a culture as relationally linked to all other constituent parts. Structuralism argues that meanings of the constituent elements of culture are only retrievable within an entire network of referents, namely the social system as a whole. Structuralism understands all actions, rituals and institutions as expressions of pre-existent binary oppositions which are embedded in all human behaviour. However, Bourdieu argues that sufficient space needs to be afforded to the complexity and creativity of ritual and symbolic practice. This will only properly be recognized within a model that can accomodate system *and* agency to a greater extent than the rigidities of structuralism.

An example of the limitations of structuralist accounts of culture is in their analysis of language. For Saussure, language is considered an objective, external reality from which the observer can distance herself. Language thus precedes speech, which is merely the enactment of the deep structures of expression. But, asks Bourdieu, are we grammarians or orators? Grammarians take language as an object of analysis, oblivious to their own position as speaking subjects: language is thus *logos*, not *praxis*, and human agency is a phenomenon to be objectified as if it were external to the process of interpretation:

> For lack of a theory of the difference between the purely theoretical
> relation to language of someone who . . . has nothing to do with
> language except understand it, and the practical relation to language
> of someone who seeks to understand in order to act and who uses
> language for practical purposes . . . the grammarian is tacitly
> inclined to treat language as an autonomous, self-sufficient object,
> that is, a purposefulness without purpose – without any other
> purpose, at any rate, than that of being interpreted, like a work of
> art.   (Bourdieu, 1992:31)

Objectivist theory therefore denies that we all inhabit culture and language as symbolic worlds over which we exert some creative leverage. Language and culture are more than a series of rule-governed speech acts; they are enacted in context and realized in speech, in history, in human interaction. Thus, Bourdieu argues that language must be seen as *habitus*: a 'system of structured, structuring dispositions . . . constituted in practice and . . . always oriented towards practical functions' (1992:52). *Habitus* regards practice as structured and value-directed but not inflexibly determined by external forces. 'Objectively "regulated" and "regular" without being in any way the product of obedience to rules, they can be collectively orchestrated without being the product of the organizing action of a conductor' (1992:53). In this respect, it differs from Farley's model of *habitus*, which seemed to allow little scope for practical wisdom as the product of human history. By contrast, Bourdieu's notion of *habitus* is that it is a cultural artefact (that is, the product of human labour) rather than some kind of self-regulating object. Practices are not merely 'rule-governed behaviour', but symbolic, purposeful strategies with many layers of meaning. Anything else is a denial of human creative agency because it presupposes that some essential structures of human culture can override any action, and reduce it to the mere epiphenomena of social laws. Bourdieu argues that the teleology of structuralism must not be allowed to predetermine the complexities of human practice.

However, to emphasize practice as the well-spring of culture is not to collapse into the opposite of structuralism, namely voluntarism. This is the notion that social order is merely the product of individual activity and consciousness. Bourdieu calls this tendency 'subjectivism'. It reflects a philosophy of action which is described in terms of strategies willed by free rational agents oriented towards calculated goals with perhaps some reference to anticipated reactions of other agents. '[J]ust as objectivism universalizes the theorist's relation to the object of science, so subjectivism universalizes the experience that the subject of theoretical discourse has of himself as a subject' (1992:46). Instead, Bourdieu theorizes an alternative model which transcends the dichotomy of 'social physics' and 'phenomenology'. He regards social reality as neither determined by impersonal structures and forces beyond our control, nor as merely the expression of individual consciousness.

Symbolic forms have an autonomy of sorts from material relations; hence the redundancy of objectivist determinism. However, society is more than the sum of individual actors or their intentions. Social structures do have a bearing on personal practice, but we must also bear in mind the 'reflexivity' of human culture as continuously practised, cultivated and renewed:

> There is an economy of practices, a reason immanent in practices, whose 'origin' lies neither in the 'decisions' of reason understood as rational calculation nor in the determinations of mechanisms external to and superior to the agents . . . In other words, if one fails to recognize any form of action other than rational action or mechanical reaction, it is impossible to understand the logic of all the actions that are reasonable without being the product of a reasoned design, still less of rational calculation; informed by a kind of objective finality without being consciously organized in relation to an explicitly constituted end; intelligible and coherent without springing from an intention of coherence and a deliberate decision; adjusted to the future without being the product of a project or plan.   (1992:50)

Bourdieu emphasizes the inventiveness and unpredictability of practice; the conventions of the *habitus* are often transformed in the very process of its reproduction. Structure and practice are thus dialectical: *habitus* is not an unchanging or static entity. Nor can we treat the social order as the outworkings of a predetermined script, and actors as automatons mouthing words written on their behalf. But equally there are structures that predispose us to certain kinds of activities and orientations which make possible some notion of a social order. *Habitus* is thus conceived as the residuum of past actions, a deposit of past knowledge and practice, but which is always available as the raw material for creative agency, or 'regulated improvisations' (Bourdieu, 1992:57). Such a perspective thus transcends the polarization between structure and agency, determinism and choice, action and reaction, individual and society. It is an 'infinite capacity for generating . . . thoughts, perceptions, expressions and actions' (Bourdieu, 1992:55). Social systems are created and recreated by everyday practices that are themselves informed by the *habitus* of cultural organization. 'The *habitus* – embodied history, internalized as a second nature and so forgotten as history – is the active presence of the whole past of which it is the product' (Bourdieu, 1992:56). A clear emphasis emerges of the *self-reflexivity* of practice; of human actors as the subjects of agency and the objects of history:

> While we never cease to experience ourselves as acting, choosing, purposeful, aspiring human beings, we also never cease to be aware of the factory gates closing behind us, the office days that are not our own, the sense of oppression by organizations nobody runs, the 'not-enough world' we are forced to inhabit most of the time.
>
> (Dawe, 1979:365)

Bourdieu's analysis avoids idealism, because practical sense always has to be transposed into physical and temporal activity. *Habitus*, memory and enactment are therefore all supremely embodied phenomena. Knowledge, custom and social relations are never independent of the bodily *habitus*. Embodied practices have meaning; but the meaning is implicit and inseparable from the practices themselves. The social structures and relations of power and difference (such as gender, social status and economic occupation) are similarly all embodied in physical and corporeal means, so they remain concrete realities rather than abstract concepts. In this respect, Bourdieu does not underestimate the importance of differentials of power: possession of material and symbolic capital will determine one's location in the 'social space' of power relations. Practice both reflects and reinforces social relations and ideologies. Whilst practice is rooted in economic and material activities, and symbolic transactions have a relationship to material transformation and allocation of power and concrete resources, the function of ideology is to reproduce and reinforce power relations by 'naturalizing' them. That is, ideology portrays cultural artefacts and economic organization as structures which exist beyond human agency, thus belying their origins. 'The most successful ideological effects are the ones that have no need of words, but only of *laissez-faire* and complicitous silence' (1992:133).

Practice and Gender

In earlier work, I identified the generation of gender relations – indeed all social relations of power and difference – as lying in human practice. Like Giddens and Bourdieu, I am using the notion of practice as a means of mediating between models of gender identity and gender relations as resting in forms of determinism (either biological or sociological) and those in voluntarism (Graham, 1995:217–18). The latter is exemplified in 'role theory' which sees gender as a series of attitudes assumed rather than embedded in structures (which are material) of power and difference. Gender is neither a matter of innate difference nor personal preference but the outcome of a network of practices which construct and sustain these dynamics. It is therefore inappropriate to think of human experience as 'programmed' either by the forces of nature or the pressures of culture. Practice recognizes the institutionalized nature of gender roles but also seeks to allow for the influence of 'choice, doubt, strategy, planning, error and transformation' (Connell, 1987:61). We are thus *self-reflexively* the creations and the creators of a gendered social order.

This reflects a sense that gender regimes and gender relations predate individual choice and agency without exercising an absolute constraint upon individual action. Quite the contrary; social systems are dependent upon calculated action and ritual or routine practices for their continuation. By opting for a theory of practice which regards the social and symbolic order as given, as materially real, as enduring through history, but also a product of human activity, it is possible to regard social relations as ordered and organized (and maintaining some degree of continuity) but not merely imposed on passive actors. There are no transhistorical or essential dichotomies of gender, but only those practices which reinforce and institutionalize difference. Structures of power and authority will give significance to practice by acting as a pattern of constraint on practice. 'The ability to impose a definition of the situation, to set the terms in which events are understood and issues discussed, to formulate ideals and define morality, in short to assert hegemony, is also an essential part of social power' (Connell, 1987:107).

Social relations are thus more accurately to be considered products or processes rather than unchanging reified structures: patterns of practices which formalize the distribution of power and meaning in material and symbolic organization. Social structure orders practice but is also sustained by custom, convention and sanction. Patterns of social relations – certain configurations of masculinity and femininity, hetero/homosexuality and race relations – are not reified in *nature* but reproduced in *culture*, their very origins in human society cloaked by certain patternings of symbolic and material practices. Particular social orders remain in place not merely through physical coercion or ideological persuasion but by virtue of persisting in networks of interlinking and mutually reinforcing practices. For gender, the institutions and patterns of child-rearing, family relations, domestic and marital divisions of labour, the operations of economy and labour market, the workings of the law and the portrayals of gender in the media, all serve to enshrine and sanction particular practices of constructing gender difference in specific contexts.

Jane Flax refers to the processes of 'gendering' practices by which social relations are both institutionalized in structures and reproduced through everyday interaction (Flax, 1993). Gender is an effect of complex, historically variable sets of social relations in and through which heterogeneous persons are socially organized as members of one and only one of an exclusionary and (so far) unequal pair – man and woman. Masculine and feminine identities are not determined by a pregiven, unchangeable biological substratum. They are created by and reflect structures of power, language and social practices and our struggles with and against these structures. Gender belies the notion of personhood as individualistic, independent and voluntaristic; instead, it is funda-mental to the experience of becoming a cultured being, and we cannot refuse its impact upon the structuring of our subjectivity, relationships, life-chances and actions. However, there may be room for negotiation, subversion and critique, because many theories of gender (such as that of classical psychoanalysis) also point to ways in which the gendering process is incomplete, contradictory or contingent.

Thus, *gendering* expresses the idea that gender is not a fixed or simple identity in the form of the possession of tangible personality traits, or even the result of a single cause. 'Gendering is constituted by complex, overdetermined and multiple processes. These processes are historically and socially variable and are often internally contradictory. The processes of gendering are provisional and must be reproduced and reworked throughout our lives' (Flax, 1993:23).

The conjunction between material and ideological practice – and the inseparability of ideas and actions – is a key precept of poststructuralist theory. For Foucault, truth and knowledge do not exist in some abstract or essentialized form; they are always exerted in and through practices of domination or resistance. At the heart of Foucault's work is the notion of the *discourses* by which regimes of power are exercised and enacted. By discourse he means the regimes, conventions and institutions by and through which particular sets of ideas circulate and gain credence in any specific context. Practice here is the necessary 'capillary' or conduit by which power and knowledge are transmitted; but power and knowledge do not exist outside the very practices by which they are conducted.

> Truth isn't outside power, or lacking in power . . . or the reward of free spirits . . . Truth is a thing of this world; it is produced only by virtue of multiple forms of constraint. And it induces regular effects of power.
> (Foucault, *Power/Knowledge*, 1980:131, quoted in Baynes *et al.* 1987:96–7)

In other words, there is no transcendent sphere of truth, no Archimedean vantage-point from which we can observe objective reality; all knowledge is implicated in the practices of domination or resistance by which it is generated.

Foucault elaborates on this perspective with regard to particular types of practice related to the historical discipline of bodies and sexuality. Both the early twentieth-century science of sexology and the medieval confessional generated a 'technology' of power and difference by which individuals were constructed and located in networks of identity and meaning: for example, particular kinds of sexual normality and deviance, or sexual sin and rectitude (Foucault, 1980). We can only understand the constant and (for Foucault) self-defeating circulation of power and knowledge as enshrined in the 'discursive practices' – ideas and material institutions, sanctions and activities – by which society is regulated and sustained. Yet power is not distributed in terms of its possession or non-possession; it is not in that sense a tangible property to be won or lost. It merely imbues all social practices which produce and reproduce prevailing patterns of knowledge which in turn reflect and enact the ubiquitous embrace of power:

> Power must be analysed as something which circulates, or rather as something which only functions in the form of a chain. It is never localised here or there, never in anybody's hands, never appropriated as a commodity or piece of wealth. Power is employed and exercised through a net-like organisation. And not only do individuals circulate through its threads; they are always in the position of simultaneously undergoing and exercising this power. They are not only its inert or consenting target; they are always also the elements of its articulation. In other words, individuals are the vehicles of power, not its points of application.   (Foucault, 1980:98)

Once more, therefore, a vision of practice emerges which insists upon individual actions as both constructed by, and transcending, relations of power: 'We live in the world, we also watch, and our living informs our watching' (Dawe, 1979:409).

Judith Butler and the Performativity of Gender

Following the post-structuralism of Foucault, in which 'foundationalist' accounts of identity and subjectivity are rejected, Judith Butler argues for a model of the gendered person as founded on *performativity*. It is, in a sense, a radical theory of practice in relation to subjectivity and agency. Her reading of de Beauvoir's adage 'one is not born a woman, but becomes one' leads her to argue that the agential self is an illusion, constructed by hegemonic and totalizing powers. This is more than the widely-accepted point in contemporary feminist theory that the intersections of class, race, nationality and sexuality render an appeal to the universal concept of 'Woman' untenable. Butler resists any idea of a coherent self who actualizes a transcendent reason via a project of consistent agency. Rather, 'there need not be a "doer behind the deed" . . . the "doer" is invariably constructed through the deed' (Butler, 1995b:142). The self is merely a series of *performances* – erased within the ceaseless interplay of signification. Any notion of selfhood representing a prediscursive identity who acts is replaced by a model of subjectivity as constituted completely by 'performative' agency.

Identity – especially gender identity – is thus an act of 'perform-ance': '[I]t constitutes as an effect the very subject it appears to express' (Butler, 1990:24). The agent behind the deed vanishes, as it were, and dissolves into no more than the effect: gender has no ontological status, but merely exists insofar as it is enacted and re-enacted. In Butler's work, the idea of a complete coalescence between will, subject, action and effect is thrown into question.

Agency is, according to Butler, merely 'resignification' of an already existing self constituted in cultural discourse, not the self-willed act of an ontologically grounded being, or the attribute of atomized individuals, prior to networks of power and structures of language. As Butler herself admits, it is 'a contingent and fragile possibility opened up in the midst of continuing relations' (1995b: 137). However, such a refusal to countenance a doer without the deed seems problematic. Is it a complete abandonment and dissolution of subjectivity altogether or merely a radical recontextu-alization of the subject within a network of social relations?

> There is no ontologically intact reflexivity to the subject which is then placed within a cultural context; that cultural context, as it were, is already there as the articulated process of that subject's production, one that is concealed by the frame that would situate a ready-made subject in an external web of cultural relations.
>
> (Butler, 1995a:46)

Butler's model does seem to offer scope to recognize within the 'web' of discourse a subject who is capable of some degree of autonomy, subversion and critical reflection. The alternative would be subjects without memories, autobiographies or consciousness, with no means of explaining individual or collective resistance, change or transformation. Subjectivity may only be effected in and through the cultural context; but it is also historical, enduring and self-aware. Otherwise, such performative identity is totally (and pathologically) ephemeral, like the patient in the neurologist Oliver Sacks' casebook, whose total amnesia condemns him to a perpetual consciousness of the immediate present. Remembering nothing for longer than a few minutes, he must endlessly reinvent himself in a constant 'narrational frenzy' of self-improvization (Sacks, 1986).

Whilst the model of identity as constituted via performative agency is evocative, therefore, it must acknowledge the enduring, systematic and sedimented nature of performances and scripts. Certain patterns of practice constitute us as subjects from the past; they form the matrix within which we come into being. Nor are these random events, but structured and systemic, as Bourdieu's concept of *habitus* well illustrates. All critical capacities are cultural by virtue of being linguistic and historically situated; but they can still be creative, subversive, inspirational and prophetic.

Certainly, as we have seen, the postmodern effect of gender is to suggest a self that is created and brought into being within a given context. But that subject is also self-reflexive: it has some capacity for acting purposefully and self-critically, albeit within the constraints of shared meanings, social structures and systems of power. Thus, to argue that one is constituted through discourse does not deny agency and subjectivity; it is merely to insist upon the cultural context of action and identity. It acknowledges the contingency of meaning, the plurality of the text, the conspiracy of knowledge and power without surrendering the thinking, acting, rational self who may be fragmented and ambiguous, but is always historically and contextually located: '[C]reation is only possible given the tools of our vocabulary, and since vocabularies are always already social, cultural, and historical products, they always speak for an interested viewpoint – though we may not always be conscious of this interested dimension' (Haber, 1994:2).

Butler herself concedes that to be constituted within language is not to be determined by it. Political strategies of the gay/lesbian movement seek to subvert dominant meanings. There is thus an agency – albeit not a prediscursive agent – that can transcend discourse. We are both the tellers and the told of our own narratives of subjectivity and agency; but, like Bourdieu, I tend to plump for a continuity of the self – albeit constituted contextually – which may not be prediscursive, but gains its substance by its coming into being in concrete, embodied, purposeful practices.

> We may be tempted to think that to assume the subject in advance is necessary in order to safeguard the *agency* of the subject. But to claim that the subject is constituted is not to claim that it is determined; on the contrary, the constituted character of the subject is the very precondition of its agency. For what is it that enables a purposive and significant reconfiguration of cultural and political relations, if not a relation that can be turned against itself, reworked, resisted? Do we need to assume theoretically from the start a

subject with agency *before* we can articulate the terms of a significant social and political task of transformation, resistance, radical democratization?   (Butler, 1995a:46)

Practice thus emerges as the process by which social relations are generated. As a working definition, we might characterize practice as purposeful activity performed by embodied persons in time and space as both the subjects of agency and the objects of history. Practice is also the bearer of implicit values and norms within which certain configurations of privilege and subordination are enshrined. Forms of practice, be they medical, therapeutic, scientific, literary – or even, as I shall argue shortly, religious – create and police the boundaries of dominance and subordination, power and powerlessness, upon which any given social order may be constructed. Practice is constitutive of a way of life, both individual and collective, personal and structural.

Such a perspective foregrounding practice is apparent in a variety of disciplines. For example, the history of bodily metaphors and representations has provided powerful, contextual and specific evidence for the intermingling of power relations, symbolic imagery and embodied practices (Foucault, 1980). The role of such representations of the body is central to the construction and maintenance of particular configurations of gender, indeed the entire social order. Another dimension of human culture, namely the study of religion, may also serve as a crucial element in an interrogation of the role of practice in the maintenance of human culture. Bourdieu's work originated in cultural anthropology in which religious ritual as purposeful symbolic practice was regarded as a crucial and fundamental activity by which the mores and myths of a culture were transmitted. Subsequent work has affirmed the importance of studying cultures in terms of the symbolic and material practices – especially rituals and rites of passage – by which core values and social relations are enacted and embodied (van Gennep, 1977).

Religion as one form of purposeful practice thus combines many of the elements noted previously as integral to the generation of human social relations. First, it is a system of symbolic meaning, both in its traditions and teaching and in the images and metaphors by which it depicts truth and safeguards knowledge. Second, it is a sociological, as well as a theological, phenomenon, pointing to the significance of religious institutions and organizations for upholding or subverting any given social order. Third, it is a personal belief-system, contributing to phenomenological and existential self-understanding, and therefore critical in the construction of identity and subjectivity. Religion therefore carries implicit values and serves to prescribe, recreate and subvert many different aspects of our cultural practices concerning human nature, knowledge, values and meaning.

Thus, critical studies of religion as a specific form of cultural practice might help to disclose its contribution in building sub-cultures of institutional and individual reality through which particular patterns of social relations are generated. Christian practice is not just the acting out of predetermined moral norms, or application of doctrinal truths. Pastoral practices, as expressions of the Christian presence in the world, may therefore be seen as the foundation, and not the application of theological understanding.

By focusing on Christian pastoral practices as the creators and bearers of the fundamental truth-claims of the Christian community, therefore, I wish to move toward a model of pastoral theology as the interpretation of the purposeful practices through which symbolic and material reality is both mediated and reconstituted. Rather as Bourdieu envisaged practice as the embodied and enacted *habitus* of cultural norms and values, I wonder whether Christian pastoral practices might be imagined as the bearers of living principles of hope and obligation. However, just as the universality of the criteria underpinning predominant notions of selfhood, truth and value were severely stretched by postmodern perspectives – particularly theories of gender – so the nature and origins of the norms informing Christian practice will require critical scrutiny.

One of the key interpretative tasks of a pastoral theology as the study of Christian practice must be to exert close critical attention to those aspects of tradition, classic texts and contemporary social analysis which constitute the 'sources and norms' for authentic pastoral activity. Chapter 6 will therefore examine different types of contemporary pastoral literature which offer various criteria for determining Christian purposeful presence and community in the world.

♣

Toward a Theology of Practice

Browning's work represents a reformulation of pastoral theology as a form of critical 'excavation' of the truth-claims enacted in the purposeful pastoral actions of the corporate faith-community. He grounds these values in a form of rationalist ethics which represent a return to Christian pastoral action as moral *praxis* but leave unanswered some critical questions concerning the constitution, origins and inclusivity of such normative principles. A critical task therefore remains to identify the possibilities of grounding Christian pastoral practice in alternative values other than those derived from rational ethical discourse.

The next chapter will therefore pursue this question more thoroughly via a survey of representative writings in contemporary pastoral theology. All claim to offer particular *sources* and *norms* for the reconstruction of Christian pastoral practice in the modern world (Young, 1990; Hodgson, 1994). Broadly, *sources* refer to the various authoritative and definitive resources which inform theological discourse and practice: the sources of Christian tradition and doctrine, experience and cultural location all contribute to constructive theological understanding. *Norms* indicate the criteria by which such sources are interpreted; the principles upon which sources are designated authoritative and binding. For example, feminist and liberation theologies identify the Exodus and prophetic strands of Hebrew tradition as a central source from which theology is to be generated. The central norm by which the diversity of theological tradition is to be judged authentic is that of liberation or the 'promotion of the full humanity of women' (Ruether, 1992:12).

My chosen sources and norms for pastoral theology in this chapter derive variously from liberation, feminist and narrative theologies. There is obviously considerable diversity to each of

112

these models, personified in different authors' emphases and preoccupations. Nevertheless, they reflect some predominant influences within contemporary theology in general, and provide the opportunity to assess their impact upon pastoral theology, as well as their implications for Christian practice.

My critique of these genres will centre upon their adequacy for the articulation of a critical, public pastoral theology as the study of purposeful Christian practice. I will also be concerned to integrate contemporary perspectives from theories of gender. I have already established that gender presents significant challenges to prevailing notions of ontology, epistemology, subjectivity, agency and teleology. Thus, attention now turns to the implicit expressions of human nature, knowledge, selfhood, action and destiny which inhabit contemporary theories of pastoral action.

The prominence of *narrative* in contemporary theology reflects, in part, a response to postmodern perspectives which refuse the grand narrative of modernity and turn instead to the proliferation of specific and particular stories which better reflect the pluriformity of postmodern culture (Lyotard, 1984). It is fitting, therefore, to consider it as one potential resource for a renewed pastoral theology. I shall examine how an emphasis on *story* as constitutive of human identity and theological disclosure is finding its way into pastoral theology. The pastoral function of telling stories, whether understood as a generic human story or the particular revelation of the Christian Story, defines the shape of the community and helps locate individual meaning and identity; but it also implies certain kinds of value-commitments concerning the nature of truth and knowledge.

The second genre of literature reflects the impact of gender as a significant site of difference, and draws upon a major component of the critical and reconstructive task of feminist theology, most notably in its emphasis on the category of *women's experience*. The critique will trace how appeals to women's experience, drawn from a variety of sources, are being used to construct new feminist norms for pastoral practice.

Chapter 3 described how the liberation theologies of the 'two-thirds' world made a significant impact on Western theology since the early 1970s and contributed to a re-evaluation of the nature of the pastoral task and the role of the laity in the world. In particular, the emphasis on *praxis* as the source and the arbiter of theological orthodoxy restores practices to the centre of theological formulation. All values, sources and norms are understood as validated and generated in purposeful action (*praxis*) toward liberation. Demands to establish forms of ministry which respond to the social context of pastoral need, and which pursue social and political transformation as well as individual care, therefore feature as a third possible source of reconstructed pastoral values and objectives.

A summary critique of these various models will reflect challenges to the sufficiency and adequacy of the prevailing categories of ontology, teleology, epistemology, agency and subjectivity implicit within the selected pastoral literature. Such critical perspectives may serve as part of the criteria by which pastoral theology might establish guidelines for Christian practices that are sensitive to human experiences of living as creatures and agents of postmodernity.

Narrative

One of the factors emphasized by Browning in re-establishing a connection between pastoral practice and identifiable moral discourse was the increasing pluralism of North American society, and the consequent loss of moral consensus. Browning attempted to recover a process of 'practical moral reasoning' by which the Church might develop an ethical framework that is rooted in Christian tradition, yet open to scrutiny and implementation within the public sphere.

The loss of moral consensus, and the need to forge a distinctive rationale for Christian practice, has exercised other writers as well. In particular, a search for a theological ethics to underpin Christian practice and pastoral ministry has led a number of writers to utilize the resources of narrative theology, and the discipline of hermeneutics – imported from biblical criticism – to provide a foundation for such a framework (Lindbeck, 1984, 1989; Stroup, 1981). The Christian community as moral agent and moral interpreter is thus paramount; but questions arise as to the extent to which such a model retains any mechanism of self-criticism, especially in the face of challenges to the authenticity of its scriptural sources and to the possibility of formulating a 'public' moral discourse.

Hauerwas on the Nature of Christian Ethics

The work of Stanley Hauerwas has been influential within this genre. Hauerwas is concerned to establish theological ethics as the discipline which fosters the development of authentic Christian character. Hauerwas argues that such moral discourse has its foundations in the stories and self-understanding of autonomous Christian communities, rather than in universal rational principles. Hauerwas rejects what he calls 'quandary ethics': decisions attempting to resolve particular dilemmas or moral crises. Rather, Christian ethics should properly concern itself with the consistent fostering of a *habitus* of discipleship, seeing virtue in the context of lives shaped and framed by moral communities.

In this respect Hauerwas shares with Browning an attention to the nature of the embodied and lived moral discourse of particular communities; but, unlike Browning, he rejects the possibility of grounding such an ethical system in publicly-accessible principles. Instead Hauerwas argues that Christian moral discourse is derived from revelation, and therefore exhibits a radical discontinuity with any moral truths that emerge from cultural or 'natural' sources. Christian moral practice is grounded in the narrative particularity of the faith-community. These are definitively the stories of the tradition as embodied in Scripture. Narrative thus serves not to describe the world but to form a community which, by virtue of its particular convictions, forges a moral context out of which moral actions will spring: 'The task of Christian ethics, then, is not to establish universal moral principles on the basis of natural law or some general anthropological claim, but to call Christians to preserve a community that tells the stories that make Christian virtues possible' (Hauerwas, 1981:122).

The disavowal of shared values between church and world, and the unique particularity of the Gospel as embodied in the stories of the Christian community, are therefore central features of Hauerwas' work. Yet his is not a sectarian or quietist vision: he has written extensively on the implications of his model of the Church as moral community for social action, particularly pacifism, and on the pastoral ministry (Hauerwas, 1983, 1985). The Church is understood as a sign of the Gospel to the world, a political institution acting in society, but drawing its core values from what it believes and claims about God. A 'Constantinian' relationship, whereby the Church simply reflects the higher values of secular society, and seeks to serve its needs without challenging or questioning the validity of them, is abhorred; instead, the Church exists to witness to a radical alternative, a 'colony of heaven' (Hauerwas and Willimon, 1989). Moral judgements thus become not blanket condemnations of those who break the rules, but the process by which the Church establishes the norms and conditions of membership. In a reformulation of the pre-Reformation Roman Catholic tradition, therefore, Hauerwas reunites moral theology and pastoral care as integral aspects of ecclesial discipline, placing the emphasis on the life of the Christian community (and not the activity or characteristics of the pastor) as the bearer and agent of moral action.

Hauerwas' emphasis on the community as moral agent rescues moral discourse from any sense of abstraction. It is truly realized (in the sense of both made a reality *and* apprehended) in human practice. He emphasizes that any ethical system, medical or theological, cannot be considered apart from its practitioners. We cannot talk generally about 'religion' or 'medicine' in the abstract, but rather the 'specific set of beliefs, behaviors, and habits embodied by a distinct group of people . . . While it is certainly true that Christianity involves beliefs, the character of those beliefs cannot be understood apart from its place in the formation of a community with cultic practices' (1988:75).

When no moral consensus exists on suffering, the technical power of the medical profession allows practitioners' priorities to become distorted; they must not offer certainties or an escape from suffering, but enable a process of living in the midst of life and death. Those who care for the suffering are impelled to teach the rest of us how to learn from it, not to shield us. To seek to avoid suffering is to deny our finitude and vulnerability to pain and death. The reality of suffering – and the witness of those, like the 'mentally handicapped', who present themselves to us in their suffering – can serve as a point of disclosure to us, and communicate moral truths which open up a world of meaning:

> The issue is not what we do, but rather who we ought to be in order to be capable of accepting all suffering as a necessary aspect of human existence. In viewing our life narrowly as a matter of purpose and accomplishments, we may miss our actual need for suffering, even apparently purposeless or counterpurposeful

suffering. The issue is not whether retarded [sic] children can serve a human good, but whether we should be the kind of people, the kind of parents and community, that can receive, even welcome, them into our midst in a manner that allows them to flourish.

(1988:167)

Caring therefore confronts us with questions of suffering and its ultimate meaning, and the authentically human task is to build a community that can live to acknowledge the significance of suffering for grasping the ultimate meaning and purpose of life. For Hauerwas, such meaning is definitively carried by the Christian narrative, and embodied in the kind of community offered to the world by the Church. If medicine is rightly understood as 'an activity that trains some to know how to be present to those in pain', then 'something very much like a church is needed to sustain that presence day in and day out' (1988:65). Christian ethics, embodied in the narrative life of the community, and enacted in its pastoral care, serves as a corrective to the rational-technical vacuity of secular medical care.

Hauerwas issues a ringing challenge to models of pastoral theology that equate it with social service and the meeting of existential needs, or to models of doctrine that regard cognitive propositions rather than a worshipping and witnessing community as the primary expression of the Gospel. By grounding Christian ethics in the narrative actions of a believing community, he circumvents problems of the relevance and truth of Christian ministry to a pluralist society. He also provides a clear bridge between pastoral practice and theological meaning, by arguing that the nature of the community is itself a living parable of the truth it proclaims. His perspective also offers a primacy to the resources of tradition (especially Scripture) which many critics of mid-century pastoral care feared had been abandoned. The building up of a faithful (and moral) community is believed to take place in the telling and retelling of the definitive Christian story.

However, Hauerwas' stance is problematic. He has yet to prove that such ideal moral communities are empirical realities. Most church congregations within the Protestant and Roman Catholic mainstream, both in North America and Britain, do not conform to his preferred model. Sociologically, the boundaries between church and world are far more blurred and fluid than Hauerwas would attest. This is especially true in the case of the Church of England, where its established position requires it to minister to all those in a given geographical area, and not simply to its own membership. Hauerwas also over-simplifies the actual construction of the biblical tradition upon which he draws: a constant process of synthesis occurred within the early Church between its own self-enclosed identity as a saved community apart from the world, and its surrounding culture. Indeed, to establish itself, it had to embrace the cultural patterns and philosophies of its day. Arguably, therefore, a sensitivity to the realities of the world as an integral aspect of its self-understanding has always been a part of theological formulation and Christian practice.

In failing to acknowledge the wisdom of the world in shaping Christian narrative, therefore, Hauerwas reveals a poor grasp of the history of doctrine. Furthermore, by designating the Christian community the guardian and guarantor of Christian narrative, he opts for a model of Christian ethics which refuses to look beyond its own self-imposed boundaries.

Gerkin and Pastoral Hermeneutics

The essentially interpretative and meaning-disclosive nature of the pastoral task is a theme continued in the work of Charles V. Gerkin, who acknowledges the influence of Gadamer. The recovery of identity on the part of pastoral theology is essentially a task of retrieving the narrative roots of the theological tradition. Narrative forms the central motif by which identity, individual and corporate, is formed; and the pastor, working out of a community of faith to address specific human need, is called to employ narrative and interpretative techniques in order to help form and nurture fundamental identity, meaning and purpose.

Gerkin is therefore concerned to develop what he calls a 'narrative hermenuetical practical theology' (1986:22), in which narrative serves as the primary bearer and interpreter of meaning. The pastoral task, to facilitate Christian living in the modern world, is to relate actions and behaviours to the deeper underlying meanings, by analyzing concrete events, their contexts and causes, their significance and desirable outcome. Pastoral actions are planned on the basis of the values and meanings thereby disclosed, the aim being to facilitate effective and appropriate pastoral practice: 'The pastoral hermeneutical effort is consistently directed toward bringing the unintelligible elements of a situation or event into a degree of understanding so that a fitting response may be made and then tested in the crucible of ongoing ministry in the situation' (1990:593). Meaning in this sense is not simply a question of coherence or understanding, but is given a normative and prescriptive status: interpretation of a pastoral situation aims at articulating a language of the good or the normative, especially in terms of human identity and ultimate purpose. It is thus teleological and ethical in nature; furthermore, it acknowledges its own contextual rootedness in time and the inseparability of interpretation and action (1986:Chapter 3).

For Gerkin, such a pastoral hermeneutic is inter-disciplinary and eclectic. A proper interpretation of a situation requires a diversity of disciplines and levels of interpretation. In this respect, he is placing himself in the tradition of the critical-correlational hermeneutics of Tillich, Hiltner and Tracy. Pastoral ministry as an interpretative and practical venture involves addressing events of ministry and life together, and in critical tension with 'the vision of life that emerges from Scripture and tradition' (1990:592). He acknowledges the complexity and delicacy of integrating different languages and disciplines, and likens such a process to a 'fusion' or 'conversation', whereby the 'horizons' of both sides will be tested. Yet ultimately, the reality of the Christian story appears primary and normative, seeming satisfactorily to resolve the tension between such perspectives:

> It is of crucial importance to ground pastoral identity in the narrative images and metaphors of the Christian story . . .
> This theological notion that our activities are permeated and given redemptive coherence and direction by the activity of God is a central theme of the Christian story. In a sense, it grounds all other themes of that story; it is what it means to be the people *of* God.   (1986:124)

Thus, whilst Gerkin may argue for a correlative and critical conversation between the faith tradition and other sources, he appears to rest ultimate criteria of authenticity upon Christian truth-claims, albeit treated with 'suspicion' (1986:72). In one sense, he does not obscure his prior commitment to the specificity of the community of faith: he has already defined 'pastoral' as representative acts of such a community (1986:18–19). Yet he never names specific limitations or flaws which might cause the tradition itself to be revised. Instead, he concludes by reaffirming a rather uncritical notion of a central, 'timeless' core to the Christian tradition, one which regards the biblical narrative as definitive.

Gerkin thus acknowledges the vulnerability of the Christian story to other narratives, but fails to identify how the content and nature of the Christian story itself is comprised. Hermeneutics, however, has not just been adopted by ethicists and pastoral theologians; feminist biblical scholars, applying similar procedures of suspicion, have cast profound doubts on the reliability of Scripture as an innocent and authentic source of 'the story of God and the people of God'. Scholars like Fiorenza have argued that what the Church conceives as 'Scripture' is by no means identical with historical practice. Rather, received traditions reflect a series of ideological interventions in authorship, editing and canonical construction, which was designed to marginalize women and undermine the earliest practices of inclusive *ekklesia* (Fiorenza, 1983).

Poststructuralist biblical scholars would recognize Gerkin's metaphor of 'conversation'; but they would deploy it as a deconstructionist strategy of undermining fixed and final authorship. The present generation of interpretation is seen as an integral element of the whole text and so there is arguably no fixed and immutable author, meaning or tradition (Williams, 1989). Thus, like Hauerwas, Gerkin assumes the unimpeachability of the Christian community, not just in asserting propositions about the existence and nature of God, but in identifying 'the Christian tradition' as definitively binding upon contemporary practice.

A Theology of Human Story-Telling

Within the British context, the re-evaluation of the identity of pastoral theology is giving rise to a discipline that is multi-disciplinary, exercised by the whole Church, and relating both to the churchly and the societal context (Selby, 1983; Pattison, 1989, 1994a; Reader, 1994). There are signs of developing relationships with the human and social sciences beyond the psychological and psychotherapeutic, and a thorough commitment to divert the allegiance of pastoral theology away from the medicalized, curative, technical mode in favour of the interpretative, existential and discursive (Lambourne, 1983). This section therefore reviews a current writer who exhibits these latter tendencies most strongly. I will concentrate on his evocation of the pastoral task as the discernment of theological potential in the telling of the generic human story.

As well as writing on the nature of pastoral or practical theology, Alastair Campbell has written extensively on medical ethics and the nature of professional care, and health care in particular. In 1989 he moved to New Zealand to pursue his concerns in biomedical ethics, but it is to his efforts to define and articulate the central character and norms of Christian pastoral care that this discussion will attend.

Much of Campbell's work is concerned with the search for a new identity and purpose to Christian pastoral care; but in the process is also concerned to recover its theological dimensions: its ability to evoke deeper understanding of God. In *Rediscovering Pastoral Care*, first published in 1981, he tackles the problems of relating contemporary practice to historical tradition in the pursuit of a renewed pastoral purpose. Many of the available resources and models seem anachronistic: current fashions in the human sciences and the secular helping professions eschew the authoritarianism and narrowness of historical practices, and appear to render many of the assumptions of the received pastoral tradition redundant.

Campbell thus echoes the concerns of writers such as Browning in identifying a breakdown of consensus and an alienation from the historical traditions, and searches for criteria by which a reconstruction of identity and purpose may be forged. Contemporary understandings of human personality do not resonate with older doctrines of sin, virtue and human wholeness, upon which traditional models of care were founded. The contemporary task is therefore to refashion a 'language' of pastoral care that can communicate the essence of human nature and destiny by embodying them in images which are accessible and appropriate to the modern context. At the same time, such a language of human care must begin to point towards the 'transcendent' aspect of pastoral activity, and attain a *theological* status as well.

The interpretative and reconstructive process adopted by Campbell is to regard the vehicle of metaphor as a powerful means of bearing the most enduring elements of the tradition, as well as allowing each new generation to reappropriate meaningful images.

Metaphor thus serves to link the tradition with contemporary practice by engaging the imagination; serving as an interpretative and disclosive device; in opening the tradition to critical scrutiny; resonating with human experience; and pointing to the nature of Divine activity in the world. In this respect, such an approach understands that human nature is essentially hermeneutical, and that acts of interpretation and understanding are fundamental to our identity, or 'being-in-the-world'.

An emphasis on the centrality of metaphor shows what sort of knowledge Campbell believes pastoral theology to be: impressionistic, engaging with the imagination, evoking the mystery at the heart of the Divine–human encounter. Metaphor is thus used as a kind of 'middle axiom', offering avenues into poetry, literature and universal archetypical models of care, but also serving to crystallize and direct theological understandings. It also serves as a vivid vehicle for discussions of pastoral agency, expressing qualities of the carer, the relationship between carer and 'client', and the means by which care is exercised. Thus, the 'Shepherd' embodies the image of God guiding, nurturing and healing the people, of strength and courage and self-sacrificial love. The 'Wise Fool' discloses a simplicity, non-conformity and skilled spontaneity. The 'Wounded Healer' portrays vulnerability, emphasizing mutuality, not expertise, in the exercise of care, and God's redemptive healing in the midst of suffering (Campbell, 1981).

Campbell thus reflects a shift of concern in pastoral theology away from 'care' as directed towards healing, the ending of suffering or even normative models and ideals of human growth. It is to be conceived as a *mode of enquiry* which recognizes in the concreteness of human behaviour (which of course itself needs explanation, analysis, contextualization) particular avenues into Divine disclosure. Hence the importance for Campbell of the human metaphors as bearers of care and meaning.

Campbell articulates a highly incarnational theology, in which the ordinary struggles of human beings to make sense of their lives serves as the fabric of Divine revelation. The community of faith serves not as a privileged guardian of special theological language, but merely as the vehicle for the articulation of the Divine dimensions already made immanent through the human search for meaning, and the articulation of the confidence that God is to be found at the heart of the human condition. The dizzying complexity of (post)modern knowledge is not rejected or counter-posed to theological revelation, but accepted as the very medium of human–Divine encounter.

In claiming the ultimate congruence of art, literature, psychology and theology, Campbell offers no model for the revelation of God as radical disjuncture, as knowledge that is 'Other' to rational human discourse. His is not a tradition of theological understanding which speaks of a decisive *kerygma* by which a new relationship with, or awareness of, the Divine is occasioned. But more crucially, perhaps, nor does his perspective allow for a critique of secular disciplines as reflecting partial and sectional accounts of human experience, and of their possible participation in sanctioning models of human nature that are androcentric or misogynistic.

Campbell therefore omits to declare whether his project is one of recovery, or reworking, of tradition. He appears to believe that traditional images – bearing with them particular assumptions about pastoral agency and models of God – can be recreated at will, and that such a reconstruction can be effected merely by the renewal of language. He does not bargain for the degree to which all human agency is caught up in a complex web of interpretations. No individual 'shepherd', for example, is entirely free to reinterpret that metaphor on his or her own: the language of theology has a public and historic status. The deployment of time-honoured, often scripturally-based metaphors may well link contemporary practice with timeless insights into the human condition and Divine reality, but some discrimination is also needed in order to deter-mine the respects in which the experience of this age is not identical with the past. Thus, Campbell's endorsement of shepherding has to be viewed alongside other more critical responses, sceptical of the desirability or even the relevance of a metaphor which is often more resonant of authoritarian leadership and clerical domination than of shared discipleship (Jones, 1983). This lack of realism in the face of entrenched meanings rather compromises the claims Campbell makes for his reclamation of images of pastoral care from historical anachronism and 'antiquarianism' (Campbell, 1981:1), by failing to offer a sufficiently critical hermeneutic to the 're-discovery' of the metaphors that guide Christian pastoral care.

The sources and norms which inform the communitarian narrative of Hauerwas and Gerkin and the generic human story of Campbell present a model of practice that is orientated towards interpretation, and of forming faith-communities within the parameters of the meanings borne by stories. This affirms a contextual and situated model of the human subject as a non-essential inhabitant of discursive culture, creating and reformulating meaning. However, it is in adjudicating on ultimate truth that the perspectives diverge. Hauerwas and Gerkin pose the Christian Story as absolute and definitive, refusing new situations to reformulate the central symbols of the tradition. Human practice recycles truth, but cannot break in with new revelation, or contradict the points at which occlusive perspectives have been privileged. Their perspective is especially vulnerable to a feminist critique which regards the received tradition as androcentric, and unable to accommodate difference and heterogeneity. Yet Campbell is a mite too indiscriminate with the sources from which the Christian might draw authoritative judgements, and the possibility of opposition between the claims of theology and other truth-claims is discounted.

This is not to argue that Christian pastoral ministry may not usefully draw upon the resources of story-telling or that the truth-claims of the community are not borne in the embodied and incarnational medium of narrative. It is, however, salutary to remember the argument of the deconstructionists: that dominant scientific, medical and political narratives tend to rationalize and naturalize coercive regimes of power and difference, and serve to categorize and exclude subordinated groups as the 'Other'. Thus, the 'hermeneutical suspicion' of the writers discussed is not sufficiently radical or extensive.

Women's Experience

Since the mid-1980s there has been a growing impetus to correct women's invisibility within the pastoral care tradition – especially as active agents – by reclaiming their history and articulating a 'theology of women's experience'. The inclusion of 'women's experience' has therefore informed a wide range of pastoral literature. It encompasses considerations of the impact of women upon the pastoral ministry; reflection on 'feminine' religious experience and its distinctive nature; questions of inclusive language; feminist reconstructions of care, growth, human identity, relatedness and community, and their implications for pastoral practice. However, the analysis of these various issues is by no means unified in its perspective; it would be inaccurate, for example, to assume unanimity in adoption of a 'feminist' perspective, and certainly understandings of the nature of women's experience as a category vary considerably. Critical attention to selected examples of this particular field serves to identify how underlying assumptions about gender identity and difference are being characterized, and how that might challenge the norms by which Christian pastoral practice is conceived.

Women and Pastoral Practice

I have already identified some of the contours of feminist critiques of pastoral care (see Chapter 2). Christian pastoral care is understood to be informed by prescriptions of pastoral need and by models of human development which do not reflect women's lives. This is identified in two main ways: first, in terms of their contribution to pastoral ministry as agents of care; and second, out of changing priorities in terms of women's pastoral needs, hitherto obscured by androcentric practices and institutions. Writers are therefore seeking authoritative sources from which an alternative epistemology might be drawn. One such source has been the psychology of women, informed by the political and theoretical precepts of feminism.

In the collection of essays entitled *Women in Travail and Transition*, Maxine Glaz and Jeanne Moessner offer a series of perspectives, informed by psychology, by which pastoral care might be transformed. They see the psychology of women as the primary source of information by which norms of human identity, fulfilment, healing and community might be discerned. A range of perspectives is presented, deriving from many schools of modern psychology. They all affirm women's experience as socially constructed, embodied, relational and psychosexual, and provide information, especially about the psychodynamics of women's development through the life-cycle, upon which more informed and considered pastoral responses can rest. There is an evident faith in the powers of rational debate and consciousness-raising in effecting more egalitarian pastoral care (Ramsay, 1991:121–2).

The essays in *Women in Travail and Transition* encompass general observations about the counselling of women to more specific discussions of issues such as sexual abuse, sexuality, the tension between economic and domestic responsibilities, depression and gynaecological problems. This is consonant with an overall aim of bringing into the open issues of pastoral concern that have previously been invisible and hidden in discussions of pastoral care. The pastor and the church have a role to play in listening to women's experience, in breaking the taboos of silence which surround issues of abuse, sexuality and nonconformity, and in rethinking harmful and oppressive images and church teachings in order to achieve greater justice and mutuality.

Theology must take its share of responsibility for reinforcing male domination and women's acquiescence in such relationships; so a pastoral response requires the issuing of a challenge to patriarchal prescriptions and the development of more positive images of women. Pastoral practice thus becomes proactive, seeking to change the ideological and material conditions which cause such hurts, refusing to adopt a model of containment or conformity.

Women in Travail and Transition succeeds in bringing to the fore women's experiences and occasions of pastoral need. The theological task is less apparent. Psychological perspectives abound; but, with one exception, are not subjected to sustained critique in terms of the implications of adopting one model over another (Miller-McLemore, 1991). Yet even feminist and woman-centred aims, ends and methods of care still represent implicit understandings of women's nature and selfhood. There is no discussion of the theological response to this, or whether the Church's care of women must simply adapt to the feminist models of therapy and counselling proposed by the psychologies of women.

At points where more specific challenges are levelled at the androcentric legacy of theology, they generally concern the imagery, language and symbolism of patriarchal concepts of God and humanity. It is agreed that such teachings reinforce the self-abnegation and poor self-esteem of women, imprisoning them in abusive relationships and sanctioning subordinate gender roles and stereotypes. There is clearly a theological dimension to the pastoral task. As Nancy Ramsay states in her essay: 'The pastor's role includes listening for and inviting reflection on the religious or theological significance of women's experience' (1991:116). Part of the 'recovery' from abuse will involve confronting and exorcizing traditional images and teachings which caused the woman survivor to feel shame, guilt and self-hatred. There will be a journey through issues of evil, trust, embodiment and theodicy in order to make sense of the experience. Ramsay's essay comes nearest to offering concrete patterns of care that allow theological reformulation to take place; however, they still come over as abstract, existing in debate rather than in examples of practice. Pastoral care is envisaged as 'connection with God's gracious love' (1991:120), but the links between care and theology are not completed.

It is assumed that the theological tradition is authentically inclusive, resting in the iconoclastic ministry and *kenosis* of Jesus. Accounts of his life portray him as nonconformist, and therefore the Gospel affirms the marginal and neglected woman today; but this rests uncomfortably alongside everything else that is said about the patriarchal nature of theology which informs the negative treatment of women by the Church. Thus, ultimately, although the contributors to *Women in Travail and Transition* frequently claim that the sources and norms for the pastoral care of women must be theological, their principal authority still remains that of psychology. One essay insists that 'the pastoral situation focuses theological reflection' (Glaz, 1991:193); but the simultaneously pastoral and theological task of rehabilitating the central doctrines, symbols and ultimate values of the faith, in order that renewed patterns of care may truly embody the Gospel, is not achieved.

There seems to be a kind of dualism to the transformatory project proposed by Glaz and Moessner. On the one hand, new patterns of care can implement the evidently more inclusive and rational visions of empowered and self-actualized women, taking their rightful place in an inclusive and egalitarian Church. However, such renewed relationships are not of themselves the sources of theological disclosure. Changes to the androcentric tradition may occur through the provision of inclusive and affirming God-talk, but the source of its regeneration and the medium of its delivery remain unspecific. When it comes to the pastoral task in facilitating change, the predominant model is one of the Church thinking its way into reform.

There is therefore a question of whether feminist pastoral ministry can assemble its own theological norms – a feminist *telos* – rather than relying upon imported models of psychological growth and empowerment. If not, it will never develop a critical hermeneutic by which it may engage with the established norms of human destiny and need. Although the contributors to *Women in Travail and Transition* recognize the theological vision at the heart of pastoral care, they offer little in the way of practical strategies by which patriarchal theological symbolism and doctrine might be reformed. The establishment of an alternative set of norms for gender-sensitive pastoral practice thus remains abstracted from the actual concrete sphere of the Christian community, failing to heal the rift of theory and practice.

Feminist Theological Anthropologies

From its beginnings, feminist theology has engaged critically with traditional theological understandings of human nature. Valerie Saiving was one of the first to introduce a feminist critique into theology, by arguing that normative notions of sin, love and grace reflected men's experience alone (Saiving, 1979). 'Pride' – excessive self-love and selfishness – is not a universally applicable quality in a culture where women have a less defined and autonomous sense of self. Women's flaw lies in their tendency to practise self-abnegation; but their lived experiences provide the counter-sources by which established norms of ethics and theological anthropology may be corrected.

A number of studies have followed Saiving's early critique and argued that theological understandings of the nature of human destiny, relations between body and soul, prescriptions of virtue, teachings about human sexuality, marriage and gender roles have been conceived from a distorted perspective; one which assumes a particular male norm to be universal. The role of such androcentric accounts of human nature, need and destiny in informing the anthropological norms of pastoral care is therefore of direct concern; as are the processes by which alternative, more inclusive, models might be constructed.

Justes (1978) examines the anthropology of Karl Barth, in particular its relationship to his theological method, and thereafter to ways in which the pastoral practice of the Church 'bears' these messages about God and humanity. Barth's claim that truth comes to us exclusively via the revealed 'Word' of God means that an understanding of human nature and destiny is drawn by analogy from revelation about the nature of God. Barth understood relations between women and men to be modelled on God's relationship to humanity, so that male is to female as God is to humanity. Thus Barth endorsed the primary role of men and the separate and complementary differentiation of the genders. To be male or female is in accordance with the divinely created order – thus sex and gender are ontological – but is also witnessed to in redemption by the relationship of God to humanity, as proclaimed by the Word. Justes challenges this on the basis of Barth's assumption that the Word as mediated to us is undistorted by androcentricism.

Justes also traces the interplay of theological 'ideology' and pastoral practice, arguing that if a pastor believes women to be inferior to men, this will be embodied and enacted in his or her pastoral work. Pastoral practice is thus a key agent in communicating theology to the world, but also a potential channel for theological revision in the light of experience:

> Theology as a study struggles to understand and articulate what it understands about God, and about the relationship between God and humanity . . . Theology is both the Church seeking to understand and express its message to the world and to itself, and a means of self-critique for the Church. In worship and sacrament, in ministry and mission, the Church expresses its theology. And in doing so the theology offers to the Church a critique of these expressions of theology.   (Justes, 1978:42)

Thus, patterns of pastoral ministry may derive directly from dominant understandings of the human person based on distorted or ideological appreciations of human nature, often mediated by norms of virtue, Christian maturity and pastoral need. The anthropological, theological, ethical and pastoral become intertwined, and ultimately are expressed as much in pastoral practice as in the statements of codified doctrine.

As I have argued earlier, the postmodern perspective on ontology and subjectivity does not perceive human nature as above or beyond history and human agency. This represents an affirmation of the importance of human history and agency within culture as the bearers and generators of truth and redemption. Human institutions, like the Church, can bear negative or positive anthropologies. Redemption has to be enacted. Theology is borne by human actions, texts and practices, as Justes argues in the passage quoted above. Barth's mistake was to believe that clues to human relations were pre-existent in creation, so failing to see the redemptive possibility in a world yet to come fostered in accordance with God's will by human effort.

Versions of feminist theory that overvalue either fixed biological and essential differences, or deny the diversity of sexual and embodied existence, refuse the complexity and lived reality of difference. Mary Buckley has identified what she calls a 'transformative' model of human nature that aims to change personal gender stereotypes and their social and cultural contexts (Buckley, 1979). This model recognizes the social context of anthropology, countering an ahistorical or essentialist model of ontology and subjectivity.

Supremely, therefore, the role of choice and strategic agency is affirmed, as practice is placed at the centre of the process by which human nature is realized and transformed. Clearly, human agency is exercised within the constraints of history and culture, which is comprised of structures, ideologies and cultural prescriptions, themselves the result of historical practices. Theological anthropology must therefore recognize the contextual and agential nature of human identity.

This is firmly a future or agency-orientated understanding, both of revelation and of the dynamics of human personhood. God is not restricted to overseeing fixed laws of creation; revelation can work through human affairs. Nor is human nature a fixed entity awaiting an unveiling independent of a given context. Nature and culture are dynamic and interactive, and form both the context and the constituents of human identity. The norms for Christian practice may have been guided by distorted and ideological notions of what it means to be human; but new strategies, which fuel and enact alternative visions, may be forged out of the old.

Pastoral Praxis in a Global Context

The theologies surveyed so far have originated from a Western context, and Britain and the United States in particular. However, a broadening of vision is necessary to take account of the global dimension of pastoral theology. As I have already suggested, developments within Latin American liberation theology were instrumental in the emergence of new perspectives on the theological and ecclesiological status of Western pastoral theology. In particular, the emphasis upon the 'pastoral' as denoting the experiential, contextual and lived situation of an entire community of faith represents a significant movement in theology, and this will be reviewed in more detail, looking in particular at sources and norms of this genre.

Liberation theology has developed its own distinctive methods and claims to knowledge, breaking decisively with traditions of Western theology. It arose out of a specific pastoral and political context, namely a growing awareness by members of the churches, and the Roman Catholic Church in particular, of the social conditions of the people. The societies of South and Central America displayed extremes of wealth and poverty, with millions of peasants forced to give up their lands to grow 'cash crops' for export, and driven into the cities where unemployment was high, labour non-unionized and wages low. In Chile, Argentina, Brazil, El Salvador and Somoza's Nicaragua, military governments enforced repressive political regimes, outlawing political opposition and arresting, torturing and murdering thousands of dissenters. Church workers and members were themselves experiencing such conditions at first hand, as a result of a gradual process of greater engagement with social and political issues during the 1950s and 1960s. Some of this impetus was undoubtedly due to the popular mobilization of political dissent, articulated by an emergent middle-class intelligentsia, and inspired by the success of the Cuban revolution in 1959 (McGovern, 1989).

However, there were also stirrings within the Church which prompted a greater engagement with social issues. Statements emerging from the Second Vatican Council encouraged an understanding of the Church as a community of faith, and the vocation of the faithful as expressed in pastoral work for social justice; and social encyclicals such as *Populorum Progressio* (1967), reflected a sophisticated economic and social analysis which identified structural and political causes of human suffering and injustice. Major portions of the Roman Catholic Church in Latin America responded to the spirit of change, and many people, lay and religious, were mobilized into programmes of evangelization and education amongst the urban and rural poor (McGovern, 1989:4–15).

Such first-hand exposure to the realities of poverty and political powerlessness contributed to the development of politically conscientized individuals. The Medellin Conference of 1968 set out three priorities for the Church in Latin America: the establishment of 'basic ecclesial communities'; becoming the church of the poor; and the pursuit of justice and peace. These objectives further encouraged models of pastoral practice which focused on grass-roots activism and political solidarity with the poorest of the poor.

Liberation theology began to emerge, therefore, as a response to the pastoral needs of the poor requiring more than individual acts of charity, or exhortations to the poor to have greater faith; instead, Christian pastoral concern was understood as demanding purposeful action in pursuit of social change. Following Marxist theory, in which the end of proper knowledge is held to be revolutionary practice in the pursuit of freedom and human liberation, the authentic expression of Christian faith was understood to be that of *praxis*: 'a transforming activity marked and illuminated by Christian love' (Gutiérrez, 1988:xxx).

Liberation theology thus offers a radically different definition from the Western tradition of theological truth as intellectual assent to the philosophical precepts of Christianity, and right belief as the true test and end of faith and the criterion for inclusion in the faith-community. Instead, liberation theologians emphasize the centrality and necessity of right actions. The 'preferential option for the poor', adopted at the Bishops' Conference in Puebla in 1979, affirmed the ethical core of the Gospel as the advancement of the dignity and full participation of the poor. Any aspects of the tradition which deny or preclude this are considered inauthentic. The role of theology, its epistemological status and the norms by which such sources are validated, is determined by its ability to transform the world. *Orthopraxis*, the proper living out of faith – in the service of the poor – becomes the central norm by which theological 'truth' is determined (McGovern, 1989:43–6).

This, therefore, identifies one distinctive characteristic of liberation theology: a commitment to *praxis* as the overarching goal of theological knowledge. A second, methodological, feature has been to lay bare the contextual origins and authors of theology, thereby challenging the claims of Western theology to reflect universal and abstract truths. Liberation theologies succeed in reminding all theologians that their truth-claims have authors, contexts and practical implications.

Thus, the pastoral care movement in Central and South America pursues social transformation as the appropriate pastoral response to human need (Rosa, 1990). Economic and political affairs are a priority for most churches, although many of the conservative evangelical Protestant denominations concentrate on individual salvation and pastoral care. Within the mainstream tradition of liberation theology, however, Christian pastoral practice in the base communities is guided by the norms of *praxis*, as the enactment of faith towards social transformation. Pastoral care is understood as synonymous with emancipatory *praxis*; and for theologians like Leonardo and Clodovis Boff, the 'pastoral' constitutes the context of human need to which *praxis* is the appropriate response. In considering the epistemological status of liberation pastoral theology, the emphasis is upon truth as serving the ends of emancipation; and indeed, of theology itself generated only within a context of engagement and action.

> Reflecting on the basis of practice, within the ambit of the vast efforts made by the poor and their allies, seeking inspiration in faith and the gospel for the commitment to fight against poverty and for the integral liberation of all persons and the whole person – that is what liberation theology means. From all this, it follows that if we are to understand the theology of liberation, we must first understand and take an active part in the real and historical process of liberating the oppressed.   (Boff and Boff, 1987:8–9)

'Very Third World, Very Asian, Very Women'

The work of Chung Hyun Kyung from Korea serves as a powerful example of liberation theology within a feminist perspective. She echoes the emphasis of all liberation theology on emancipatory *praxis* as the key arbiter of epistemological validity: for her, theology is pledged to the creation of an identity for Asian women, which is free of the bonds of colonialism, economic exploitation, racism and sexism. Protest against the oppressive social conditions of Asian women – as 'Han of han', or the poorest of the poor – forms the social context; but the theology which is to emerge must authentically reflect women's aspirations and experiences, and must not be couched in the alien tongue of a dominant culture. Thus women look for a theology that will affirm and advance their 'womanity': a full humanity that values their 'gender specificity', rather than subsuming it under a universal (but covertly androcentric) human anthropology. Chung thus identifies this emergent theology as 'very Third World, very Asian and very women'.

An appeal to the distinctive character of women's experience and knowledge is prominent: an analysis of oppression on gender, class, ethnic and national lines will be combated by a renewed spirituality and theology. These will reflect women's political, economic, cultural and psychological situations; affirm a spirituality that rests upon holistic, corporate, ecological and cyclical patterns; and name women's creative and nurturant capabilities as part of the nature of God. However, women's experiences are identified as grounded in the context of a cultural and political struggle; the project is that of naming their own experience for themselves. Thus, Asian women resist romantic evocations of 'culture' and 'tradition' – especially concerning the supposedly submissive and gentle characteristics of Asian women, embodying 'complementarity' and 'harmony' – which make women the bearers of (Western-imposed) fantasies about Asian culture and the 'Eternal Feminine' (Chung, 1990: 24–32).

Chung's understanding of theological method and epistemology is worthy of note. This nascent theology, as she relates in *Struggle to be the Sun Again*, owes its development to its corporate nature, out of various networks and collectives of women theologians. The community is the chief agent of theological construction, and it is 'inductive, collective and inclusive'. Such a theology must be conceived as 'God-praxis' not 'God-talk': primarily a commitment to struggle and social transformation. It comes from women's experience and is articulated out of reflection upon Christian traditions; but it is ultimately validated by participation in practice. However, Chung insists repeatedly on the specificity of this theology: women's experience is primary and authoritative, and the efficacy of such transformatory knowledge is judged according to criteria of 'womanity'.

Another interesting feature of Chung's account concerns the knowledge claims of theology in relation to cultural and religious pluralism. The mingling of Western missionary Christian culture with indigenous traditions, especially concerning the status of women, figures prominently in other sources emerging from women within the world Church; the question of how the resources of the faith are to be expressed and embodied within a culturally specific milieu in response to human need is frequently debated (Kanyoro,

1991:57). Chung wishes to extend conventional notions of what might be authentically Christian by insisting that the demands of the struggle may require significant revision of the given tradition. The syncretism of Christian theology with indigenous Korean spirituality is a necessary and welcome enrichment of *praxis*. Finding vibrant sources of emancipatory practice – like the harnessing of shamanistic techniques of exorcism, the 'Han pu-ri' of breaking the bonds of social injustice, and assimilating an ancient cultural heritage in the name of dignity and liberation – takes precedence over maintaining an irrelevant and narrow orthodoxy:

> In their struggle for survival and liberation in this unjust, women-hating world, poor Asian women have approached many different religious sources for sustenance and empowerment. What matters for them is not doctrinal orthodoxy ... What matters to Asian women is survival and the liberation of themselves and their communities ... Syncretism has been such a 'dangerous' word for Western theologians ... Syncretism, for them, is the lazy and irresponsible way of combining different religious heritages without any principles. They talk as if Christian identity is an unchangeable property which they own. Any radical break of Asian theologians from orthodoxy in an effort to dive deep into our Eastern traditions and be transformed by them has been considered suspicious by Western church leaders. Traditional Western theologians seem to say to us that they have the *copyright* on Christianity: 'All rights reserved – no part of our teaching may be reproduced in any form without our permission.' (Chung, 1990:113)

This highlights the tension between a view of Christian tradition as immutable and timeless or always changing in its interaction with human sciences, diverse cultures and different world-views. Along with it goes the question of authority in relation to 'orthodoxy': Chung is advocating a model that draws its authority from the *Minjung*, or people's liberation struggle. She thus renders theological epistemology and authority as resting within, and relying upon, *praxis*; and of its being provisional and mutable. Yet clearly, as she is only too aware in the above quotation, there must be normative criteria for *praxis*, even if its guiding principles can no longer be seen as fixed and absolute propositions. The challenge of theological claims to truth, relevance or authenticity as posed by pluralism thus acquires a further dimension of particular concern to pastoral theology: that of developing an adequate notion of *orthopraxis* which can survive rapid social change, diversity of human need and cultural pluralism, without collapsing into an anti-theoretical or anti-epistemological account of pastoral care.

Liberation Theology and Pastoral Care

Recently, a number of Western pastoral theologians have attempted to adopt the methods and values of liberation theology as a model for pastoral care. Under the transformative influence of the liberative model, the objectives of pastoral activity are translated into those of social transformation: of action for justice. In contrast to the therapeutic model of twentieth-century Western pastoral care, which liberationists characterize as privatized, élitist and individualistic, pastoral practice as liberation takes place in the public, political domain: in medical and other welfare institutions, or via social policy measures, political intervention or maybe community development. Salvation embraces the entire inhabited universe, not merely disembodied souls; nor is the Gospel a consolation in the next world for social injustices in this one.

Stephen Pattison's argument in *Pastoral Care and Liberation Theology* is that contemporary pastoral care is individualistic, apolitical and ameliorative, failing to identify or act against the underlying dynamics of injustice. Pattison indicts the discipline, and most pastoral practitioners, as neglectful of any critique of structural and policy dimensions to human need. In this respect, he is seeking to transpose the insights and methods of Latin American liberation theology into a local context, and uses the field of mental illness as an illustration of his intentions. He offers an account of mental illness – its ontogeny, diagnosis and treatment – which emphasizes the interrelationship between low socio-economic status and ill-health, the comparative power of the medical and psychiatric professions to determine patient treatment and the influence of gender, race and class discrimination (1994:83–170).

Pattison presents a formidable array of evidence to indicate massive – and ever-widening – inequalities of access and provision in health care, personal social services and welfare benefits. Thus, it is appropriate to think of 'the poor' as constituting a significantly dispossessed class in Britain today, and those who have experienced mental illness, of whatever type or severity, as further disadvantaged and marginalized by the standard of care they receive. The greater preponderance of mental illness amongst women features in the discussion: Pattison integrates many of the feminist critiques of women and mental illness and the role of the Church in reinforcing models of feminine passivity and self-abnegation. In response to this neglect, Pattison seeks to reconstruct pastoral care according to criteria based upon the principles of liberation theology and liberating *praxis* (1994:223).

On the one hand, the reader gains a graphic account of the abuses of institutionalized and impersonal psychiatric regimes; but if the alternative is to cast vulnerable people into the void of 'care in the community' where resources and support are cut to a minimum, then there may be something to be said for the benefits of benign institutions. Therefore, more work is needed to develop a pastoral care which is reconstructive as well as critical and prophetic. In particular, the question arises of how pastoral care may be guided by a set of values that are both politically-aware and theologically-informed; and how pastoral practitioners can work to achieve these ends in concert with clients and user groups as well as health care professionals and policy-makers.

Pattison gives a very persuasive and thorough account of the *politics of pastoral care*: that policies affect and shape our lives, and that the relationships of giving and receiving care are also trans-actions of power. However, liberation theology does more than simply politicize Christian practice. It presents us with an entirely new model of theological formulation that privileges the poor as theological agents. It also identifies the experiences and interests of those on the 'underside' – be it of the economic order or the mental health system – as the most authentic perspectives against which *praxis*, or value-directed transformation, is to be judged. I wonder whether the radical implications of this have properly permeated our consciousness. It may suggest that the experience of mental illness warrants more than mere patient consultation, towards regarding the condition, and the compassionate response it elicits, as in some way indicative of the dynamics of suffering and redemption. It challenges our preconceived notions of personhood to suggest that experiences of brokenness and fragmentation need to be integrated into our dominant notions of self, community and value. This is of far-reaching consequence: not least because it still seems to beg the question of how to build sources and norms of care that resist labelling or pathologizing difference whilst promoting human wholeness. In other words, we are still short of a way of valuing the insights into suffering and salvation elicited by accounts of vulnerability and illness whilst being able to distinguish those forms of mental illness that express themselves in religious delusion and distorted spirituality.

Conclusion

The critique of various genres of pastoral theology has focused on the sources and norms which inform their chosen patterns and objectives of pastoral practice. One critical question to emerge concerns the relationship between tradition and contemporary context; in particular between old and new theological images, prescriptions and norms and their respective authority in informing pastoral practice. The perspectives rooted in the psychology of women and the telling of stories recognize the inadequacy of the established sources; but they are insufficiently rooted in material practice to effect a concrete transformation of the dominant tradition. They fail to identify the specific steps by which the values and metaphors of care are actually realized in the midst of human regimes and relations.

In contrast, the narrative emphasis of Hauerwas and Gerkin is that values are always already embodied in the practices of community. However, the changing circumstances and contexts of such value-directed communities are insufficiently acknowledged, with the result that the truth-claims to which the communities were living witnesses are never exposed to critical scrutiny or reformulation. Such a model proposes an enacted and contextual model of human nature, and a narrational and situated notion of knowledge. However, Christian Story as definitive source posits an essentialized and ahistorical view of revelation which refuses to regard the ultimate claims of faith as contingent upon human authorship.

Appeals to the authority of the Christian community are rejected as too sectarian in a pluralistic society where theology must be available as public truth. Similarly, appeals to the authority of Scripture are insufficiently critical of the ideological nature of such texts, and the extent to which a model of human nature as hermeneutic must take account of the connections between knowledge and power. Anthropological or feminist appeals to pastoral sufficiency as resting in the discovery of a 'true self' are also inadequate in the light of the postmodern and post-psychoanalytic 'decentering' of subjectivity as fragmented, socially mediated and coerced. It is more satisfactory to opt for understandings of human identity as forged in and through practice, glimpsed in the process-orientated perspectives of feminist theological anthropology.

The evocation of women's experience represents an attempt to revise existing sources and norms toward a more inclusive definition. The aim is to rethink patterns of care to conform more accurately to women's needs and natures, as identified in psychology and anthropology. The theological tradition, conceived as primarily symbolic and metaphysical, is then adjusted to portray images and ideals which are more affirmative of women. The Christian community exhibits patterns of care because of its commitment to gender equality; but this is asserted *de facto*, without attention to the problems of reformulating an androcentric tradition. The enactment of care and the reformulation of theology are effectively regarded as separate processes.

Criteria for authentic Christian pastoral practice as determined by a model of liberatory *praxis* locate human identity within history, and identify theological knowledge as arising from a specific context and harnessed to transformatory and political ends. Models of Christian pastoral practice within liberation theology ground the normative principles for social transformation in a model of action and reflection upon experience and social context. The criteria for authentic practice – the values of liberation – are both the sources and the objects of pastoral practice. Priorities for the Church's pastoral activity rest upon critical reinterpretation of sources and norms only realized in concrete situations. This reflexivity of values is consistent with many of the perspectives from theories of gender; but this very contingency renders critical attention to the selection of sources and norms for *praxis* all the more important.

Therefore, when considering what kind of sources and norms are required for an adequate pastoral practice in a contemporary context, one conclusion to emerge is that such values arise from, and inform, purposeful practices. What is normative and authentic for the Christian community is enacted and embodied in *praxis*. It is these diverse pastoral practices that reveal, and construct, the dominant frameworks of meaning and truth. The activities of fostering moral ways of life, story-telling, promoting human development, and pursuing gender equality are undertaken because the community has inherited, and inhabits, a particular set of truth-claims. These claims are fundamentally theological; Christian pastoral practice has particular aims and ends because of what Christians proclaim and experience concerning God. However, although God is understood as transcendent reality, the theological values of practice are only manifested in the concrete *praxis* of the community in a given context.

Browning's vision for the guiding sources and norms of Christian practice argues that the objectives of pastoral care are to foster the expression of human rational moral principles. The life of the community enables Christians to live out those moral norms; patterns of believing and belonging aim to fulfil the precepts of moral reasoning. Browning argues that the Christian community and its pastoral practice are organized in order that Christians may be moral and truthful; pastoral actions are expressions of rational moral reasoning. Patterns of believing and belonging aim to fulfil the precepts of moral principle. However, an alternative model may be developed in the light of the above critique. This would argue that a principled way of life exists only in human *praxis*. Christians act in ways they believe to be good, just and true because they inhabit a community which aspires to realize a particular vision of ultimate value – in their case, the reality of God. In effect, this perspective on the dynamics of pastoral practice turns Browning's argument on its head. Rather than congregational life being the expression of ethical principles and pastoral actions the outworking of moral reasoning, I want to assert that faithful and purposeful practice springs from participation in a value- and vision-directed tradition. The *practical wisdom* of the faithful and practising community is the medium by which truth-claims and value-commitments come into existence.

Therefore, the focus for principled and theologically-informed pastoral practice rests upon the ordering of the life of the faith-community, but must be an analysis which resists appeal to ultimate values enshrined beyond the *praxis* of that same community. The task of the pastoral theologian, in articulating the values by which such faith-communities practise, is therefore not to construct *a theology of pastoral care* which regards action and value as separate. Instead, pastoral theology is *critical phenomenology*, studying a living and acting faith-community in order to excavate and examine the norms which inhabit pastoral *praxis*.

As this chapter has related, contemporary pastoral practices of all kinds are informed by a diversity of sources and norms which constitute the prescriptive and evaluative core of *praxis*. The criteria generated by critical theories of gender offer an interpretative framework by which the adequacy of these models may be assessed. The contextuality of human community, the non-essential nature of identity and experience, the necessity of identifying biases inherent in epistemological claims, and the strategic nature of ultimate aims and ends suggested that models which locate their prescriptive values in the contingency of practice were more consonant with human experience as gendered and allow the possibility of creative transformation. Effectively, gender challenges pastoral practice to refuse any system of sources and norms which lies in metaphysics or beyond human agency or mediation. However, this is not to say that Christian practice cannot derive from religious experience; merely that such theological precepts must always be grounded and enacted in concrete situations.

If the normative values of the faith-community are indeed constructed in value-informed and value-directed practice, and if perspectives from postmodernism and gender theories favour contingent and situated notions of human identity and destiny, then the normative criteria for such practical reasoning lose any fixed or metaphysical properties. The norms of history and tradition become embodied in the accrued experience of the past, and attain binding status only insofar as they validate current purposes. With no external or absolute prescriptive values, judgements concerning the finality of any particular truth-claims are rendered problematic. What is needed is a critical theory of pastoral action by which reliable and verifiable norms can be established from within the reflexivity of *praxis* and community. Social theory after postmodernism is grappling with a similar dilemma, and so, in the next chapter I will investigate some of these debates in order to develop critical criteria for a satisfactory model of Christian practical wisdom.

CHAPTER 7

Community and Alterity

Reason is not a faculty or capacity that can free itself from its historical
context and horizons. Reason is historical or situated reason which gains
its distinctive power always within a living tradition. (Bernstein, 1983:37)

One of the themes of my discussion so far has been the search
for articulating a basis for post-postmodern ethics and politics:
criteria for transformative action that does not wish to abandon the
imperatives of hope and obligation. One possible solution, already
identified in Chapter 5, has been to turn to the various theories of
human action which place *practice* at their heart. These theories
regard prescriptive norms for transformative *praxis* as defined not
by metaphysical norms but as inhabiting the discursive and concrete
practices of communities. Such theories reject foundationalist
claims to identity and knowledge, in that they deny the intrinsic
neutrality of a knowable world, but instead offer a model of reality
as the outcome, and not the precondition, of human knowing. They
start from the basis that knowledge and agency do not involve
the collection of facts about a world 'out there', apprehensible
via rational thought. Instead, they take the notion of human practice
as constitutive of identity, meaning and knowledge, and extend
it into attempts to take the discursive, the practical and the performative as the basis for moral and epistemological foundations,
whilst refusing to collapse back into extra-discursive or pre-cognitive
criteria.

Whilst such theories of practical wisdom de-essentialize the
conditions for prescriptive reason in the service of politics and
ethics, and admit that knowledge is the contingent product
of human action, they insist that the potential exists for a 'post-
metaphysical' *phronēsis*. This chapter will therefore undertake a

142

critique of some theories of human action and practice which seek to move epistemology and ontology beyond the postmodern impasse in the name of an anti-foundationalist ethical discourse and political action.

In their various ways, all theorists discussed have a commitment to keeping faith with post-Enlightenment notions of rationality, freedom and value, whilst seeking to engage critically and constructively with postmodernism. For that reason, I shall not consider theorists who wish to reject the insights of post-Enlightenment philosophy and social theory; so the communitarian basis of rationality and morality proposed by Alasdair MacIntyre (1987) will not be discussed here.

By contrast, the writers discussed here are mindful of, and sympathetic to, much of the anti-foundationalist project. Nevertheless, all are concerned to retain a vision of ethics and politics by developing frameworks of rational discourse upon which practical responses can draw. This is also pertinent to the task of constructing a critical theology of pastoral practice which is sensitive to postmodernity, because all regard the process of the legitimation of knowledge as a practice, sustained by particular, situated human communities. However, they replace the principle of objective reason with the establishment of *conversations* between members of localized communities as the benchmark of sustainable norms of truth, value and morality.

Habermas and Critical Theory

> The project of modernity, the hope of Enlightenment thinkers, is not a bitter illusion, not a naive ideology that turns into violence and terror, but a practical task which has *not yet* been realized and which can still orient and guide our actions.   (Bernstein, 1985:31)

Critical Theory shares with poststructuralism a thorough critique of the claims of modernity and a suspicion of universalizing reason. It insists, however, upon the possibility of a critical reinterpretation and reconstruction of the nature of subjectivity and political agency under modern capitalism, and it argues for the viability of an *emancipatory reason* which transcends the authoritarian, totalizing ideologies of hegemonic institutions. Critical Theory thus has the potential for the articulation of prescriptive norms for a *praxis* of resistance and change. Many critics of the postmodern tendencies identified above have therefore found an affinity for their concerns with the work of contemporary inheritors of the Frankfurt School, and with Jürgen Habermas (1929–) in particular.

Whilst critical of modernity, such a reconstructive project does not attempt to resort to a wholesale rejection of the fruits of the Enlightenment, especially a commitment to the emancipatory potential of human reason and agency. Similarly, Habermas is understood as sharing many of the preoccupations of poststructuralism, especially its concern with language as both constitutive of human relations and as the vehicle of interpretation and meaning. He stresses the possibility of forging rational values out of collective speech communities, whilst still subscribing to a radical critique of empirical and positivist epistemology (Bernstein, 1983).

Habermas' work is characterized by its eclecticism. His influences include American pragmatism and Freudian psychoanalysis as well as Marx, Heidegger and the Frankfurt School of Adorno, Horkheimer and Marcuse. Habermas' central concern is whether the processes of modernity as exemplified in the Enlightenment have been irrevocably distorted and discredited by the tendencies of late capitalism, or whether it is possible to realize an ideal society in which social relations and individual subjectivity are not alienated.

Critical Theory starts with a critique of positivism. Modernity has narrowed and distorted human reason by affording a primary and privileged epistemological status to the norms of empiricism and objectivism. In the spirit of Max Weber, the Frankfurt School saw the Enlightenment as representing both the liberation of human reason from traditional and authoritarian control, but also its enclosure in the pervasive assertion of *Zweckrationalität* (instrumental-technical rationality). As the dynamics of modernity come to dominate all spheres of public and private life, so a 'disenchanted' social world is stripped of the premodern charisms of traditional and affective rationality. The result, according to Weber, is the inevitability of the 'iron cage' of bureaucracy: a society entrapped by instrumental-technical reason, with its claims to universality and objectivity, which obscure questions of value and prevent dissent from the dominant notions of acceptable knowledge and truth. The work of Theodore Adorno in particular reflected this sense of the inevitability of authoritarian State domination as a condition of modernity, not only in the economic sphere, but also in the repressed subjectivity of the individual (Kearney, 1994; Baynes, 1987).

Adorno presented an analysis of late capitalism as a society of 'total administration': the alienation inherent in the appropriation of the fruits of workers' labour had been further systematized and extended into all areas of society, including leisure, consumerism, sexuality and the family. Beneath the rhetoric of liberal democracy, welfare rights and personal freedom lay a coercive State which pursued its hegemonic practices into the most intimate areas of life. For Herbert Marcuse, the State endorsed sexual freedom whilst reducing sexuality to a commodity by which gratification is marketed and controlled, denying human creativity and autonomy and settling instead for alienated acquisitiveness. Thus modern society advocates tolerance, personal freedom and the pursuit of pleasure, but these are ideological values, claims to a superficial equality which mask the underlying relations of domination. Production, consumption, knowledge and culture are all manufactured and homogenized with no real content beyond encouraging society to accept the commodification of human satisfaction. The transformation of such alienated consciousness will only occur through the actions of those who rebel against such repressive hedonism in the name of a creative consciousness which transcends instrumental and technical domination.

However, although early figures in the Frankfurt School concentrated on tracing the 'negative dialectics' of alienated consciousness, Habermas was also concerned to move beyond a mere critique of modernity. He draws upon Hegelian and Marxian notions of History as possessing an emancipatory and enlightening Spirit (*Geist*) which challenges the monopoly of *Zweckrationalität*. He seeks to identify the nature of such emancipatory reason, and the conditions within which its expression can be generated and its authenticity guaranteed.

In his first major work, *Knowledge and Human Interests*, published in 1971, Habermas developed a central theme of his work: namely, rationality and principled knowledge as practical, contextual and dialogical. Knowledge is the reflection of material interests rather than abstract ideals; therefore all knowledge reflects particular kinds of human interests as expressed in social relations. Habermas identifies three kinds of knowledge: practical, emancipatory and technical. Modernity has signalled the encroachment of the latter over the other two. However, this represents a distortion of human reason, which Habermas regards as finding its most authentic and liberatory expression in the non-coercive, mutually-revealing exchanges of human communication. Habermas is enough of a historical materialist (after Marx's inversion of Hegel on history) to stipulate that ideal discursive communication is only possible in conditions of non-oppressive social relations. The aim is thus to begin generating normative practices, however distorted and partial, that can realize such a community of discourse.

In his subsequent work, Habermas develops his understanding of practices of communication which would constitute values capable of exposing and dethroning the hegemony of instrumental rationality. This is the central theme of his *Theory of Communicative Action*, published in 1981. The corporate and communicative nature of language, and the human encounter this entails, is for Habermas the ethical heart from which political norms and policies will emerge. The nature of language and its relationship to human culture and meaning is paramount: thus, like the poststructuralists, Habermas understands identity and selfhood as constructed by language and mediated in 'speech-acts', thereby repudiating an essentialist view of the subject. However, unlike the poststructuralists, Habermas deploys his 'linguistic turn' in the service of a defence of the possibilities of purposeful, principled action, by arguing that the very existence and use of language guarantees some kind of faith in the possibility of rational discourse and human community. Language entails and ensures sociability: any speech-act implies a desire to communicate and a commitment to the possibility of the creation of mutual understanding and shared meaning. Such conversations can be harnessed in the service of emancipatory principles and practices, by acting as the testing ground for rationality and political strategy. Speech therefore establishes relationship and reveals an intention to forge *moral-practical* or *aesthetic-practical* reason, which can serve as a source of political practice other than the *instrumental-technical* rationality of the ruling class (Bernstein, 1985:17ff).

Thus, in his assertion that shared coherent meaning is possible, Habermas is talking about the possibilities for establishing a vision of human community. He points towards the means of its generation, in intersubjective communication. He is not denying the reality of coercive, alienating and totalizing rationality, or descending into a metaphysics of presence concerning the availability of external sources of truth and universal reason. Habermas thereby implicitly challenges the assumption at the heart of poststructuralism's dismantling of reason: any notion of truth as undistorted communication necessarily implies an intolerance of the free play of *différance* in the name of denying the plurality and polyversity of the subject. Rather, Habermas argues that intersubjectivity establishes rational conversation – presumably because it has some degree of rule-governance – which can underwrite truth not as absolute, which is where it does become totalizing, but as enacted consensus, albeit fallible and contestable.

Habermas is alert to the dangers of evoking romantic or nostalgic notions of community. He is aware of the difficulties of actually creating the conditions for such intersubjective communication, when all is distorted by hegemonic institutions and belief-systems. The consensus which underwrites emancipatory reason may never actually exist: it is arguable that if it did, all dialogue would cease and another totalizing system of knowledge would result. However, Habermas proposes the notion of the 'ideal speech situation', free of any external coercion or distortion, in which all participants could assent to the rightness of the argument (Dews, 1987:192–9; Bernstein, 1983:182–9). Such a consensus might never exist in actuality. However, Habermas argues that it does in a phenomenological sense, because human encounter is based around the assumption that some consensus exists, even though the participants simultaneously realize that they are 'bracketing' or suspending their doubts. Habermas calls this a 'universal pragmatics', in which our everyday acts of communication are the performative 'achievers' of knowledge and value:

> As a matter of fact we can in no way always (or even often) fulfil these improbable pragmatic pre-conditions, from which we nevertheless begin in communicative everyday practice, and indeed, in the sense of a transcendental necessity, *must* begin. For this reason socio-cultural life-forms stand under the structural limitations of a communicative reason which is *simultaneously denied and laid claim to.*
>
> (J. Habermas, *Der Philosophische Diskurs der Moderne*, 1985, quoted in Dews, 1987:221)

Critical Theory has been influenced by classical psychoanalysis. Marcuse's notion of alienated consciousness echoed the struggles between Eros and Civilization, in the form of restrictions upon desire imposed by the repressive technical reason of modernity. Habermas also utilizes a model of psychoanalytic therapy to elucidate the core of his critical and emancipatory method. Hegemonic and coercive knowledge are forms of distorted communication, which in individuals appears as neurosis, and in societies as ideology. Psychoanalysis attempts to name the distorting processes and thus distinguish between appearance and reality. Our conscious words and actions have meaning only in terms of their differentiation from unacknowledged and repressed structures in our unconscious. By revealing these factors, we understand the dynamics of our distorted condition, because 'difference' has revealed the disjuncture – and the violence done by the assertion of the dominant 'truths' – between surface and suppressed meanings. *Praxis* is thus guided by the task of probing the significance of that which is hidden or deferred. By revealing the origins or authorship of social theories, or competing versions of reality, it is possible to see what versions or voices are absent, and what has been repressed in order to establish dominant truth as unequivocal (Habermas, 1970).

Habermas combines the insights of psychoanalysis with Gadamer's notion of the collision of epistemic horizons to forestall criticisms of ethnocentrism in his evocation of communities of communicative action. The ideal speech situation may appear to be some sort of projection of consensus into a future *telos* beyond human intervention, thus serving to absolutize and totalize all over again. However, Habermas insists that the ideal speech situation is a goal rather than an end, a process rather than an ultimate state.

The provisionality and dynamism of intersubjectivity is also safeguarded by the tensions inherent in his notion of 'broken subjectivity', or the non-identity of persons under repressive state and hegemonic institutions. We all experience ourselves as distanced from others, and as fragmented within ourselves; but this search for unity in difference underwrites a plurality of meaning. Misunderstanding and dissonance in any intersubjective encounter ensures our discomfort with the inexactitudes of the conversation; yet the communicative possibilities themselves maintain our commitment to continuing such discourse. The ruptures of dissonance and non-identity serve to break the coercive power of totalizing and absolutizing knowledge. Thus, difference actually serves to prevent fixity and absolutism in intersubjective communication, whereas for poststructuralism it means only complete fragmentation:

> If deconstruction prevents us from asserting or stating or identifying anything, then surely one ends up, not with différance, but with indifference, where nothing is anything, and everything is everything else?
>
> (R. Kearney, 'Dialogue with Jacques Derrida', quoted in Dews, 1989:229)

Thus Habermas does not adopt Foucault's position, that dominant discourses of power and knowledge render notions of the self nothing but a passive and coerced captive of those discourses' foreclosure of undifferentiated subjectivity. His theory of intersubjective communication recognizes the fragmented and alienated condition of the self, but insists also upon the subversive potential of autonomous and purposeful human agency.

Roy Bhaskar (1989) has challenged Habermas on the question of the agents of communicative action and emancipatory practice. He argues that Critical Theory's revision of Marx relinquishes the notion of transformatory *praxis* as resting in the political struggles of the proletariat, and shifts it to an indeterminate group of the dispossessed in a non-specific historical period. However, there are signs in Habermas' work that radical and marginal groups, such as the feminist, ecological and other alternative social movements, might be considered agents of the subversion of the 'pathologies of modernity' by acting as the guardians of communicative rationality. Ideally, they would invite society to examine and converse about its underlying mores by pointing to alternative visions of human needs and interests via their emancipatory practices. This presupposes that mainstream society is prepared to respond openly and positively to such challenges, and admit them into legitimate political discourse.[1]

Therefore, the organized and systematic potential of communicative action is still questionable. It is dependent upon the localized and isolated protests of fringe groups becoming translated into more widespread political action; but this may require a greater theoretical and philosophical grounding, in class-based or other solidarity. It is debatable whether the modern technical bureaucratic State can be fundamentally subverted by sporadic epistemic skirmishes on the borders of civic society. Certainly, it is arguable that the informality of such groups runs the risk of revolutionary agency collapsing back into the possession of individual consciousness or life-style, rather than the material attribute of class. A public and universal transformatory imperative is not necessarily guaranteed simply by the existence of speech acts attesting to the discontinuities and contradictions of capitalism: ideal speech-communities have to embody purposeful and self-conscious *praxis*, or else remain forever transient, marginal and privatized.

The boundaries of the ideal speech community, and the locus of communicative action, have also excited controversy, especially amongst Habermas' feminist critics. They argue that Habermas persists with an unreconstructed Marxian division between the public – productive – world ('System') of economic labour, the State and technical-instrumental rationality, and the private – reproductive – sphere ('Life-world') of domestic labour, the family and affective and aesthetic-moral values. Critics of Marxist class analysis say that this grants no status to human practices other than the economic as constitutive of social – and especially gender – relations. Over-concentration on the autonomy of the economic thus distorts understanding of the role played by the private/ domestic relations of production and reproduction in the shaping of human action and rationality (Nicholson, 1980).

The theory of communicative action does attempt a more complex analysis which partially acknowledges the separation of public and private in modern capitalism, but also offers a means of reconciling them. Habermas' evocation of the 'material' and 'symbolic' realms, respectively 'food and object production' and 'socialization and cultural transmission', recognizes the divorce under modernism between the public and systemic, and the private and interpersonal. In his analysis of the development of late capitalist societies, Habermas has argued that welfare provision has been extended and made more democratic, but with ambiguous results. It has established a language of rights and individual welfare within public policy, but it also represents a further encroachment of principles of bureaucratization and commodification into private, especially familial, concerns. Feminist critics such as Fraser

(1987) argue that Habermas ignores the gender implications of this: that welfare legislation and service provision reinforce gender divisions by controlling and stereotyping women, and rely on gendered divisions of labour and essentialist discourses of women as natural carers to maintain the public/private dichotomy.

Habermas attempts to resolve this paradox by arguing that philosophy is the discipline which brings together fact and value, and can therefore heal the schism between the systemic and the life-world. Anything that reintroduces the communicative rationality of the life-world into the public technical realm is a prefiguration of the ideal speech community; and insofar as the affective tasks at the heart of domestic labour resist the intrusion of wage labour and instrumental values, they act as exemplars of emancipatory action. He thus defends the autonomy of the familial life-world, but at the risk, as critics point out, of romanticizing symbolic values and retreating into an essentialist treatment of them as inherently feminine (Soper, 1989; Fraser, 1987). The marginalization and devaluation of women's work might be rectified by its assimilation into the public sphere, but this will do nothing to undermine gender divisions which are justified on the basis of an appeal to a naturalized, and gendered, public/private distinction. Rather, it is necessary to undermine the bifurcation of economic and domestic labour, of public and private – in short, that of reason and desire – and this is the same project which Habermas defines as lying at the heart of communicative action.

Feminist commentators therefore identify the promise of Habermasian Critical Theory in providing a *via media* between economistic Marxism and poststructuralist nihilism. As Chapter 1 highlighted, feminism is itself divided on the question of whether fundamental Enlightenment principles like equality, justice, rationality and freedom are so thoroughly entangled with the roots of gender difference as to be rendered redundant. This begs the question whether gender bias has so infected the epistemological, moral and ontological norms which guide principles of human practice as to be insurmountable. Alternatively, it may be possible that theories of enacted and communicative knowledge can exert sufficient critical leverage as to dislodge androcentric models of truth, rationality and emancipation, and recreate less coercive and essentializing metaphors and narratives of gender. The experience of feminist emancipatory action, around issues of sexuality, child-care and reproduction, may thus serve to inform a shared prescriptive vision of the ideal speech-community in concert with the formal precepts of public economic justice as represented by traditional Marxist-Hegelian theory. In this respect, gender difference actually augments and extends the normative vision of Critical Theory's *praxis* by deliberately introducing formerly hidden perspectives from the 'life-world'.

The emphasis on communication as constituting speech-acts and language in Habermas must also be understood as an attempt to recast logocentric notions of rationality in favour of reason as 'practical wisdom', or *phronēsis*. Culture must therefore not merely encompass subjective ideas and beliefs, but a pluriformity of concrete utterances and symbolic practices that can further a diversity of knowing, communicating and acting. Thus, Habermas holds out the critical project of philosophy as articulating criteria by which emancipatory knowledge and practice may be guided; but in order to escape the totalizing discourse of modernity, such a rationality must be aesthetic, playful and symbolic as well as logocentric and propositional:

> A theory of reasoning proper to creatures such as we, a theory of how we arrive at and maintain agreements subject to later revocation through persuasion rather than through force, will have to include an account of the essential functions of myth and metaphor, narrative and interpretation.   (Baynes, 1987:14)

Habermas' model of *ideal speech communities* thus begins to resolve the conflict between a complete surrender to atemporal and reified teleologies on the one hand, and total relativism on the other. The normative nature of communication acts to underwrite a social critique. This does not rest on an external or transcendental truth, but one validated by the very integrity of the human community. Thus, no abstract notion like 'democracy' can replace the human encounter as the normative point of communicative *praxis*, because this represents rationality as existing in an ideal and abstract state or consciousness beyond the material, historical and social context. It is possible to extrapolate from Habermas that any truth-claims not identifiably generated in a real conversation in which both sides are communicating to some degree on shared and mutual terms would be categorized as pathological and totalizing, thereby invalidating the conditions of the ideal speech situation.

However, Habermas is vulnerable in terms of defining and defending the boundaries of such communities. Arguably, his system risks over-privileging traditional Marxian-Hegelian notions of class, without fully integrating those groups – such as women – who are marginalized in the public sphere. Thus, even a Habermasian model of consensus still presumes a notion of impartiality, even complacency, in which no group necessarily has to surrender interests in order for another to gain. However, if the *praxis* of a community is to rest upon the norms of human emancipation and solidarity, it must address the issue of how to adjudicate between competing, perhaps incompatible, accounts of justice, truth and goodness. A model of *phronēsis* may therefore have to privilege some sets of specific, concrete needs as worthy of greater obligation than others. For instance, the vision of consensus within the ideal speech community may have to be undergirded by an explicit commitment to the needs and motives of 'Others', and all they represent.

'Concrete' and 'Generalized' Others

For Seyla Benhabib, a feminist writer also committed to Habermasian social ethics, this very question of the nature of community is central. She defends communicative ethics against charges of utopianism and false consensus by making a clear distinction between communicative ethics and communitarianism. Both perspectives share a scepticism towards modernity, and an awareness of the limitations of the political projects of liberalism and Marxism. For communitarians, modernity has fractured moral continuity and shared values; for postmodernists, modernity abused the free play of difference by imposing instrumental logic and repressing diversity and otherness in the name of a 'grand narrative' of history, progress and humanism. The heirs of the Frankfurt School echo such disillusion with modernity by exposing the fragility of economic growth and scientific progress. They also challenge atomistic and individualistic models of personhood and protest against the autocracy of instrumental reason: both features of the alienation of the self under late capitalism (Benhabib, 1992:76).

Both communitarianism and communicative ethics look to renew a moral and political project in a revitalized sense of community;

but they diverge on two important counts. For communicative ethics, the fairness of moral norms can only be discerned via a process of communicative negotiation. The model of the disinterested and formalized reason by which we discern the moral good is questioned: persons are intersubjective and concrete beings. Thus, the moral stances under debate arise not from formalized or hypothetical descriptions of interest but from actual dialogue. In contrast, communitarians do not allow for such perspectives and contexts to be subject to self-scrutiny (precisely the hallmark of modernity) – they are rather seen as fixed and given. Communicative ethics assumes that one's own identity rests upon debate and dialogue with the other; communitarianism rests on conformity and homogeneity – and is therefore guilty of repressing the specific claims and interests of women, minorities and dissenters. Thus, for Habermas and Benhabib, the very possibility of communicative ethics rests on a strong definition of *difference* and *alterity*.

Communicative ethics is not, as sometimes depicted, a formalistic theory of consensus. It is rather 'the open-ended procedure of an "enlarged mentality"', which emphasizes the situatedness of participants in mutual dialogue, the necessity of reaching beyond the boundaries of finitude and contingency towards the horizons of hermeneutical and dialogical encounter. The ability to empathize with the standpoint of the other is the goal to be pursued and effected; and for Benhabib, the essence of communicative ethics is not in some ultimate consensus but the procedural aspect: 'The emphasis now is less on *rational agreement*, but more on sustaining those normative practices and moral relationships within which reasoned agreement *as a way of life* can flourish and continue' (1992:38).

Benhabib develops this by use of the concepts of the 'generalized other' and the 'concrete other'. The former is the classic model of liberalism which sees each individual as rational being, neutral and interchangeable. Justice rests on treating others as one would wish to be treated in return: thus morality is based on similarity and equality. The notion of the 'concrete other' regards everyone as specific, diverse and heterogeneous. It is less about assertion of abstract rights and duties, and more about interaction, encounter and reciprocity.

However, Benhabib argues that these two must exist on a continuum: because a moral system based on concrete others would favour private relationships of care and would risk relativism and discrimination. The two are needed to complement each other: universalism requires us to be consistent whilst exemplifying our shared moral integrity in the face of the concrete other. But the irreducible difference and mystery of the other (their 'alterity') reminds me that a moral community is heterogeneous and pluralistic, rather than merely assuming a universal set of needs and qualities that actually turn out to be a projection of my own subjectivity as the norm.

> Admittedly, rationalistic theories of the Enlightenment ... were based on the illusion that a perfect consensus was possible; but the dialogic model of ethics ... envisages a continuous process of conversation in which understanding and misunderstanding, agreement as well as disagreement are intertwined and always at work. The very commitment to conversation as the means through which the enlarged mentality is to be attained suggests the infinite revisability and indeterminacy of meaning.
>
> (Benhabib, 1992:197–8)

Communicative ethics works for Benhabib because it posits just such a procedure of interaction and dialogue 'among actual selves who are both "generalized others" considered as equal moral agents, and "concrete others", that is individuals with irreducible differences' (1992:169).

The insistence of communicative ethics is therefore that communication and dialogue are the very guardians of value, although nothing about the substance of such values themselves is predetermined. Ultimate value rests in the acknowledgement of the 'Other' as significant, not incoherent, despite the boundaries of difference. Habermas is aware of the captivity of the self in hegemonic discourses, but also affirms identity as defined in relation to an Other as the source of an active and differentiated, if problematic, subjectivity. It is in the integrity of that subjectivity, an individual's quest for intersubjectivity and the contradictions of the discourses and exercises of power, that totalizing knowledge will be challenged. Habermas thus expresses a model of communicative action that is both dialogical and dialectical: norms emerge out of practice but also undergird such action in a process of hypothesis and revision; and this process of constant re-evaluation takes place through the encounter with the unfamiliar and dissonant 'Other', with whom creative and constructive dialogue can be effected.

Feminist Knowledge and Situated Practice

Feminist theories of practical reasoning experience similar problems and limitations to those already identified in the work of Habermas and in earlier surveys of postmodern challenges to human nature, knowledge, ethics and purposeful action. Identity and knowledge as grounded in practice brings into focus a method of being, acting and reflecting that is self-reflexive, yet still maintains ethical and political integrity. In the absence of transcendent truth-claims, the purposeful practices of a community may be held to constitute epistemological and normative standards; but a further critical perspective is still required in order that a claim to political identity does not result in a self-serving vision. Donna Haraway expresses the desire for a theory of human action with special reference to programmes of gender equality which will meet such criteria:

> Feminists don't need a doctrine of objectivity that promises transcendence, a story that loses track of its mediations just where someone might be held responsible for something, and unlimited instrumental power. We don't want a theory of innocent powers to represent the world, where language and bodies fall into the bliss of organic symbiosis. We also don't want to theorize the world, much less act within it, in terms of Global Systems, but we do need an earthwide network of connections, including the ability partially to translate knowledges among very different – and power-differentiated – communities. We need the power of modern critical theories of how meanings and bodies get made, not in order to deny meanings and bodies, but in order to build meanings and bodies that have a chance for life.   (Haraway, 1991:187)

Questions of positionality and situation have occupied feminist theorists. Since claims to universality and objectivity have been exposed as ideological supports for patriarchal, Western, technical-rationalist schemes, alternative accounts of the production and validation of knowledge have been required to confront their own particularity and contingency at the same time as wishing to assert the legitimacy and authority of these vantage-points for reliable and responsible action.

In her discussion of 'situated' as against 'disembodied' knowledges, Haraway therefore develops further the debate about the possibility of both affirming the specificity and positionality of claims to knowledge and value, and of avoiding relativism. She advances a notion of 'vision' for resolving this challenge: vision serves as a metaphor for the practice of generating and facilitating 'situated knowledges'. The danger of objective knowledge is its ability to cloak its own origins under the rhetoric of universalist reason masquerading as correspondence to the truth. It is a pretence to infinite vision which denies the specificity and particularity of its perspective. What is needed is an understanding of vision as situated and embodied: 'a usable, but not an innocent' account of knowledge (1991:187). All knowledges come from somewhere, and are reliant on particular – human and technological – forms of mediation.

Haraway stresses that 'location', or situatedness, guarantees an awareness of the limitations (or horizons) of our own perspective. However, her commitment to the ethical and political priorities of epistemology leads her also to insist upon the irreducibility and concretion of any situated experience. Vision implies perspective; but, by virtue of this, it also entails 'the embodied nature of all vision' (1991:188), or what I have already termed a 'vantage-point' (Graham, 1995:211), which invests a perspective with both authority and positionality. These very experiences of location are in themselves precautions against the totalizing 'god-tricks' of universalism and objectivism. Only those who pretend to talk from nowhere or everywhere are to be feared as 'playing God' and claiming the power of life and death by appealing to universal and totalizing vision and knowledge:

> [S]cience becomes the paradigmatic model not of closure, but of that which is contestable and contested . . . The only way to find a larger vision is to be somewhere in particular. The science question in feminism is about objectivity as positioned rationality. Its images are not the products of escape and transcendence of limits, i.e., the view from above, but the joining of partial views and halting voices into a collective subject position that promises a vision of the means of ongoing finite embodiment, of living within limits and contra-dictions, i.e., of views from somewhere.   (Haraway, 1991:196)

This grounds questions of what constitutes adequate knowledge in concrete worlds. Haraway debates the implications of committing oneself to a positional situated knowledge. Far from undermining any rational enterprise, such a view recasts notions of what it means to know, and what is available to be known: 'Positioning implies responsibility for our enabling practices' (1991:193). Given that those in subordinate positions have experienced the extent to which knowledge is implicated with power, they are more inclined to appreciate the dangers of absolute claims to truth and interpretation:

> The standpoints of the subjugated are not 'innocent' positions. On the contrary, they are preferred because in principle they are least likely to allow denial of the critical and interpretive core of all knowledge. They are knowledgeable of modes of denial through repression, forgetting, and disappearing acts – ways of being nowhere while claiming to see comprehensively. The subjugated have a decent chance to be on to the god trick and all its dazzling – and therefore, blinding – illuminations. 'Subjugated' standpoints are preferred because they seem to promise more adequate, sustained, objective, transforming accounts of the world.   (1991:191)

Rather than characterizing different truth-claims in dichotomous or oppositional terms to one another, we can see them in terms of resonance and relationship. This is particularly relevant in talking about forms of knowledge pertinent to gender: difference here can be either dichotomous and fixed, or associated with 'tensions, resonances, transformations, resistances, and complicities ...' (1991:195).

Hawkesworth (1989) also turns to practice as the root of cognition; critical epistemology must attend not to the qualities of the potential knowers, but to the methods by which knowledge is forged, assessed, validated and implemented. It also sees cognition as a communal and hermeneutical activity. The human practice of cognition is guided by certain historical conventions and some theoretical presuppositions about procedures and validation. In this respect, Hawkesworth allows for an already existing context within which knowledge is contested, and an access into historical convention which seemed to be denied by poststructuralism.

Postmodernism's ability to jettison the Enlightenment model of subjectivity as unitary, essentialist and autonomous is also welcomed by Linda Alcoff (1988). However, she questions whether feminists are in danger of appropriating another form of essentialism in their enthusiastic adoption of plurality, multiplicity and difference. The anti-humanism of poststructuralism, whereby the subject is merely constructed amidst a web of conflicting and coercive discourses, makes notions of transformatory and resistant agency problematic.

Alcoff's solution is to propose a model of 'positionality' in order to recharacterize women's subjectivity and epistemology. Identity becomes relational, contextual and performative. Patriarchy often defines women in relation to a fixed norm – androcentric humanity, or perhaps women's relationships to men – but positionality acknowledges that everybody inhabits a variety of social situations, roles, historical locations and institutions. We inhabit such places via what Alcoff terms 'concrete habits, practices, and discourses' (1988:433), which are both specific and mutable. As Lorraine Code comments, the articulation of positionality involves a person in claiming a located and contextual identity for herself, and acknowledging her relationality via the recognition of alterity. Such positionality enables the development of strategic visions that are situated, responsible and transformative:

> These articulations . . . are open to social and political critique, remapping, renegotiation. Yet they designate positions that are, at the same time, sufficiently stable to permit active political involvement. Positions are at once loci for the active construction of meaning – meaning that is neither simply discovered nor imposed, but constructed – and foci for sociopolitical critique. The positionality proposal draws on specifically located beginnings in and elaborations of the second-person relationships that are pivotal points in any life history. It creates a political space for reinterpreting and engaging critically with the forms of authority and expertise that circumscribe women's control over their lives. (Code, 1991:180–1)

Location, positioning and historicity therefore define the language by which we can understand our experiences. Interpretation does not take place from a position of abstraction, but *in media res*, in a fusion of theory and practice. Critical self-understanding – and hence the nature of *phronēsis* – is formed within a material network of relationships, values and practices out of which meaning is constructed and acted upon. However, such positionality does not denude such discourse of all possibility of value. In particular, it should not be seen as a surrender to relativism, which Haraway characterizes as the inverse 'god-trick' of totalization, 'promising vision from everywhere and nowhere equally and fully' (1991:191). Relativism is thus implicitly nihilistic because it believes purposeful practices to be – literally – neither here nor there.

However, situated knowledge affords full recognition to the positionality and contextuality from which statements of meaning and value derive their coherence. It is an epistemology designed to resist 'closure': absolute, disembodied and oppressive prescriptions which represent some sort of deathly and pathological denial of alternative and dissonant knowledges. So for Haraway, 'location is about vulnerability; location resists the politics of closure, finality, or to borrow from Althusser, feminist objectivity resists simplification in the last instance' (1991:196). She therefore establishes links between domination, pathological uses of 'absolute' knowledge and the 'closure' represented by such claims to objectivity. 'True' knowledge therefore becomes, to extrapolate from Haraway, a *disclosure*: that which entertains dissonance, tolerates and celebrates plurality, but above all is a way of knowing which respects all knowledge as situated in human contexts.

Haraway's evocation of 'closure', and my suggestion of truthful and good knowledge as entailing disclosure, offer a perspective both on the nature of knowing and the nature of human identity as gendered and situated; limited and constrained by social contexts, but not ontologically absolute or unable to transcend the horizons of its own particularity. If an epistemology claims its own absolute foreclosure and finality, then its own introversion means a denial of other 'vantage-points' and an inflated sense of its own self-sufficiency. The bench-marks of responsible and disclosive *phronēsis* therefore display many of the qualities of contextuality, embodiedness and provisionality, thus disputing and replacing conventional models of objectivist standards of knowing.

Hawkesworth develops this emphasis, insisting upon a diversity of cognitive practices, in order to reflect different ways of knowing; thus logical reason is not necessarily privileged. However, although this would allow for the validity of feminist claims to embodied or intuitional knowledge, it would not absolutize them (1989:547). All knowledge is provisional, and, like Haraway, Hawkesworth does not retreat from the implications of this partial and specific nature of knowledge; nor does she feign a form of utopianism that believes there is an 'ideal' knowledge to which it is possible to aspire, a danger in the notion of 'ideal speech situation'. Nevertheless, some informed judgements can be made in order to assert interim cognitive claims by which further practices are informed and guided. Thus, accounts of knowledge are verified by what they prove capable of doing; and such strategic knowledge can bear out the validity of the norms to which such practices are directed.

Situated knowledge may be considered a form of pragmatism, which regards knowledge as adequate insofar as it fulfils practical objectives, however provisional. But Hawkesworth and Haraway mediate between the realism of Critical Theory and the relativism of pragmatism, in that they recognize practical utility as a necessary, but not sufficient, condition for epistemic adequacy. The merging of 'visions' and the mutual accountabilities of situated knowledges protects a community from absolutizing its own particularity:

> A critical feminist epistemology must avoid both the foundationalist tendency to reduce the multiplicity of reasons to a monolithic 'Reason' and the postmodernist tendency to reject all reasons *tout court* . . .
>
> In the absence of claims of universal validity, feminist accounts derive their justificatory force from their capacity to illuminate existing social relations, to demonstrate the deficiencies of alternative interpretations, to debunk opposing views . . . For those affronted by the arrogance of power, there are political as well as intellectual reasons to prefer a critical feminist epistemology to a postmodernist one. In confrontations with power, knowledge and rational argumentation alone will not secure victory, but feminists can use them strategically to subvert male dominance and to transform oppressive institutions and practices.
>
> (Hawkesworth, 1989:556–7)

Such a theory of practical knowledge and identity, therefore, would rest upon an interrogation of its own claims to conversation, whilst still having faith that ethical and epistemological values can be so generated. In the absence of 'extra-discursive' or transcendent criteria, the representations generated by 'situated practices' serve as the grounding for political and strategic commitments.

Haraway, Hawkesworth and Alcoff thus sketch a 'situated' or 'positional' hermeneutics which begins to establish some criteria for a critical *phronēsis*. However, their proposals for such an interpretative model do not entail any accounts of actual scientific or political practices. They may form an agenda for a feminist *phronēsis*, therefore, but remind us that such theories of knowing, however attractive and plausible, need to be tested in concrete situations. Otherwise, the danger is to reproduce the abstraction and detachment of objectivist theory; to believe that critical and hermeneutical study takes place from a neutral location, and that transcendent principles can be distilled from a concrete situation in order to be 'reapplied' into the situation under scrutiny. However, a consistent commitment to the reflexivity of knowledge suggests that such theorizing from a disengaged place of safety is untenable. Thus, a model of situated knowledge which regards itself as in some way immune from the very conditions of positionality which it demanded of the actors and knowers under observation, would be completely contradictory. In order to be true to the contextual and situated nature of human experience, I would insist that such a model should be as heuristic and provisional as the conditions which it seeks to interpret. Critique cannot take place without the specificity and concretion of a vantage-point.

Disclosure and Foreclosure

Therefore, it is essential to emphasize the phenomenological nature of studying the situated practices of any community. It characterizes practical wisdom as heuristic, not criterial; so theory and epistemology assume no deterministic or absolute status beyond their own context. It reminds us of the reflexivity of experience and knowledge; that subject and object are bound in a mutual relationship, and that self-identity is inextricably associated with the formation and expulsion of the 'Other'. These considerations – of identity and knowledge as positional, provisional and reflexive, of the inseparability of theory and practice and of the corrective presence of 'alterity' to exclusive or essentializing truth-claims – have already been identified as the hallmarks of hermeneutics and situated epistemologies, but must also be the dominant mood of any gender-sensitive critical analysis.

In constructing criteria for excavating and evaluating the prescriptive norms of communitarian practice, the dominant values must therefore be to foster models of being, acting and knowing which affirm and realize these qualities of positionality, provisionality, reflexivity and alterity. In order to achieve this, I want to develop the concept of *disclosure*. For practical wisdom to be guided by the dialectic of 'disclosure/foreclosure' would mean that its evaluative criteria remain contextual, but consistent in its questioning of the fundamental implications of any enacted claim to truth or value.

To ask of any practice – 'What does it disclose/foreclose?' – is to attempt to identify the values and preconceptions by which such practices are informed. This enables a critical renewal of such values in the light of changing contexts, but honours the strategic nature of any dimension of practical reasoning.

Despite the paucity of phenomenological or ethnographic material within available accounts of positional and situated epistemologies, the following critique will attempt to give some flavour of the critical analysis of feminist *praxis* which adopts the perspectives of disclosure/foreclosure. In particular, it should be noted that recurrent themes emerge concerning the implications of 'disclosive' practices for our notions of human nature, knowledge, action, experience and ultimacy. These are the dimensions of human experience already rendered problematic by critical theories of gender, and it has already been established that our conceptions of ontology, epistemology, agency, subjectivity and teleology are best seen as provisional, situated, embodied, non-essential and contingent. Thus, an emphasis upon *disclosive* practice as a responsible, authentic and reflexive way of inhabiting culture returns to earlier conclusions concerning the nature of gendered human experience.

Anne Seller's reflections on the interplay of epistemological, moral and political claims in the campaign against nuclear weapons stress the inseparability of knowledge and agency. Both are positional and specific; practice and wisdom proceed in a mutual dialectic. Purposeful, value-directed agency has a capacity to disclose value; and the critical interpretation of action illuminates new values, aims and ends. Seller also highlights the strategic nature of knowledge, defying a reified or abstracted set of truth-claims. Such renewed truth-claims are only realized – in the sense of being apprehended *and* being made real – and sustained by committed practices:

> Neither knowledge *nor* political solutions are final, they consist rather in continual doing. This is not a coincidental similarity; the two are inextricably bound up with each other. Knowledge tells us how to make sense of the world, how to adapt to it, what demands realistically to make of it . . . Politics too is trying to make sense, to live with, adapt to. Put another way: we won't so much finally achieve peace as continuously make it, and that will mean continuous efforts at understanding . . . In doing these things we will

doubtless discover previously unimagined meanings to peace and
equality. I say 'discover' because they will be implicit in, or
prompted by, previous understandings and decisions. In that sense
they lie beyond the individual, are not simply an arbitrary choice
... What peace and equality are discovered to be will depend on
the decisions that various communities have taken. Through our
decisions with a community, we decide how we want to belong to
the world, how we want to set about understanding it, living in it
and changing it.   (Seller, 1988:180–1)

However, such a process of 'discovery' does not take place in an
historical vacuum; but it does highlight the extent to which the
purposeful practices of a community are conditioned by the
resources of the historical tradition. This may apply especially to
a faith-community which appeals to historic texts and conventions
as normative for its current practice. Such resources may inform
the sources and norms of prejudgement, and have determined
prevailing patterns of practice; but insofar as renewed experience
and reflection upon a contemporary positionality may lead to new
insights, then the community must arbitrate on the validity and
authenticity of new meanings. One criterion for that assessment
could be that of disclosure: contemporary experience – such
as that of a feminist movement – may reveal the foreclosures
and fault-lines of historic practices. However, the contextuality
and positionality of the subject, and its agency, is firmly rooted in
historical tradition as well as contemporary social relations.

Debates about the relative weight of experience and tradition
are further challenged by such understandings of the necessarily
transformatory nature of knowledge. Existing understandings of the
relationship between experience and tradition have tended to regard
the latter as normative and prescriptive, whereas 'practice' elevates
the status of experimental and transformatory knowledge into a
real source of revelation (as 'disclosure'). Practice, as a situated
knowledge in the here and now, presents a profound recasting
of notions of historicity. The hermeneutical circle, establishing
a critical movement between understanding, interpretation and
application, would suggest that our interpretation involves a constant mediation of tradition and current experience. Historical texts,
events and practices are consistently reappropriated in the midst
of this meeting of horizons, and disclose a plurality of possible
meanings. The past is therefore not a fixed and concrete event, but

the enduring availability of possible meanings available for reinterpretation. Similarly, Derridean notions of 'intertextuality' reject a fixed meaning; thus the 'truth' of the past rests only in a tradition which constantly re-awaits practical reappropriation.

Nancy Fraser talks about changes in political discourse and policy arising out of 'runaway' needs: the issues that are categorized as appropriate to the private realm, but enter the public, political sphere through the activities of subordinate groups for whom these issues are more than personal. Self-help groups, tenants' associations and women's health groups have all articulated questions of domestic or private concern as policy issues. In this way, she argues, feminism has redrawn the boundaries between 'political', 'domestic' and 'economic' on a number of issues: child-care, sexual harassment, housework and 'date rape' (Fraser, 1987).

Fraser's account is in part a critical analysis of Habermas' theory of communicative action and its relevance for feminism. As my critique earlier in this chapter argued, the division between public and private realms reflected an historical-materialist analysis which privileged the realm of production at the expense of the sphere of reproductive labour. In asserting the legitimacy of their (hitherto unacknowledged) needs, the women in Fraser's study exposed the inadequacy of such an account. Thus, they performed a *disclosive* function in identifying the dissonance between their perspectives and established meanings, and challenged the 'foreclosive' tendencies of public policy which marginalized their economic position. Furthermore, such a reorientation of emancipatory priorities is undertaken 'communicatively'.

Questions about what constitutes 'basic human need', and how particular issues are defined as priorities for political or public concern, must therefore be seen as contested and contextual, not essential or ontological. The cultural representation of certain needs as axiomatic, and the corresponding silencing of others forecloses the gender bias inherent in the organization of policies which reflect sectional interests and privilege certain aims. For example, the assertion of women's bodily and gynaecological needs has been discouraged in some schools of feminist theory for fear of 'essentializing' the female body. However, an appeal to policy needs around sexuality and embodiment may actually 'disclose' the extent to which such definitions are socially and politically constructed, and release social meanings of bodies with a feminist *telos*. Thus, the assertion of need as fundamental does not necessarily 'enclose' women in difference, but allows them to identify, and act upon, emancipatory values.

The risks of ontological identity politics are also viewed differently from the vantage-point of 'disclosure'. Here, the assertion of fixed, given, innate identities subverts social strategies of containment which may defuse oppositional subjectivity by a strategy of denial. Judith Butler's assertion of a 'non-essential essentialism' in relation to gay and lesbian politics is a case in point. To assert that one's experience as a lesbian or gay man is categorical – not the result of childhood seduction or social conditioning, but an integral part of one's identity – is to establish an irrefutable political platform. However, Butler argues that such a superfically essentialist ontology is actually highly strategic and subversive. Viewed positionally, as a piece of inventive, performative practice, it serves to disclose the integrity of same-sex love as a rightful aspect of human behaviour, and forecloses discourses that label it as 'unnatural'. Practices such as cross-dressing and 'drag', which 'parody' and call into question fixed and dichotomous gender characteristics, founded upon heterosexual logic, also disclose the constructed nature of all gender identity. The *performative* character of gender implied by such 'subversive bodily acts' serves to reveal that all subjectivity is fundamentally enacted and agential:

> The foundationalist reasoning of identity politics tends to assume that an identity must first be in place in order for political interests to be elaborated and, subsequently, political action to be taken. My argument is that there need not be a 'doer behind the deed', but that the 'doer' is variably constructed in and through the deed. This is not a return to the existential theory of the self as constituted through its acts, for the existential theory maintains a prediscursive structure for both the self and its acts.　(Butler, 1990:142)

Thus, the nature of a community's ontological assertions must be viewed not as abstract, categorical claims to fixed essences, but as purposeful forms of strategic naming, and must be assessed according to the criteria of *disclosive practice*.

Conclusion: Alterity and Practice

I have been arguing that the recognition of contingency, historicity and alterity stand as generic conditions for the construction of an anti-foundationalist regulative practical wisdom by which purpose-ful communitarian practices may be guided and assessed. Bernstein's comments on the qualities of a 'hermeneutical turn' within theories of practical wisdom resonates with many of the conditions for adequate *phronēsis* already identified:

> A false picture is suggested when we think that our task is to leap out of our own linguistic horizon, bracket all our preunderstand-ings, and enter into a radically different world. Rather the task is always to find the resources within our own horizon, linguistic practices, and experience that can enable us to understand what confronts us as alien. And such understanding requires a dialectical play between our own preunderstandings and the forms of life that we are seeking to understand. It is in this way that we can risk and test our own prejudices, and we can not only come to understand what is 'other' than us but also better understand ourselves.
>
> (Bernstein, 1983:173)

Such a science of understanding is not regarded as the ultimate clarification of pure meaning, but as a contextually-grounded encounter of multiple perspectives. We attend to the human agency behind knowledge and meaning, regarding claims to truth as the contingent product of human practice, rather than the foun-dation. We are the properties and objects of language, tradition and culture just as much as they are our properties, in turn, as speaking and acting agents. Abstract and objective theory is thus recast as interpretative practice; the fundamental feature of human 'being-in-the-world' is its interpretative and linguistic nature.

Habermas' theory of communicative action affirms the contextual and non-essential character of human nature, emphasiz-ing the linguistic foundations of community and human values. It insists upon dialogue and practical discourses, such as in the pursuit of scientific competence, as the activities which forge the definitive accounts of rationality and adequate knowledge by which ethical and political projects might be guided. This allows us to acknowledge that certain ethical and political discourses may be authoritative and binding, without denying their contingent and strategic status. It casts theory as a performative and heuristic discipline:

> It would involve giving up the grand-narrative idea of a single truth, without giving up the idea of truth as a *regulative ideal* – something we should attain to in all our behaviours and critical responses . . .

It would acknowledge the constructed nature of subjectivity without supposing that this makes all humanist questions of ethics and agency redundant.   (Soper, 1990:128)

Thus, value-commitments may be made with some conviction, but only as norms created by human practices. Nor are values separate from the world they have helped to create; and as the critical interpreters of such values, we are both their creators and creatures. Thus, in the absence of Kantian 'pure reason', we understand ourselves as the embodied agents of human values; but critical scrutiny of such norms will necessarily be self-reflexive and situated.

A critical phenomenology of social action assists the process of rendering transparent and publicly-accessible the values which fuel the actions of any community. Critical attention to the origins of such prescriptive norms, to their strategies of justification and to their final aims and ends, would consider such interpretation and analysis as itself context-dependent, unable to adopt an objective extra-discursive standpoint from which to give a verdict. Rather like the fact of our embodiment, we use our communities of value as 'vantage-points': situated, not innocent, but nevertheless reliable locations from which to attempt a social critique.

The notion of *alterity* is one way of regarding human identity, meaning and community as both singular and interdependent, and reflects the necessity and contingency of 'Otherness'. Alterity expresses the paradox at the heart of human experience, that identity is founded on solipsism and individuation, of experiencing the Other as completely alien and inaccessible, but that the boundaries of identity are dependent upon the existence and particularity of others. As individuals, we encounter the Other as an equivalent being to ourselves, interpreting, reacting and acting as we act. The existence of the Other in poststructuralism represents both the negated non-meaning through which stable identity is attained and the force which threatens to subvert that very stability and coherence. Any community which attempts to adopt a totalizing claim to knowledge and truth would therefore be denying the fundamental condition of alterity by destroying the 'Others' of non-meaning, provisionality or occluded groups and perspectives.

Alterity provides the impetus to seek a more formalized recognition of the 'Other', which can both honour the integrity of our own situated contingency and not collapse into epistemic isolation. Thus, my next chapter will explore the prospects for a theory of practical wisdom which is true to the situated nature of identity, value and agency, and yet does not absolutize that which is specific, provisional and contingent.

A criterion of *disclosive practice* is central to the recognition of *alterity*: to what extent do practices create 'Others' and what do the truth-claims subtending our boundaries look like from their perspective? As Sandra Harding argues, Western androcentric science is most effective in the creation of 'Others' out of its epistemic and technological practices (Harding, 1991: viii–xi, 268–95). However, such a model rests upon the sovereignty and autonomy of the knower, and denies the 'situatedness' of the knower in a social context. Alterity, however, testifies to the necessary relationship between knowers and known, and agents and clients, of any practices.

Be it the boundaries of a discursive community or the essentialist and determinist prescriptions of rigidly-dichotomized schemes of gender, therefore, alterity and difference point to the instability and coercion at the heart of claims to final and ultimate enclosure. Truth and falsehood, normality and deviance are interrelated but heuristic; it is important to recognize that such categories only become real in their deployment in conversation and *praxis*. In stating our truth-claims we also assert the interdependence and shared nature of truth – its intertextuality – because independent or stable meaning is created out of a more extensive pluriformity of truth.

The possession and pursuit of value implies some notion of choice: the good only has meaning in relation to something else, the one accepted and the other rejected. The notion of truth and falsehood as two necessary sides of a dichotomous relationship therefore extends into the realm of truth-claims and value: truth is seen not as an absolute, but something forged out of the human exercise of choosing certain values as they are embodied in social relations.

Thus theories of human action which emphasize difference as the dynamic which structures human subjectivity also rest upon communication, discourse and dialogue as the central mediations of normative action. In particular, those perspectives which insist on the plurality and intersubjectivity of human identity and communication have proved fruitful in honouring a model of practice which refuses rigid dichotomies, as in essentialist and determinative gender identity, or between notions of truth and falsehood, knower and known, fact and value. It is this disclosive identity expressed by alterity which therefore serves as the guiding principle of judgement.

Another dimension of our subjectivity which is emphasized in hermeneutics and situated epistemologies is the *reflexivity* of experience. The principles of positionality and prejudgement envisage a self that is neither innocent nor extracted from the processes of its own knowing. Similarly, just as knowledge is never innocent of context, it is not immune from the social relations from within which it emerges. In particular, any account of practical wisdom must take account of the relationship between knowledge and power, and regard epistemological authority as always contested.

Fraser's evocation of 'runaway needs' also draws attention to the disclosive power of what Gadamer termed 'breaches of subjectivity'. The dissonances and crises which a community might experience serve as an opportunity to re-examine the values upon which such assumptions, now disrupted, have rested. Anne Seller also argues that many people identify their entry-point into the peace movement as being an experience of disquiet at the national security rhetoric of the State, and of struggling to articulate this feeling of dislocation (1988:181). To extrapolate from Seller, perhaps such ruptures throw into relief the fault-lines between competing discourses about national interest, official secrecy or attitudes to foreign powers. Thus, they require us to re-evaluate our values in the light of new evidence, causing a realignment of allegiance and political activism.

Alternatively, such breaches may be the expressions of crises, causing a reassessment of formerly taken-for-granted values. The fault-lines between foreclosure and disclosure therefore reveal the point at which the unitary, substantive and normative expels the chaotic, multiple and deviant. In order for positive values and strategies to be asserted, alternative avenues are occluded; critical analysis would thus attend to the options thereby foreclosed, and the implications of such a decision.

Having identified some principles for a critical practical wisdom from the natural and human sciences, I shall now attempt to define a similar working emphasis for pastoral theology. I will do this with reference to actual accounts of Christian pastoral practice which identify themselves as seeking specific aims, informed by – feminist – values, pursuing concrete strategies and drawing normative criteria from particular sources and norms. This is an attempt to demonstrate a critical investigation of actual Christian *praxis*: how the pastoral theologian might excavate the 'fault-lines' of such purposeful actions and also identify authentic sources and norms for future strategies and goals. Chapter 8 will therefore reflect on three analyses of feminist pastoral practices – in liturgy, spiritual direction and preaching – in order to elaborate the prospects for a *critical theology of pastoral practice*.

Notes

1 Many social theorists would argue that the political processes of liberal democracy do not allow for the open expression of dissent and opposition, but that debate is managed and suppressed, thus preventing serious challenges to the power of the ruling elite. See Lukes, 1974.

♣

CHAPTER 8

Transforming Practice

> The presence of God may indeed be a function of our ability to speak
> meaningfully of God . . . The location of theology has changed. Where is
> God? we ask. Look to the underside of history and the emancipatory
> struggles of oppressed peoples everywhere. Or look to the ecological
> quest for the wholeness and integrity of life. Or to the dialogical creation
> of common though shaky ground in the midst of cultural and religious
> differences . . .
>
> My thesis is that the answer to the challenge of postmodernity – how to
> speak meaningfully of God's presence and action in the world – is already
> implicit in these practices.   (Hodgson, 1994:65–6)

One of the central arguments of this chapter will be that a *critical
theology of pastoral practice* cannot be pursued without close reference to concrete examples of engagement. Thus actual examples
of pastoral practice will be discussed as the bearers of a renewed
theological sensibility. In the process, I hope to identify some
evaluative criteria for the practical pastoral reasoning of faith-
communities sensitive to human experience as gendered.

The aim of the following critique will be to identify the nature of
the values which inform specific forms of feminist pastoral practice.
By adopting the commitments of feminism, such practitioners
are therefore directing themselves towards values of gender equality
and inclusion. All forms of *praxis* also seek in various ways to
reappropriate and recast traditional forms of Christian pastoral
activity in the name of affirming the full humanity of women and
correcting androcentric distortions.

The diversity of practices reviewed is also consistent with trends
identified in Chapters 3 and 4, which departed from narrow
definitions of pastoral care as equated with individual cure of souls,
toward a more eclectic discipline concerned with the purposeful

172

actions of a gathered 'intentional community'. Thus, the pastoral task is rendered as those pursuits directed towards the development and administration of Christian faith and practice, and therefore transcends the traditional sub-disciplines of homiletics, organization, catechetics, pastoral care and liturgics. Moreover, these activities – and the concomitant discipline of pastoral theology – are not confined to the person of the individual pastor. The emphasis is rather on collective *practical wisdom*, and how this is disclosive of theological value.

The three chosen examples therefore represent a breadth of Christian practices in relation to women: the proclamation of the Gospel within public worship, from the perspectives of the lives of women; the formation of women's character and spirituality in the context of the struggle against sexism; and the liturgical expression of a gender-inclusive community. My critique of these case-studies will aim to expose the practical wisdom of each set of practices, and the nature of the prescriptive values thereby expressed and enacted. I shall be relying on written texts for the illustrative material, although a phenomenology of pastoral practice might also involve a greater ethnographic emphasis. However, the following study may be regarded as a way of 'reading' pastoral practices for what they reveal about the values which underpin Christian *praxis*, and in particular, what may be distinctive about feminist pastoral practice and *phronēsis*.

I shall be applying critical criteria of gender perspectives to the study of the three examples. The perspective of human experience as gendered serves as a constant critical force upon the values at the heart of feminist Christian *praxis*. The criteria drawn from Critical Theory and feminist situated practice represents a rejection of coercive and deterministic values in favour of *disclosive practices*. These sought to forge notions of human identity and agency, and of ultimate truth, as provisional and situated, yet grounded in a pre-commitment to a common humanity and the possibilities of ethical action. This chapter will therefore evaluate the potential of pastoral practices relating to women as lived and historically real examples of Christian disclosive practices.

My critique will focus on the manner in which three specific *horizons* of feminist *praxis* are approached: women's experience, the faith tradition and the community of faith. All these in some way constitute primary *sources and norms* for pastoral practice.

Attention to the manner in which these horizons are formulated and deployed in informing and directing the pastoral tasks will be the core of this critique. This will reveal the presuppositions and values of each of these forms of feminist *praxis*, and especially their characterizations of human nature, action, ethics, knowledge and experience. The model of practice as favouring situated, contextual, provisional forms of human experience is consistent with the disclosive function of *practical wisdom* as outlined in Chapter 7.

Women's experience is a primary source and norm for feminist theology. The patriarchal nature of theology is challenged by the critical protest against the exclusion of women and other occluded groups as theological subjects. Many feminist theologians also argue that Christianity is only redeemable from its patriarchal past insofar as the tradition can be transformed by women's experience to reflect more authentic values of liberation and wholeness (Young, 1990:35–7, 49–69). However, such an appeal cannot remain unexamined, and in my critique of feminist pastoral practices I shall ask how women's experience is privileged within feminist theology and what this represents in terms of its implied authority. Much of the impact of the three examples rests upon their claims to render visible and vocal the dimensions of women's lives made hidden and silent. I shall examine the significance of this in the light of Christian *phronēsis* as a cultivation of ways of knowing and acting which foster 'disclosure'.

If an appeal to women's experience serves as a corrective to androcentric *tradition*, then the status of Christian doctrine, Scripture and history in providing sources and norms for feminist *praxis* is problematic. Some feminist theologians create a category of 'usable tradition' (Ruether, 1992), but the criteria by which that is characterized may reflect notions of the nature and function of tradition which require further examination. How does tradition reflect the Christian past and the accumulated witness of faith, and how reliable and authoritative is it in the conduct of contemporary Christian *praxis*?

The relationship of the three specific examples of feminist pastoral practice to a *community of faith* is also of concern. Some models of practice root themselves exclusively in a woman-centred community; others define themselves in some oppositional or critical symbiosis with official churches and religious institutions.

Is there a necessary contradiction between self-professed feminist communities which draw upon patriarchal models of practice, or can renewed forms of Christian *praxis* emerge from the re-appropriation of traditional forms? I shall argue that intentional communities of pastoral practice are necessary to safeguard the embodied, situated and public nature of Christian practical reasoning; but the relationship of dissenting communities to powerful institutions is not easily resolved. However, I shall argue that the theological nature of pastoral practices rests in the ability of the pastoral encounter, via its appreciation and cultivation of the mystery and provisionality of alterity, to apprehend the presence and agency of the Divine.

Feminist Preaching

Gender as a factor in the preaching of sermons has attracted little attention, despite historical evidence of women preachers throughout Christian history. However, in the past ten years a growing body of material has emerged: volumes of published sermons by women and works on the role and significance of women's preaching for feminist theological practice have appeared (Smith, 1989; Milhaven, 1991; Durber and Walton, 1994). In one sense, the immediacy of such sermons is diminished because the texts cannot be heard, only read. Nevertheless, it is possible to attempt some assessment of the claims of feminist preaching in its re-appropriation of traditional forms and the extent to which it offers a model of *disclosive* pastoral practice.

Naming Women's Experience

The potential of women's preaching to disclose new areas of theological understanding is the theme of Annie Lally Milhaven's collection of sermons on themes 'seldom heard'. The invisibility of women's experience, and especially of unaddressed areas of pastoral need, seek some redress; but as women speak about previously unspoken lives they redefine the nature and function of pastoral preaching. The authority of the preacher is used not to reinforce her own status but to expose new areas to our considered attention, to establish them as pastoral priorities, and facilitate disciplined theological reflection and analysis.

Many of the sermons therefore emphasize the power of women's *naming* of hidden experiences. Brewer argues that the Church itself has complied in the silencing of incest survivors by upholding so-called 'family values' and refusing to admit to the complexity, anger and pain inherent in situations of conflict or abuse (Brewer, 1991). The Church's structures of care are designed to control, repress and deny such pain and confusion in the name of reconciliation, tolerance and forgiveness. However, appropriate and authentic care is that which hears, and believes, incest survivors. Such honouring of experience is essential to the process of healing.

The disclosure of women's pastoral needs also challenges the foundations of moral and pastoral decision-making. Ansara argues that, instead of insisting on absolute criteria of right and wrong, exposure to the truth of people's lives calls forth a greater generosity (1991:145–56). Morality which insists upon strict distinctions between right and wrong, or law-abiding and deviant, rests upon definitions of difference and otherness which refuse to acknowledge the integrity and autonomy of the 'Other'. If those in possession of the power to enforce moral boundaries are confronted with the dissident horizon of difference, and are able to admit to its validity, and to accept it as constituting a moral claim upon the entire community, she argues, the rigid lines of difference erected in the pursuit of domination begin to blur and fade: 'Stone-throwers rarely ask to hear their targets' stories. They seldom try to see the world through their victims' eyes. They are too busy to listen – too obsessed with collecting stones' (Ansara, 1991:146).

The dogmatism engendered by abstraction is undermined by the immediacy and concretion of hearing, and sharing, another's situation. Ansara argues that this is the first stage in a mode of ethical judgement which acknowledges that no moral choice is ever perfect or absolute – due to the presence of sin – but that a situational emphasis honours the complexity of human experience informed by a plurality of sources, including reason, tradition and experience.

The disclosure of such experiences takes place within a social context: the pastoral needs exposed have often been created by patriarchal exploitation or domination. Thus the challenge to the feminist preacher is not simply to deliver a personal testimony, but to trace the intersection of the individual and the structural or collective. The *situated* nature of disclosive *praxis* may thus entail an acknowledgement of individual particularity in relation to the horizons of social and political contexts. A concern of feminist theory and practice has been to honour women's shared experience of gender oppression, but also to respect the specificities of race, colour, ability, class and sexuality. Such an interplay ensures that experience as a category resists narcissism and introspection; it also sustains a perspective upon human agency as both creative and voluntary yet culturally grounded and socially structured.

In women's preaching, the process of telling others' stories is an example of conversational practice: matching the personal with the collective; of inviting the hearers to place their stories alongside those of others. Some of the sermons in Milhaven's collection do consider the implications of the divisions of sexuality, race and culture for fragmenting a single and indivisible notion of women's experience. This attention to difference as a challenge to the indivisible authority of any one preacher thus serves to highlight how the testimonies of hidden 'Others' can challenge patterns of exploitation and speak of the disclosive impact of hearing such *alterity* into speech.

For example, the analysis and exposure of the ideologies of homophobia is the purpose of Mary Hunt's sermon. Non-conformist love reveals the fears underlying exclusive and foreclosive notions of human sexual desire (which assume that there are only a few prescribed and acceptable expressions of love), and thereby opens to our view a more expansive vision of the love of God which knows no boundaries and counts no cost. The difference of same-sex love thus acts as a disclosure of the risks and mysteries of God's presence amongst us. Hunt argues that the 'radical' life-styles of sexual non-conformists lose some of their Divine potential if they shrink from a creative, loving confrontation with those who seek to deny and expel them. Thus, part of the disclosive character of difference is generated in the creative tension between conformity and non-conformity: 'Theological power structures fall into self-contradiction in the face of same-sex love. Yet we stubbornly refuse to let them off the hook so easily by leaving their folds. We know their fear of love, and we graciously offer them a way beyond it' (Hunt, 1991:163).

Definitions of self-worth and dignity that reflect racist standards and foreclose black women's integrity can be subverted by a deliberately self-affirming posture of those thereby rendered 'Other'. This is the theme of Taylor-Smith's sermon. By celebrating their beauty as persons formed in the image of God, black women expose the standards of a beauty industry which excludes them. Smith uses Psalm 139:13–14 – 'For you created my inmost being; you knit me together in my mother's womb. I praise you because I am fearfully and wonderfully made; your works are wonderful, I know that full well' – as a powerful instrument of self-affirmation and resistance (1991:243).

Speaking out of difference therefore becomes a positive and powerful strategy. The pride of womanist testimonies and the struggle for racial justice undermines the hegemony of the universality of white feminism within sexual politics. Such work calls upon the unveiling of difference, both as a means of exposing the reality of black women's oppression, and also to provide a vantage-point from which such specificity can be translated into common visions of justice. To occlude difference ignores such specificity, risks missing the points at which women's experiences are bodily and material, and precludes true encounter with those who are different, whether in an oppressing or an oppressed role.

The Use of Tradition

Preaching requires an encounter with the historic truth-claims of the Christian faith, as affirmed in its various sources: Scripture, tradition, Church teaching and the historic forms of liturgy within which preaching has been founded. The manner in which feminist preaching effects such a process of interpretation raises questions about the use of tradition as an hermeneutical resource for feminist Christian *praxis*.

Engagement with tradition within the sermons in Milhaven's collection is used to support and confirm the normative horizon of women's experiences. This is consistent with the overall project, of naming the repressed and silenced perspectives of women; and thus the emphasis is on the impact of such a proclamation of experience, rather than the task of engaging with normative texts. However, the authority of the biblical and historical traditions to determine women's destiny is challenged, as in Ansara's exposure of the androcentric paradigms of teaching on sexuality and abortion (1991:150–1). In other sermons, the inadequacy of the tradition is identified as one element that a renewed feminist *praxis* would address and correct; but this remains a rhetorical claim without any indication of the proposed strategies by which texts and traditions might be transformed:

> It is time for the church to allow the Scriptures to live in the lives of incest victims and survivors . . . As women knock on the door of the church, asking to be heard, the door must be opened. It is time the church stopped contributing to the silence . . . If the church cannot open its doors to these daughters, then they will be forced to seek solace elsewhere. Most do not want to leave the church. Most want the words of Jesus to live for them as well as others. The church must let these words bring the healing that Jesus intended.
>
> (Brewer, 1991:26)

The potential of the homily to witness to new perceptions of divine agency and salvation is featured occasionally. Mary Hunt locates the fear of love in a tyrannical model of God, punitive and overbearing; there is thus a close relationship between renewed models of self-love and alterity, social relations of mutuality and trust, and reconstructed metaphors for the Divine who is the source of such love and self-disclosure:

> The love of a merciful, tender, maternal God/ess pales by comparison in a culture in which power is prized. The image of a macho God-father, with his amazing Son and their sidekick Holy Spirit has so dominated the Christian consciousness since the Middle Ages that we have had few other images. Without a change in the concept of God I am convinced that there is little hope for overcoming heterosexism/homophobia.   (Hunt, 1991:159)

A public declaration of experience is therefore placed in the context of the gathering of the community for worship, and a challenge concerning the nature of belief is issued. Hunt uses an occasion of pastoral practice – the sermon – to express new perspectives and to pursue their implications for the core values of the faith-community. Its willingness to entertain the controversy and generosity of non-judgemental community is an expression of the Divine nature; theological claims are embodied in the standards of love and justice by which Christians are prepared to live.

Preaching in the Community of Faith

Within an ecclesiastical and theological tradition of women being silenced, a silencing engendered of subordination, the presence of women preaching is of itself a radical act. It symbolizes the inclusion of women into a renewed community and affirms the right of women to exercise the authority of teaching and interpretation in handling, and communicating, the Word. Physically as well, by occupying the space accorded the authoritative speaker – the pulpit – women assert their power to reappropriate tradition, as a physical presence and in terms of engaging with sacred texts (Durber and Walton, 1994:1–4).

Feminist sermons emphasize the promise of change, of the unexpectedness of the Gospel, of an exposure to a vision which defies hierarchy, authoritarianism and nostalgia, preferring renewal and transformation. For women to preach in contemporary faith-communities is to maintain a continuity with the first witnesses to the resurrection, and to reaffirm women's role as witnesses and bearers of the Gospel. Yet this is taken as symptomatic of a Gospel which refuses finality, closure and legalism in favour of the 'great surprise' of a resurrection morning (Hilkert, 1987:69). Rebirth, forgiveness, reconciliation and exodus are themes in many of these feminist sermons which reiterate the breaking open of old patterns and relationships and the promise of new life in Christ.

Thus, the medium and the message are considered synonymous: women's proclamation of the Gospel is itself a sign of the Good News at work, and women preachers serve as agents of a Gospel which speaks of the overturning of established and conventional patterns. This allows for a radical notion of Christian *praxis* as embracing novelty, theological innovation and creative revelation, as well as continuity with received tradition. The Eucharist is for many Christians the moment at which the faith-community is most truly itself, as it meets to remember the suffering and redemption of Jesus. But this is not a repetition of the Passion, but the *anamnesis* which constitutes the present and future hope of the good news. As Mary Hunt says, the Eucharist frees Christians to look to new signs of hope without needing to recreate the past:

> Jesus died once for the sins of the world; it is not necessary to repeat his performance. It is time to flesh out the notion of Eucharist so that it really means bringing together a community to give thanks

and praise for the fact of new life after death. Without some deep affirmation of this basic Christian notion of the sacramentality of the whole of creation there is no way to admit newness, diversity, fresh revelation. (1991:160)

For such an acclamation to be delivered within the context of public worship underlines the degree to which Christian purposeful practices – in this case, liturgy and preaching – maintain a continuity with the values of historical tradition whilst re-enacting them anew in changing circumstances.

A significant number of the sermons in Milhaven's collection have not been delivered in the context of public worship, because their authors, as women, were not allowed to preach them. Others have only been preached to 'Women-Church' gatherings, or specific women's liturgies. Thus, the degree of impact of such sermons upon the institutional church is still problematic, and many of the contributors acknowledge the controversial nature of their testimonies.

However, the public and institutional context of such sermons is insistent. The decisive impact of feminist preaching may well arise from the contrast between the personal and particular nature of such preaching and the conventions of sermons which universalize and totalize limited androcentric experience. The naming of experiences 'seldom heard' places demands upon church congregations to consider issues of concern to women; but the cumulative effect may also be to shift the Church's priorities altogether in terms of the nature and purpose of preaching. In this respect, Milhaven's collection may be misleading, in that it features women preaching about 'women's issues': an important example of the naming of difference, as I have indicated, and a proclamation of the particularity of such testimonies. But, as Fiorenza suggests, women's preaching, in engaging with controversy, non-conformity, embodiment, exclusion and justice, may also shift the very paradigm of preaching as a Christian theological and practical task. In particular, it deflects the act of preaching away from bolstering the unquestioned authority of Scripture or doctrine, the universalization of male clerical experience as universal and definitive, and the nature of preaching as forbidding counterargument or dialogue. It moves instead towards a proclamation of 'the richness and fullness of G-d's liberating presence in our struggles today' (Fiorenza,

1991:ix). The sermon seeks to expound and evoke the liberating *praxis* of the community.

Preaching as feminist *praxis* portrays the acts of proclamation and reception as efficacious and theologically authentic not by virtue of unquestioned authority derived from outside the context, but in terms of the sermon's disclosive and liberative impact upon the life of the community and its related contexts. Authority is something which acts within the situation, rather than acting upon it; and the truth-claims by which the orthodoxy of preaching is assessed are entirely practical:

> The truth of God-language and of all theological claims is measured not by their correspondence to something eternal but by the fulfilment of its claims in history, by the actual creation of communities of peace, justice and equality. The criterion of liberation faith and liberation theology is practice, or, more specifically, the process of liberation in history.   (Welch, 1985:7)

Thus, preaching may well have an expository dimension, but this is still orientated to transformative living and renewed practice. In many Reformed traditions, the centrality of the Word is contrasted with that of the Sacrament; but in this perspective the sermon is very much sacramental in a classical sense. It is a form of human encounter, purposefully directed towards the articulation, exploration and recapitulation of the values underpinning Christian community and practice. However, the sermon becomes also a doorway into the transcendent, and is therefore sacramental. Divine grace comes as the words and meanings expressed are heard and then enacted by the whole people into something more than surface experience.

Feminist Spiritual Direction

Kathleen Fischer's contribution to feminist pastoral theology is in the field of spiritual direction. Feminist values shape her practice:

> Feminism provides a new way of seeing reality. It is an alternative world-view which replaces the divisions intrinsic to sexism with models of wholeness for both women and men. Feminism is a vision of life emphasizing inclusion rather than exclusion, connectedness rather than separateness, and mutuality in relationships rather than dominance and submission. Feminism also entails the conviction

that full individual development can take place only within a human community that is structured in justice. And so feminism works for social change. (Fischer, 1989:2)

A collection of familiar themes within feminist theology cluster into Fischer's statement: the opposition between feminist and sexist views of being and relationships, the latter based on dichotomies and hierarchies, the former upon holistic, interconnected patterns of being. Feminism as a transformative vision, fuelling change not only for women but men too, is also present; as is the rejection of individualistic models of self-realization, in favour of an integration of individual welfare with corporate and socio-political pro-grammes. It thus offers a classic feminist vision, but one generated within a context of feminist politics and imported into the practice of spiritual direction.

Women's Experience and Spirituality

Fischer's programme for spiritual direction offers affirmation and empowerment for women, and includes the personal and the political. Spiritual direction deepens women's comprehension of their oppression and enhances self-esteem. It is thus inherently healing and transformative, by simple virtue of disclosing formerly hidden and ignored experiences. Women's experience is 'the authoritative starting-point for spirituality' (1989:6): feminist spiritual direction honours the integrity of women's experience in the context of a patriarchal society which excludes women's perspectives and needs from what is normative, and prescribes oppressive and inauthentic models of self-knowledge, self-esteem and personal growth. The emphasis informing Fischer's method is therefore one of the contradiction between the portrayals and definitions constructed for all women by patriarchy on their behalf, and women's own inchoate but none the less innate and authentic self-understanding. There is a gulf between the images and pre-scriptions offered by society, and women's own quest for integrity and identity. Salvation consists of women being freed to name their own reality, in whatever ways are appropriate. Thus women's ways of knowing and naming are contrasted with the prevailing norms of a sexist society.

Fischer's model of women's identity is somewhat ambivalent. She emphasizes the socially-constructed nature of subjectivity and gender traits. She rejects determinist versions of gender identity, choosing instead to stress the cultural constructions. Institutions and structures of power condition women's experience and communicate negative messages to them. However, Fischer also returns to the theme of an authentic self, emerging from spiritual direction to affirm her intrinsic wants and deepest integrity instead of conforming to societal expectations and pressures. Fischer adopts a position which contrasts social perceptions and treatment of women with their own identity, thus suggesting that women have a 'core' and authentic self that is buried by sexism. This is the role of spiritual discernment, to be fostered in the service of building an autonomous sense of self. Reclaiming bodily experience, and integrating it with spirituality in the face of traditions that deny physical and embodied experience in the constitution of individual subjectivity, is not for Fischer a deterministic claim that women are more bound by, or to, their bodies than men: it is rather that sexism has reduced women to mere bodies, and now their reclamation must declare that bodies are active agents in forming and mediating all experience (1989:31–6).

Fischer argues for a unity and integration of women's experiences to extend to the psychological, spiritual and socio-political. This reflects her feminist commitment to the embodied, interdependent, integrated nature of reality. However, this ignores the extent to which women's exercise of power and the forging of new models of relating may also be problematic. They are assumed to be automatically benign and mutual (1989:137–8). In this respect, Fischer veers towards a form of essentialism, regarding women's oppression as socially and culturally contingent, but their liberation and growth as axiomatic, and devoid of historical, cultural or contextual difference:

> Women find the exercise of power more satisfying if it simultaneously enhances the lives of others. Roles and careers traditionally assigned to women presuppose such attention to developing and nurturing others' gifts: motherhood, teaching, nursing. Enabling others is a central goal of women in ministry. Yet this is real power ... These models affirm women's ways of becoming attuned to others' emotional states, their capacity for understanding and being understood by others.   (1989:142)

Thus, there is a contradiction between Fischer's model of women's oppression and false consciousness as socially conditioned, and their growth and empowerment as essentialist. Liberation and human growth result from the 'stripping away' of the layers of patriarchy from inauthentic experience and tradition. The notion that the helping relationship between women could be anything but benign and reciprocal is not an issue for Fischer; but it represents a fundamental contradiction in her models of experience, selfhood and agency.

Spiritual Direction and Christian Tradition

Fischer's norms for pastoral practice rely on feminist reappropriations of the tradition to supply renewed understandings of salvation, community, female role models and new ways of talking about God, the person and work of Jesus and the Holy Spirit. The recovery of the tradition of 'Sophia', as embracing wisdom, overcoming divisions and dualisms, provides an amenable and empowering model for women. It is present within the biblical testimony, is identified as the focus of Jesus' ministry, and it can serve to inspire contemporary practice. Thus, again, there is a retrieved tradition of Christian maturity and holiness independent of the androcentric strand, which validates and fuels feminist practices.

The dominant model of tradition as embodied in Scripture and the historical faith is one of 'message' which has the power to change consciousness and attitude. The tradition is one of 'knowledge' and apprehension of truth, leading to transformation, self-confidence and empowerment. The practices of feminist reinterpretation are characterized as 'alternative ways of viewing theological truths' (1989:165) or 'seeing the Bible in a new way' (1989:161). As with notions of selfhood and identity, therefore, the tradition is inherently liberative, but has been distorted by patriarchal presentation and misrepresentation. Fischer gives, through her exercises, plenty of examples of reinterpretative practices, all of which retain the text at its face-value, expressing a 'message' rather than reflecting the *praxis* of faith-communities. Thus, although women's experience and imagination serve to correct the distortions, Fischer's aim is to restore the tradition to its authentic, original meaning.

Creative agency, the use of imagination and interpretation feature more prominently in reshaping metaphors for God, where women's spiritual experiences and discernments augment the received tradition. Fischer recognizes that experience is structured by language, but also that pastoral practices can foster new metaphors and models. However, such renewed images cannot be sustained in abstract; they are enacted in the process of their usage in the context of pastoral practice. Habits of prayer and contemplation serve to cultivate such images; through regular use, they become consolidated and begin to assume a power and efficacy in fostering women's spiritual awareness: 'Contemplative prayer is a way of discovering God, ourselves and other persons. Continual encounters with God in prayer have power to transform our established images of the divine, whatever they may be' (1989:56).

Thus there is a dialectic between discourse and practice, affirming the material and enacted basis of theological metaphors. Traditional models of Divine language may be transformed by the faithful inhabitation of pastoral practices; and such renewed images are then embodied in actual relationships:

> [A] symbol or image achieves power in the spiritual life by gradually unfolding its significance . . . As new images are integrated into one's spiritual life, old images are changed in light of them . . . Integration of an image into the spiritual life does not happen if we remain outside observers, studying the metaphor from a detached distance. We must interact with the symbol in some way, establishing a relationship with God through the symbol, and drawing out its meaning in terms of that relationship. (1989:66)

The Community of Faith

I have already identified the strong emphasis in Fischer's work on the social context of women's empowerment and spiritual direction. She is concerned to resist any stereotypes of spiritual direction as individualistic or narcissistic. The inclusion of exercises at the end of every chapter also serves to integrate theory and practice, and exemplifies the practical realization of her arguments. The mutual and non-hierarchical nature of direction also challenges the traditional notions of spiritual direction; Fischer discusses how 'circles' of women might exercise corporate direction. The community context of spiritual growth is therefore stressed, as is the necessity of grounding the quest for individual holiness and wholeness within the struggle for a just society.

In another sense, however, spiritual direction also seeks to proclaim ultimate truth, in terms of understanding its potential as a vehicle of Divine disclosure. The cultivation of new images of God and the routine habits of faith as the instruments of reappropriation have already been discussed. However, the pastoral encounter as a revelation of the Divine is also a recurrent theme, and significantly, this resides in the apprehension of God as 'Other'. The denial of alterity, the exclusion of difference, vulnerability and the stranger, are deemed part of the foreclosure of dualism and polarization. A spirituality which fosters a generosity to others, and breaks down the exclusive distinctions of us/them, affirms the unity of creation and the recognition of the Divine in all things. By going beyond – transcending – the margins of our own security and certainty, we encounter a Divine presence at the heart of otherness:

> Inclusiveness is not merely a human gesture of acceptance; it is an experience of transcendence which discloses a deeper understanding of God. Love of the outsider leads to a deeper vision of who God is . . .When we are pulled outward toward transcendence we learn more of God . . . We find God in the otherness of the other.
>
> (1989:44)

Such an experience of transcendence has the power to heal and inspire; and this vision of God embedded in human encounter and renewal informs the theological understanding of Fischer's work. The experience of God is one of wholeness, hope, resurrection and solidarity; and spiritual direction facilitates and encourages the conditions within which such a process of healing and disclosure can be effected.

Liturgy and Women-Church

One of the most tangible expressions of feminist Christianity, especially in the United States and Britain, is the prevalence of alternative liturgical communities which seek to celebrate women's experience as sacred and devise new forms of worship and ritual outside the prescriptive constraints of the patriarchal institution. One of the strongest movements is known as 'women-church', which has attained prominence through the writings of the feminist theologian Rosemary Radford Ruether. Ruether writes about actual communities of women and men, illustrating with reference to a broad range of liturgical material the practical expressions and enactments of pastoral strategies which articulate women's experiences, restore them to the canon of visible and 'usable' tradition, and seek to transform the Church. She argues that a separate space is necessary to enable women's 'exodus from patriarchy' (1985a: Chapter 4), a strategy designed to give women space to frame liberative practices and criteria for themselves on their own terms. Women therefore form themselves into a critical culture, articulated in ritual, liturgy and worship, which will ultimately release the whole Church from patriarchal hegemony.

Women's Experience and Women-Church

In resistance to androcentric traditions of Christian worship which devalue the body, women-centred liturgies reappropriate embodied experience as a doorway into the numinous and transcendent. One aspect of this is the ritual affirmation of bodily change and transition; feminist liturgy therefore represents women's repossession of somatic and personal integrity in the face of patriarchal objectification. One of the rites of passage in *Women-Church* expresses such an affirmation:

Puberty Rite for a Young Woman

My eyes are not objects of control over me. My eyes are the way I see the world. They enable me to look in all directions, to take in the beauty and the excitement of all visible things.
My lips are not objects of control over me. My lips are the way I speak and sing and eat and kiss and express my love and delight.
My legs are not objects of control over me. My legs are the way I walk and run and dance and move wherever I wish to go.
My breasts are not objects of control over me. My breasts are the way I express my mothering powers, to make milk, perhaps someday to feed a baby with my milk.
My body is not an object of control over me. My body is me. It is my being, my acting and my being present wherever I want to be. Let my body always be the joyful expression of myself. Let it never be used as a means of power and control over me.

(Ruether, 1985:188)

However, feminist communities must be wary of limiting the ambitions of such communicative dialogue by remaining too churchly. Some feminist liturgies have concentrated on creating a 'haven' or 'oasis' (Fageol, 1991:25) for the worshipping community and so risk failing to engage with and understand the outside world. In their concentration on the reappropriation of tradition and the maintenance of dialogue with the institution, such movements may foreclose the possibilities of communicative dialogue with 'secular' feminists in search of authentic *praxis*-based spiritualities, with women of other faiths, or even with men alienated from the established Church.

For Ruether, however, the rituals of healing, the life-cycle and the seasons are integral aspects of the revaluing of women's experiences. However, liturgy also has a function to constitute women-church as the community of liberation from patriarchy and mark its continuity with historical 'spirit-filled' communities of prophecy and renewal. In this respect, she sees the critical protest of feminist women and men as necessarily rooted in the purposeful pastoral activities of 'intentional communities of faith and worship' (Ruether, 1985:3) and communities such as women-church as the crucible of theological regeneration and renewal. The formation of feminist liturgical communities thus involves the naming of experience as a strategic activity. Women-church communities not only serve as prefigurative expressions of inclusive relationships, but, according to Ruether, also as sources of a wealth of practical wisdom – symbolic, sacramental and pastoral – which will renew the tradition.

> It is not enough to hold an ideology of criticism and social analysis as an interpretive base, nor to participate in protest and action groups and organizations of nurture to guide one through death to the old symbolic order of patriarchy to rebirth into a new community of being and living. One needs not only to engage in rational theoretical discourse about this journey; one also needs deep symbols and symbolic actions to guide and interpret the actual experience of the journey from sexism to liberated humanity.
>
> (Ruether, 1985:3)

Tradition

The early chapters of *Women-Church* trace 'the idea and reality of the ecclesia of women throughout history'. Thus, Ruether argues for two important principles in terms of the relationship of contemporary feminist liturgical communities to historical tradition.

First, she stresses the principle of a continuity of women-affirming *praxis* throughout Christian history. Second, she insists upon the legitimacy of such spirit-filled communities as the fulfilment of the essential themes of exodus, justice and inclusiveness found in the Christian Scriptures. Thus, Ruether's account of Christian history is one of a constant dialectic between an official institution veering between cycles of corruption and renewal, spurred by the corrective and reforming charism of spirit-filled *praxis* embodied in alternative 'prophetic' movements.

The engagement of feminist liturgy with tradition represents a reinterpretative task in pursuit of redemptive and disclosive strategies. In particular, there is a commitment to replace exclusive forms of language and practice – especially exclusive or hierarchical patterns of sacramental ministry – with notions of shared and mutual ministry of the community of believers. In this respect, there is a clear commitment that the practice of the worshipping community is a sign of its most authentic intentions, and that the practice itself constitutes the liberative promise:

> All the functions of church – the repentance by which we enter it, the Eucharist by which we commune with it, and the ministry by which we mutually empower it – are simply expressions of entering and developing a true human community of mutual Love . . . The whole concept of ministry as an ordained caste, possessing powers ontologically above nature and beyond the reach of the people, must be rejected. Instead, ministry must be understood as the means by which the community itself symbolizes its common life to itself and articulates different aspects of its need to empower and express that common life.   (Ruether, 1985:87)

Feminist liturgy displays how innovative creation of new forms and symbols in worship may be consciously deployed to echo older forms. However, they are reframed in ways that cancel out their oppressive power and enable the misogyny of such traditional forms to be confronted and expelled. Such practices implicitly regard tradition as malleable, and creative liturgy as re-enacting and reappropriating conventional texts, practices and rituals:

Exorcism of Patriarchal Texts

(A small table with a bell, a candle, and the Bible are assembled in the center of the group. A series of texts with clearly oppressive intentions are read. After each reading, the bell is rung as the reader

raises up the book. The community cries out in unison, 'Out, demons, out!')
Suggested texts in need of exorcism:

– Leviticus 12:1–5 . . .
– Exodus 19:1, 7–9, 14–15 . . .
– Judges 19 . . .
– Ephesians 5:21–23 . . .
– I Timothy 2:11–15 . . .

(At the end of the exorcism, someone says, 'These texts and all oppressive texts have lost their power over our lives. We no longer need to apologize for them or try to interpret them as words of truth, but we cast out their oppressive message as expressions . . . and justifications of evil.') (Ruether, 1985:137)

Women-church therefore invokes contemporary forms of liturgy, language and sacred texts to remake tradition creatively in response to new demands. However, women-church does not merely rest content to define itself as outside the mainstream, but to redefine notions of orthodoxy in keeping with the spirit of the Gospel:

> The only legitimate discussion of church polity concerns not apostolic policy, but whether polity is capable both of assuring responsible transmission of the tradition and, at the same time, of being open to new movements of the Spirit by which the meaning of the tradition can come alive . . .
>
> Tradition, to remain alive, must be open to this continual reshaping of interpretive culture by new spiritual experience . . .
>
> Christian feminism does not revive any literal past form of Christianity, but uses material from the tradition to make a significantly new interpretation and development. (1985:34–7)

This is the point at which Ruether's evocation of history and tradition appears contradictory. She portrays the real and enacted practices of the faith-community as the source of generation of new theological images and metaphors. However, she also wants to claim that such renewed expressions are simply the re-establishment in contemporary discourse of enduring themes of liberation and justice. It is not therefore clear whether the prior existence of such a 'golden thread' of tradition defines and authorizes the contemporary community, or whether, more radically, the emerging practices of spirit-filled communities are sufficient to reorganize and recast

the claims of the tradition in new ways. The former risks essentializing the tradition, and reduces history to an abstract message.
However, the latter option would wrest the authority and orthodoxy
of the tradition from the past and the reiteration of half-glimpsed
themes of liberation, and invest the contemporary community with
the responsibility for proclaiming the truth and validity of liberation,
empowerment and salvation as they rest in the life and witness of
the faith-community in the world.

Women-Church and Magisterium

For Ruether, critique and reform of the institutional Church
occurs via a dialectical relationship with basic communities such as
women-church. The historical Church lays exclusive claim to
salvation, but must recognize that its authority is only validated by
an openness to new movements of the Spirit. Similarly, radical
spirit-filled communities cannot survive without the institutional
structures. Neither group can claim to be the only vehicle of
salvation for all time, in final terms. This would represent a descent
into 'repression and separation', rather than the disclosive interplay
of 'optimal creativity' (1985:32).

Women-church insists upon remaining open to dialogue with
traditionalists, seeing its innovative and disclosive power as resting
in the exploration and definition of difference-in-relation with the
institution. This is an interesting expression of *alterity*, but one
wonders whether the dominant institution would reciprocate. The
nature of traditionalism, like fundamentalism, is to deny plurality
or ambiguity, even within itself, let alone the legitimacy of the
dissident. However, perhaps the vocation of the Other is to remain
in defiance of the negating self-sufficiency of the dominant
institution by celebrating and affirming a dissident identity that will
not be denied or totalized. The fact that such an identity exists in
concrete practices and communities proclaims in lived experience
the viability of such alternative discourses.

Ultimately, women-church exists as a witness to the provisionality
and situatedness of experience, serving to disclose new avenues
and expressions of Divine action in symbolic, embodied and
corporate practices. Feminist liturgy may be seen therefore as a
form of Christian practice which expresses the relationships, commitments and truth–claims underlying the corporate life of the faith

community. Such guiding values of the Gospel are given their enactment in material practices which are located within the human and metaphorical, and which articulate the experiences of the present. Liturgy may begin with the concrete expression of human solidarity, but by articulating and reappropriating the root metaphors of faith, seeks to give shape and form to the disclosive possibilities of a transcendence within which the values of human destiny and purpose are afforded ultimate meaning.

Conclusion: Feminist Praxis

Women's Experience as Source and Norm

All three examples of feminist pastoral practice have emphasized the distinctive function of such activities in the recovery and naming of women's experiences and needs, which have been hitherto undervalued, misrepresented or pathologized by the patriarchal Church. In the process, healing, reconciliation and empowerment can take place as women articulate in ritual form the sacredness of embodied experience, exorcize the oppressions of injury, violation and abuse, and celebrate the landmarks of the menarche, childbirth, menopause and other social and morpho-logical transitions. The implicit values of such disclosure are remarkably akin to psychoanalytic and hermeneutical practices: by exposing and recovering the unvoiced and repressed dimensions of experience – of individual consciousness, of a community or of history – a greater truth and authenticity is made possible. The healing value of correcting such distortions is regarded by such feminist writers *ipso facto*; but it also makes sense in the light of perspectives on gender which regard the naming of women's experience as the epiphany of alterity and otherness. The repressed 'Other' is created by the assertion of a unitary and dominant perspective; thus the ethical authority of the recovery of such hidden identities rests in the end of unequivocal and totalizing identity. Thus, the naming of women's needs and experiences serves as a disclosive practice in that it reveals the distortions and universalized prescriptions of androcentric pastoral practices, and serves to reorder the fundamental values of such practices toward the celebration of the complexity of human experience.

Pastoral practices which celebrate new ways of naming oneself and one's experiences may subvert coercive and repressive patterns; yet such evocations of experience take place within a system of structures which pre-exists and transcends individual choice. Thus, 'speaking from difference' must include a realization that *personal* identity is constituted within a *regime* of differences. Feminist theology can learn here from womanist writers and theologians from the two-thirds world, who automatically place their personal and individual experience within a broader political and economic context of polarization, sexual exploitation, neo-colonialism and material struggle (Chung, 1990; Tamez, 1989; King, 1994).

This rendition of women's experience is not essentialist. It must be regarded as emerging from a social and historical context. The emphasis on women's experience as source and norm within feminist theology, and exemplified in the three cases of pastoral practice, is largely a corrective to universalizing androcentric experience. In this respect, it may be understood as a plea for all theological discourse to recognize itself as *situated*, or as theologians more usually term it, *contextual*. It is therefore a strategic assertion of experience; but the signs of contradiction within the work of Fischer in particular warn that feminist appeals to *women's experience* as the foundation of critical interpretation and action cannot rest unexamined. Such appeals must be seen as proceeding from, and constituting, a particular *vantage-point* that is itself constructed, rather than essentialist. A 'hermeneutics of suspicion' must be injected into the conditions under which experience is formed, and in particular to the transparency of accounts of knowledge and selfhood.

This does not mean that experience claims no authority for itself; but the postmodern condition affirms the specific and the located as the place within which human identity is forged, and as the nexus of pastoral/theological practice. Thus, human practice is to be seen as the source of ontology and identity; and pastoral practices, given their enacted and public nature, may be in a position to embody and situate the expression of specific experience within the continuities of purposeful action, story, community and history.

Theories of postmodernity also stressed the non-rational nature of personal identity and subjectivity. The potential of all forms of pastoral practice to express value and meaning through the imagination, the bodily, the sensual, and to challenge the logo-centricism of Western patriarchal constructs of knowledge has been demonstrated by the previous case-studies. Fischer's exercises in spiritual direction deploy the powers of the unconscious and the creative imagination; the liturgies of women-church celebrate the embodied, symbolic and ritualistic spheres of being and agency.

Renewed pastoral practices therefore have the capacity to disclose a model of human nature which is committed to the recovery of alterity, and which celebrates the complex and polyverse nature of experience. The recognition of such diversity and plurality within ourselves also helps to create a new ethical and theological sensibility, based on a toleration of difference and alterity. What would it mean to hold this model of human nature as a paradigm for the Divine nature? The hypothesis that humanity bears the mark of Divine nature would therefore be revealed in a theology which discards notions of God as fixed and immutable and adopts a model of God as dynamic entity, experienced in relationship and alterity, changing as creation changes:

> I suggest that we start by holding our God lightly, letting her go and evolve rather than guarding a tight-fisted faith. This way we can be more flexible in our worldview, shifting as we must with new knowledge and insight. If our God/ess is not big, elastic, and embracing enough to make the change then I wonder what we mean by the divine. (Hunt, 1991:159)

Tradition as Source and Norm

Critical engagement with the tradition informed the practical reasoning of all three examples of feminist pastoral practice. Part of the critical trajectory of feminist pastoral practice involves exposing the extent to which the norms of tradition from which Christian values are constructed reflect patriarchal, limited and particular perspectives, rather than neutral and universal experience. It resists the foreclosure of unquestioning obedience to Scripture, and regards the act of constructing alternative knowledges as interpretative, critical and reconstructive.

Milhaven's collection tended to use biblical tradition as a selective endorsement of perspectives already accorded authority by their origins in women's experience, and therefore did not grapple with issues of the status of Christian tradition in any generic sense. The other two examples, however, illustrated more clearly the ambivalence and contradiction with which much of feminist theology approaches the Christian tradition. Fischer's use of imaginative participation with Scripture encouraged a creative engagement with what Phyllis Trible (1984) has termed 'texts of terror', but left the essential structure and origins of the text unexamined. Ruether's insistence upon the historical continuity of women-church with prophetic values within the tradition also reveals the extent to which feminist theology is in thrall to the past. Reinterpretation of the tradition is undertaken by representing negative teachings as a distortion of an essential 'message' or 'principle', which can be distilled independently of its historical or textual medium.

However, Fischer and Ruether also suggest alternative methods of reclaiming the past other than by reference to *usable tradition*. In the reworking of the conventions of liturgy, and the 're-visioning' of Divine metaphor, Ruether and Fischer respectively practise strategies of 're-reading' tradition in ways which reopen texts, established patterns, received authorities and models and start to redraw their parameters. Rather than merely recovering and revising the past, therefore, such practices recreate and rewrite it. This is in keeping with many deconstructionist strategies which seek to exploit the hidden and marginal meanings and characters upon which a coherent and unitary surface text is contingent. Similarly, to regard all religious language as provisional and metaphorical enables the received tradition to be treated as the product of historical and contextual agency and knowledge; it is thus flexible enough to incorporate new experiences and perspectives. Feminist theologians do not therefore need to prove that the tradition has always been sufficient and complete – which is a theological argument about the nature of revelation – although they do need to establish for their sceptics and opponents that their contemporary experiences are worthy of inclusion into the canon – an epistemological and political argument.

Feminist hermeneutics has strongly challenged the self-evidence and unity of traditional sources; but criteria for authenticating the usable tradition vary. This question of *authority* is debated by Carol Christ as she assesses the implications of postmodern perspectives for feminist theology (Christ, 1988). The absence of an objective, external standard by which a feminist vision may be validated has already been encountered in my earlier critiques of feminist epistemologies. Christ chooses the work of Elisabeth Schüssler Fiorenza as an appropriate model of feminist hermeneutics.

Fiorenza's method derives its core criterion of validity from feminist *praxis*: that termed authentic in the text is that which testifies to the pastoral and evangelical practices of first-generation Christians, which proclaimed the values of *agapē*, radical equality and redemption, inaugurated originally in the life, death and resurrection of Jesus, and embodied in the faith and works of the '*ekklesia* of equals' (Fiorenza, 1983:349–51). The existence and viability of such communities acts as a hermeneutical hypothesis which guides her reading of the canonical texts, and thus informs Fiorenza's judgement of the authenticity of the tradition in reporting actual practices. *In Memory of Her* is effectively a sustained study of the extent to which that authentic, inclusive practice can be retrieved through the surviving textual traditions, and how these early practices can be maintained as more definitive and genuinely Gospel-centred. Ultimately, such a judgement involves a return to the contemporary situation, and an understanding of how the example represented by the practices of the earliest churches *discloses* a more inclusive and just Christian community today.

However, not even the canon of Scripture thus inspired is definitive for all time. It is not 'archetypical' but 'prototypical'; foreclosure is resisted in that no text embodies the truth absolutely and finally, but is merely a blueprint for, and prefiguration of, a reality still to come. The contemporary experience of the Christian community in its quest for justice and mutuality in the world remembers the initial redemptive acts of Jesus, but attests to its constant renewal and re-enactment in the *ekklesia*. Thus, Fiorenza's hermeneutic rests its authority on the practice of the Christian community, historical and contemporary, as rooted in its profession of faith. Scripture is one source of guidance, but has been subject to patriarchal distortion. Inasmuch as gender equality and feminist transformation are normative – derived from the decisive events associated with the Christ – Scripture is itself judged according to its conformity to such a vision and its ability to inspire the contemporary renewal of disclosive relationships.

Fiorenza's understanding of tradition and truth as resting in the practices of faith and purposive liberation offers a model which is both public (openly accessible to debate) and feminist (committed, strategic and located). The possibilities for a public theology concern not so much its claims to cognitive credibility as it mirrors the facts of human experience, as its contribution of questions of theological value and policy to public debate. Admitting to their location in specific communities, such values are also rendered available to public and secular scrutiny. However, these public values or mores are not in any way divorced from the stories, strategies, relationships and principled actions of the faith-community. The validity and veracity of this is guaranteed, without recourse to essentialism or foundationalism, by locating those 'ultimate' values in the activities and concrete possibilities of a self-critical community.

The boundary of the tradition – the fault-line which distinguishes orthodoxy from heresy – is therefore always defined in terms of the parameters of a faith-community's practical theological wisdom. Tradition is seen as alive and organic, to be reappropriated in the pursuit of *praxis*. The role of tradition is thus to be indicative, but not definitive, and liberates feminist theologians from the task of being required to justify contemporary practices as in keeping with shreds of tradition, however muted, marginal or ephemeral. If tradition is the result of historical practices, then this invests the present with a greater status. Theology is an experimental and hypothetical discourse, seeking to reorder and reinterpret the past in all its plurality.

Therefore, as well as emphasizing that tradition itself as the accumulation of historical practices, such a process of interpretation also allows free interplay between the past and the present. The authority of the past rests in the fruits of its interaction with the present, and thus in what it leads to – discloses – in the present. Potentially, this epistemology also acknowledges that history does not contain all that is necessary and sufficient for building the values and principles from which inclusive Christian communities draw their sense of purpose.

It is therefore in the engagement between the horizons of past, present and future that a true apprehension of tradition emerges, not through the distillation of eternal principles independent of the living reality. In this respect, the epistemology of pastoral theology is akin to forms of scientific practice which operate through the development of experimental hypotheses rather than the absolute application of fixed claims to truth. Ultimately, the authenticity and validity of accumulated tradition is never finally exhausted, because the judgements of the present necessarily await further testing and verification in the projects of the future. Interpretation of tradition is forever open and eschatalogical in focus, because its validating focus is embodied, situated and purposeful practice. However, in order to maintain the disclosive nature of such a validating focus, and to protect its public, collective face, I would argue that a practical wisdom which synthesizes past, present and future must be grounded in some kind of intentional community of *praxis*. Thus, the community of faith and practice becomes the pivotal agent in the articulation and enactment of a postmodern gender-sensitive Christian pastoral theology.

Communities of Faith and Praxis

A community may see itself as the bearer of tradition only insofar as its purposeful practices disclose patterns of authentic living. Its situatedness, both in history and in embodied practice, enables it to live out its truth-claims with integrity and yet retain a posture of openness and dialogue. The faith-community therefore derives its epistemic authority from *praxis*; and theology, as the reflection and systematization of such practical wisdom is rendered as *thinking* (itself a form of practice) rather than thought (a form of abstraction and disengagement):

> How do we present our views in the fullness of our embodied and perspectival commitment, without falling back into a premodern universalism that has rightly been criticized as expressing the will to power of those who have been able to express their views? I suggest it is not by pretending to an intellectual neutrality which in any case is only a pose, but rather by acknowledging and affirming the conditions of time and space, which limit our perspectives as well as giving them their distinctive perspectival power . . . We should not hold our views so tightly that we cannot appreciate the perspectival truths embodied in the lives and works of others. We should think of our 'truth claims' as the product of embodied *thinking* not as eternally or universally valid *thought*. (Christ, 1988:15)

My earlier critiques of feminist pastoral practices illuminated their insistence upon the disclosive potential inherent in their purposeful enactment. First, there is the disclosure of pluralism.

The encounter with *alterity* becomes a genuine moment of disclosure, because one group or identity is confronted with the occluded parts of its own nature: it recognizes that its own exclusive claims to knowledge or stable identity are destabilized by the existence of other situated beings. Thus fixity and absolutism are also displaced.

In a second respect, also, difference serves as disclosive, in that a deeper and larger truth is revealed as resting in diversity and pluriformity. Those who reduce 'truth' to their own image actually distort that inherent complexity and heterogeneity of human experience. Thus, embracing the Other and celebrating, not repressing, diversity, is the avenue to genuine, non-coercive identity and truth. Any institution, like the Church, thus is challenged to generosity towards other groups, because it suggests that authenticity is distorted by exclusive truth-claims. Themes to be favoured within the theological tradition would be those which affirm the heterogeneity of truth, the inability of one single system to contain reality, and the ultimate mystery and alterity at the heart of all identity.

Just as there is a pluriformity of practice, so perhaps there are many ways of knowing – a *pluridoxy* to match the *orthopraxis*! Pastoral practices need to encourage the development of human imagination, embodiment, spirituality and conviviality; all of which may be understood as vital aspects of experience and avenues of personal and collective development. Fundamentally, all these characteristics evoke the core metaphor of conversation: an ever-widening dialogue between different voices, sources and modes of thinking and being. Pastoral care must therefore be diverse in form, encompassing and harnessing all aspects of rational and non-rational faculties.

The examples of feminist *praxis* also stressed the theological disclosure inherent within the pastoral encounter. Fischer's evocation of the Divine as disclosed in the celebration of the 'Other' affirms that transcendence is to be encountered in the immediacy and concretion of the pastoral event, not within a metaphysical realm. The transcendent becomes a dimension beyond the certain and the known, but attainable only through the recognition and cultivation of alterity. The practices of intentional faith-communities therefore represent the creative synthesis of past and present in the service of future imperatives. The diversity of pastoral action within the community also acts as the guardian of pluralism and alterity, in expressing a multiplicity of ways of knowing and acting. The disclosive practices also embody the relationships which proclaim the core values of the Christian faith, and situate the truth-claims of the community in its purposeful enactment, believing also that such sacraments of human agency will elicit signs of transcendence.

CHAPTER 9

New Horizons

How can women and men present a vision of human wholeness – a vision
rooted in both Christian tradition and contemporary experience – which
will help in the ecumenical task of renewing the Church? The Community
Study was – and is – at the heart of the ecumenical agenda. It reflects the
realization that the world will come to believe not because of the clarity of
our doctrinal formulations (important as this is) but because of the quality
of our life as a loving, reconciling inclusive community in Christ.

(Crawford and Kinnamon, 1983: viii)

It is now possible to move towards a resolution of the question posed
at the beginning of this book: that of the challenges posed by
postmodern culture for Christian conduct and theological understanding. The anatomy of postmodernity has been sketched in
Chapter 1. Broadly, I assumed the loss of any 'grand narrative' of
hope and obligation and the deconstruction of foundationalist
thought constituted vital challenges to contemporary Christians.
In particular, I used human experience as gendered to exemplify
the contrast between modernity and postmodernity. Perspectives
from feminism and gender theory destabilize core categories of
selfhood and community: ontology (what it means to be human);
subjectivity (the ontogeny and development of consciousness and
self-identity); agency (the processes by which human activity transforms material reality and interacts to effect interpersonal change);
teleology (the sources and norms of moral wisdom in the absence
of fixed appeals to truth); and epistemology (the relationship
between 'knower, knowing and known' (Hawkesworth, 1989)).

Contemporary theories of gender posit human material and
symbolic practices as the generating sources of gender identity and
gender relations. Accounts of the formation of gendered personhood emphasize the interplay of bodily experience, the material

202

transformation of the 'natural' world, practices of *cathexis* and child-rearing and the acquisition of language as generating social relations characterized by patterns of power and difference. These various human practices constitute the arena within which gender differences and resulting regimes of power and domination are forged and maintained.

Such a perspective denies the possibility of universal principles such as 'truth' 'objective reason' or 'human nature' upon which to found a renewed ethics and politics. Instead, transformatory sources of meaning and value must be generated from within the very scientific and political practices which they fuel. A perspective that acknowledges the situated and interpretative nature of human experience, and honours the 'vantage-point' of positional claims to truth, also offers an epistemology which reflects the contingent, reflexive and contextual nature of gendered identity, agency and subjectivity. Attention to the oppressive power inherent in the assertion of definitive meaning and identity also alerts critics to the importance of affording *difference* and *alterity* a privileged position in their knowledge-practices. These principles foster a sensibility which seeks ethical and authentic human practice in the criterion of *disclosure*: a refusal to universalize one's particularity or to absolutize the boundaries of any single community or culture.

A commitment to the contextual and situated nature of human experience, if taken seriously by pastoral theology, therefore means that the only vocabulary available to Christian communities in articulating their truth-claims is that of pastoral practice itself. In their relationships and actions of care, social change, adult formation, worship and stewardship, communities of faith enact their core values of human being, truth, destiny, knowledge and obligation. The faith-community acts as the guardian of *practical wisdom* by which such purposeful action gains its authenticity and credibility, and serves as the medium by which truth-claims are forged and publicly articulated. The community of faith and *praxis* is therefore afforded primacy by such a pastoral theology, in common with other postmodern theologies:

> A religion is a communal phenomenon that shapes the subjectivities of individuals rather than being primarily a manifestation of those subjectivities. It is a linguistic medium that *makes possible* the description of realities and the formation of beliefs rather than being a catalogue of those beliefs.　(Murphy and McClendon, 1989:206)

To regard all theological discourse as grounded in human agency is resonant with perspectives on human identity and experience as constituted through practice, and therefore as enacted, contextual and provisional. Theology now becomes not an abstract series of philosophical propositions, but a performative discipline, where knowledge and truth are only realizable in the pursuit of practical strategies and social relations.

The unity of theology, therefore, is located in the study of the practices of intentional faith-communities. The *praxis* of the faith-community constitutes the character and wisdom of theology: it is the means by which Christians purposefully inhabit the world, and the vehicle through which the community itself is formed and ordered. Pastoral *praxis* is not aimed at retrieving an essential self, but at creating the purposeful habits by which disclosive encounters with *alterity* can be fostered in human history. Pastoral theology is the particular study of Christian practices and the normative truth-claims they express. It seeks to excavate and evaluate the sources and norms of practice, and the values and visions thereby disclosed.

According to this view, therefore, pastoral theology breaks out of the 'clerical paradigm' and locates itself as the 'critical inquiry into the validity of Christian witness' (Wheeler and Farley, 1991:15). It studies the whole mission of the Church, as expressed in its diverse practices of ordering the faithful, engaging in social justice, communicating the faith, and administering Word and Sacrament. This is increasingly the emphasis that characterizes contemporary Roman Catholic pastoral theology, influenced by liberation theologies and by the theological anthropology of Karl Rahner (Rahner, 1968, 1969; Duffy, 1983:10, 85–115). The Church exists not for itself, but to proclaim and enact the Gospel in human society; and thus pastoral practice is the living expression of the Church's mission to the world:

> Pastoral theology deals with the action of the Church. It is pastoral because it engages concrete circumstances, it is theological because it reflects systematically on the nature of the Church and analyses the circumstances which confront the Church today . . . The work of pastoral theology begins only when Christians here and now and at a local level incarnate the Church's nature.   (Rahner, 1968:25)

Here, Rahner gives due primacy to practice, and to pastoral theology as the study of Christian practice, but is effectively arguing that it is the Church which determines the nature and priorities of that practice. This suggests that the structures and values of the Church are still in some way independent of history, and that human action is merely the expression of an *a priori* ordering of faith. However, if practice actually *constitutes* human identity and meaning, then action is not the outworking of faith, but its prerequisite. Ultimately, the norms and values of practice give shape to the faith-community, and not the other way around. Thus, although I wish to emphasize the primacy of the faith-community for Christian pastoral practice – as the inhabitant of tradition, the bearer and mediator of experience and the vehicle of purposeful and transformative action – my emphasis rests upon the practices, and not the institution.

One of the themes of my review of feminist *praxis* in Chapter 8 was that the Gospel is invalid – even idolatrous – if it is proclaimed by a patriarchal Church. The positive experience of those who have come to know an inclusive community, who work self-consciously within an understanding of the tradition as offering dignity and equality to women and men, who find their faith renewed by the mutuality and self-acceptance of such a vision, commends models of pastoral practice which nurture an inclusive community that understands the Church as a living sign of gender justice to the rest of society. The quality of the faith-community's relationships thus definitively constitutes the evidence for Christian truth-claims.

Thus, insofar as pastoral practice seeks to build and sustain a moral and just human community, then the integrity of its vision rests in the tangible qualities of its 'disclosive practices'. Otherwise, the normative principles for practice risk foreclosure in the predetermined patterns and self-interest of the institution. An emphasis on the primacy of disclosive practices, however, reminds the Church that the purposes of mission are to reveal the redemptive actions of God to the whole inhabited creation, and not to win members or status for itself. Once more, therefore, it impels the faith-community to see its practices of enacting and naming the Divine presence in the world as paramount, and the faith-community as merely a medium, sign and witness of such transcendence. This places the onus upon pastoral theology to ensure that the disclosive imperatives of transformatory practice determine the self-understanding of the community of faith, and not the other way around.

Alterity and Transcendence

Postmodern theologies emphasize and celebrate the provisionality and strategic value of truth, reject foundationalist notions of reality, and ground their truth-claims in the performative, enacted reasoning and purposeful practices of faith-communities. However, this development faces a similar challenge to that posed to postmodern philosophy and politics: can such perspectives sustain a theory of human understanding and existence without abandoning the imperatives of hope and obligation? Can values rooted in the specificity and concretion of the community resist the foreclosure of self-absorption and self-justification – even self-aggrandizement? This challenge is especially keen to Christian faith-communities who wish to maintain a dialogue with the public and the secular, and not retreat into (not so) splendid isolation.

I argued in Chapter 7 that a communitarian and practice-based *phronēsis* could resist the foreclosure of introspection by regarding its truth-claims as forms of *situated knowledge*. Critical evaluation of such practical reasoning would deploy the critical dialectic of *disclosure/foreclosure*: in the spirit of situated knowledges and hermeneutics, the encounter with the 'Other' presupposes a larger reality beyond the present and immediate. It thus represents an ethical imperative towards communication, generosity and dialogue: all marks of good conversation. A recognition of the factors which engender difference also exposes the extent to which our own fixity of self-possession is actually contingent upon relationality and finitude. In a similar way, therefore, through the pastoral encounter with others, participants will experience the paradox of familiarity and otherness which both situates them within, and draws them beyond, the present and immediate. Can we regard authentic pastoral practice, therefore, as that which draws us into encounter with the 'Other', towards a deeper understanding of our own identity-in-relation?

The process of going *beyond* the situated and concrete in the encounter with the Other may also serve as a metaphor for the human experience of the transcendent. It speaks of an encounter with transcendence and authentic faith occurring at the very point of loss of certainty and self-possession: divine activity and presence are encountered in the mystery of alterity. However, the paradox is that this encounter with the 'beyond' is only possible, and is forever grounded, in the immediate. Within Christian incarnational theology, this would be understood as the human and immediate being the vehicle or sacrament for the transcendent and Divine. If such a Divine and transcendent dimension is available to human apprehension, it will only be realized in the practical and concrete arena of purposeful action. Practical wisdom guided by the principles of communicative action and alterity is grounded in the hypothesis of our common humanity. The *telos* of pastoral practice, humanly speaking, is to resist the foreclosure of absolute difference and disclose the experiences and voices of the 'Others' whose presence is a living reminder of that shared human nature, despite the power relations and occlusions of separation and difference.

Implicit within notions of pastoral practice as *disclosive* is an eschewal of claims to exclusive agency: the Divine dimension of human experience and practice rests in alterity, provisionality and self-abandonment. This has far-reaching implications for Christian understandings of mission and relations with other faiths. It suggests that a Divine reality is inconsistent with notions of uniqueness or exclusivity of revelation:

> If one believes that a God of love acts for human salvation, one will be inclined to think that God will act to show what the divine nature is, what salvation is and how we may achieve it. At the same time, the divine will reveal itself in ways which interact with human powers of imagination, reflection and conceptual understanding. We will not expect one clear, decisive, certain revelation . . . God manifests in many names and forms; the divine character is shown in real acts God performs. But there may not be just one unique and normative act, clear to all and free from error. The conclusion seems inescapable; that the divine self-revelation is a prompting of human minds to come to a clearer, but never infallible, perception of the divine nature and saving action. (Ward, 1991:121)

In terms of a doctrine of the nature of God, this pastoral/practical theology effects a shift from ontology to practice. Human religious experience names the effects and traces of God rather than an essence of divinity; this renders metaphorical language for God all the more necessary and appropriate. Models of God will thus emphasize not essence and identity but action and agency, consistent with the notion of practice as the sphere of Divine–human encounter, and of *orthopraxis* as the vehicle of Christian truth-claims:

> Christians should not redefine social praxis by starting with the gospel message. They should do just the opposite. They should seek out the historical import of the gospel by starting with social praxis.
>
> (J.P. Richard (1972), Racionalidad socialista y verificación histórica del cristianismo, quoted in Segundo, 1982:85)

Pastoral Theology as Interpretative, not Legislative Discipline

My vision of pastoral theology portrays it as the systematic reflection upon the nature of the Church in the world, accessible only through the practical wisdom of those very communities. Therefore, as a discipline pastoral theology is not legislative or prescriptive, but interpretative. It enables the community of faith to give a critical and public account of its purposeful presence in the world, and the values that give shape to its actions.

I admire the work of Don Browning and Stanley Hauerwas in their vision of Christian ethics not as absolute prescriptions of right and wrong but the discipline which fosters and enables people to live moral lives. This is not situational ethics or antinomianism. It is about articulating a vision of the good and the true in concrete, if interim, practices and sensibilities. Thus the moral discourse of the community aims at ordering the community of faith in such a way as to nurture the sensibilities and habits of faith. However, unlike Browning, who regarded pastoral practice as the application and enactment of *a priori* moral principles, I have argued for a model of Christian practice which inherits and inhabits traditions of practical wisdom that are realized and re-enacted through the purposeful ordering of the community. Moral perfectibility is sought as a notion of the ultimate good – an eschatalogical ideal – by which the building up of the faithful may be guided.

Such a model of pastoral practice is thus a refutation of prescriptive pastoral care which seeks to enforce moral conformity to absolute norms on behalf of controlling and dominating interests. However, it does not abandon completely any notion of pastoral discipline or Christian perfection. In the face of uncertainty and Divine provisionality, Christian pastoral practices can still affirm some kind of (interim) truth and value by virtue of their location in the continuing life and work of the faith-community. The exact nature and purpose of ultimate reality may be cloaked in mystery; but at least a purposive and practising community meets to celebrate and realize the Divine possibility. It is within such a community that those who suffer may find support and healing, and through its celebrations and acts of compassion that healing and redemption may decisively be experienced and prefigured.

The primary mode of enquiry for pastoral theology will therefore be *phenomenological*. This respects the reflexivity of gender and the contextual nature of *phronēsis*, arising from and returning to practice, not pretending to exist outside their own culture or generation; yet ethical, in that such critical knowledge claims a principled authority arising from considered analysis. Pastoral theology as the *critical phenomenology of pastoral practice*, therefore, excavates the horizons of value embodied in all intentional practices of faith and evaluates their continuity with historic forms of *praxis*, their appropriateness for the complexity of human experience and their viability as public and communitarian forms of practical wisdom.

A notion of transcendence is therefore generated through the immediacy and concretion of pastoral encounters and practices impelling human communities to transcend their own finitude and limitation. Such a dynamic may not just characterize Christian communities, but the whole of human history. If so, salvation would rest not in the restoration of a pristine pre-Fall creation, or in the realization of some existential and metaphysical principles of human wholeness, but in human and divine actions fusing in the realization of redemption, justice and disclosure.

Thus, pastoral theology as the critical study of the values informing and directing Christian practice draws near to the traditional function of moral theology, as the discipline concerned to guide the ordering of the community of faith. However, as a postmodern, gender-sensitive and performative discipline, pastoral theology is less concerned to legislate about the application of eternal moral norms or rules articulated outside the situation, as it is concerned to act as interpreter of the resources by which the faith-community may cultivate its sensibility for disclosure. Pastoral theology does not neglect the imperatives of hope and obligation, but refuses to absolutize the epistemological foundations of pastoral response and transformative *praxis* in the interests of a larger vision yet to come.

Bibliography

Abbott, W.M. (ed.) (1966) *The Documents of Vatican II*. London: Chapman.

Adams, J.E. (1976) *The Use of the Scriptures in Counseling*. Grand Rapids, Michigan: Baker.

Alcoff, L. (1988) Cultural Feminism versus Post-Structuralism: the Identity Crisis in Feminist Theory. *Signs: Journal of Women in Culture and Society*, Vol. 13, No. 3, 405–36.

Allen, J. (1992) Post-Industrialism and Post-Fordism. In S. Hall, D. Held and T. McGrew (eds), *Modernity and its Futures*. Cambridge: Polity Press, 169–204.

Alvarez, S.E. (1990) Women's Participation in the Brazilian 'People's Church': A Critical Appraisal. *Feminist Studies* 16, No. 2, 381–409.

Ansara, K.K. (1991) Abortion: 'Throw No Stones'. In A.L. Milhaven (ed.), *Sermons Seldom Heard*. New York: Crossroad, 145–56.

Avarista, M.F. (1991) Throwaway Children. In A.L. Milhaven (ed.), *Sermons Seldom Heard*. New York: Crossroad, 67–74.

Balasundaram, F.J. (1991) Feminist Concerns in Asia: An Ecumenical Christian Perspective. *Bangalore Theological Forum*, Volume XXIII, No. 3, 39–75.

Balmforth, H., Dewar, L., Hudson, C.E. and Sara, E.W. (1937) *An Introduction to Pastoral Theology*. London: Hodder & Stoughton.

Barker, F., Hulme, P. and Iversen, M. (eds) (1992) *Postmodernism and the Re-reading of Modernity*. Manchester: Manchester University Press.

Bauman, Z. (1989) *Modernity and the Holocaust*. Cambridge: Polity Press.

Baynes, K., Bohman, J. and McCarthy, T. (eds) (1987) *After Philosophy: End or Transformation?*. Cambridge, MA: Massachusetts Institute of Technology.

Bebbington, D.W. (1989) *Evangelicalism in Modern Britain*. London: Unwin Hyman.

Belton, F.G. (1916) *A Manual for Confessors*. London: Mowbray.

Benhabib, S. (1992) *Situating the Self: Gender, Community and Postmodernism in Contemporary Ethics*. Cambridge: Polity Press.

Benhabib, S. (1995a) Feminism and Postmodernism. In S. Benhabib, J. Butler, D. Cornell and N. Fraser (eds), *Feminist Contentions: a Philosophical Exchange*. London: Routledge, 17–34.

Benhabib, S. (1995b) Subjectivity, Historiography, and Politics. In S. Benhabib, J. Butler, D. Cornell and N. Fraser (eds), *Feminist Contentions: a Philosophical Exchange*. London: Routledge, 107–25.

Bernstein, R.J. (1971) *Praxis and Action: Contemporary Philosophies of Human Activity*. Philadelphia: University of Pennsylvania Press.

Bernstein, R.J. (1983) *Beyond Objectivism and Relativism: Science, Hermeneutics and Praxis*. Oxford: Blackwell.

Bernstein, R.J. (1985) *Habermas and Modernity*. Cambridge: Cambridge University Press.

Berry, P. (1992a) Introduction. In P. Berry and A. Wernick (eds), *Shadow of Spirit: Postmodernism and Religion*. London: Routledge, 1–8.

Berry, P. (1992b) Woman and Space according to Kristeva and Irigaray. In P. Berry and A. Wernick (eds), *Shadow of Spirit: Postmodernism and Religion*. London: Routledge, 250–64.

Bhaskar, R. (1989) *Reclaiming Reality: A Critical Introduction to Contemporary Philosophy*. London: Verso.

Bocock, R. (1992) The Cultural Formations of Modern Society. In S. Hall and B. Gieben (eds), *Formations of Modernity*. Cambridge: Polity Press, 229–68.

Boff, L. and Boff, C. (1987) *Introducing Liberation Theology*. Tunbridge Wells: Burns & Oates.

Bourdieu, P. (1992) *The Logic of Practice*. Cambridge: Polity Press.

Brennan, J.H. (1967) Pastoral Theology. In W.J. McDonald (ed.), *New Catholic Encyclopedia*. New York: McGraw-Hill, 1080–84.

Brewer, K. (1991) Shattering the Silence: Incest. In A.L. Milhaven (ed.), *Sermons Seldom Heard*. New York: Crossroad, 23–39.

Browning, D.S. (1969) The Influence of Psychology on Theology. In W.B. Oglesby Jr. (ed.) *The New Shape of Pastoral Theology: Essays in Honor of Seward Hiltner*. Nashville: Abingdon, 121–35.

Browning, D.S. (1976) *The Moral Context of Pastoral Care*. Philadelphia: Westminster.

Browning, D.S. (1982) The Estrangement of Pastoral Care from Ethics. *Concilium* 156, No. 6, 10–17.

Browning, D.S. (1983) *Religious Ethics and Pastoral Care*. Philadelphia: Fortress Press.

Browning, D.S. (1985) Practical Theology and Political Theology. *Theology Today*, vol. XLII, No. 1, 15–33.

Browning, D.S. (1987) Practical Theology and Religious Education. In L.S. Mudge and J.N. Poling (eds), *Formation and Reflection: The Promise of Practical Theology*. Philadelphia: Fortress, 79–102.

Browning, D.S. (1990) Ethics and Pastoral Care. In R.J. Hunter (ed.), *Dictionary of Pastoral Care and Counseling*. Nashville: Abingdon, 364–6.

Browning, D.S. (1991) *A Fundamental Practical Theology: Descriptive and Strategic Proposals*. Minneapolis: Fortress Press.

Browning, D.S. and Fiorenza, F.S. (eds) (1992) *Habermas, Modernity and Public Theology*. New York: Crossroad.

Buckley, M. (1979) The Rising of the Woman is the Rising of the Race. *Proceedings of the Catholic Theological Society of America*. 34, 48–63.

Burck, J.R. and Hunter, R.J. (1990) Pastoral Theology, Protestant. In R.J. Hunter (ed.), *Dictionary of Pastoral Care and Counseling*. Nashville: Abingdon, 867–72.

Burkhart, J.E. (1983) Schleiermacher's Vision for Theology. In D.S. Browning (ed.), *Practical Theology: The Emerging Field in Theology, Church, and World*. San Francisco: Harper and Row, 42–60.

Burrell, D.B. (1992) An Introduction to 'Theology and Social Theory: Beyond Secular Reason'. *Modern Theology* 8:4, 319–29.

Butler, J. (1990) *Gender Trouble: Feminism and the Subversion of Identity*. London: Routledge.

Butler, J. (1995a) Contingent Foundations. In S. Benhabib, J. Butler, D. Cornell and N. Fraser (eds), *Feminist Contentions: a Philosophical Exchange*. London: Routledge, 35–57.

Butler, J. (1995b) For a Careful Reading. In S. Benhabib, J. Butler, D. Cornell, and N. Fraser (eds), *Feminist Contentions: a Philosophical Exchange*. London: Routledge, 127–43.

Campbell, A.V. (1981) *Rediscovering Pastoral Care*. London: Darton, Longman and Todd.

Campbell, A.V. (1984) *Moderated Love: A Theology of Professional Care*. London: SPCK.

Campbell, A.V. (1985) *Paid to Care? The Limits of Professionalism in Pastoral Care*. London: SPCK.

Campbell, A.V. (ed.) (1987) *A Dictionary of Pastoral Care*. London: SPCK.

Campbell, A.V. (1989) *The Gospel of Anger*. London: SPCK.

Campbell, A.V. (1990) The Nature of Practical Theology. In D.B. Forrester (ed.), *Theology and Practice*. London: Epworth, 10–20.

Carr, A.E. (1988) *Transforming Grace: Christian Tradition and Women's Experience*. San Francisco: Harper and Row.

Carrington, W.L. (1957) *Psychology, Religion and Human Need: a guide for ministers, doctors, teachers and social workers*. London: Epworth.

Chopp, R. (1987) Practical Theology and Liberation. In L.S. Mudge and J.N. Poling (eds), *Formation and Reflection: The Promise of Practical Theology*. Philadelphia: Fortress, 120–38.

Christ, C.P. (1988) Embodied Thinking: Reflections on Feminist Theological Method. *Journal of Feminist Studies in Religion* 5, No. 1, 7–15.

Chung, Hyun-Kyung (1988) 'Han-pu-ri': Doing Theology from Korean Women's Perspective. *Ecumenical Review* Vol. 40, No. 1, 27–36.

Chung, Hyun-Kyung (1990) *Struggle to be the Sun Again: Introducing Asian Women's Theology*. Maryknoll, NY: Orbis.

Chung, Hyun-Kyung (1991) Come Holy Spirit, renew the whole creation. *Women in a Changing World*. Geneva: World Council of Churches, No. 31, 12–15.

Clebsch, W.A. and Jaekle, C.R. (1964) *Pastoral Care in Historical Perspective*. Englewood Cliffs, NJ: Prentice Hall.

Clinebell, H. (1984) *Basic Types of Pastoral Care and Counselling: Resources for the Ministry of Healing and Growth*. Second edition, London: SCM Press.

Code, L. (1988) Experience, Knowledge and Responsibility. In M. Griffiths and M. Whitford (eds), *Feminist Perspectives in Philosophy*, London: Macmillan, 187–204.

Code, L. (1991) *What Can She Know? Feminist Theory and the Construction of Knowledge*. Ithaca, NY: Cornell University Press.

Connell, R.W. (1987) *Gender and Power*. Cambridge: Polity Press.

Cornell, D. (1995a) What is Ethical Feminism? In S. Benhabib, J. Butler, D. Cornell, and N. Fraser (eds), *Feminist Contentions: a Philosophical Exchange*. London: Routledge, 75–106.

Cornell, D. (1995b) Rethinking the Time of Feminism. In S. Benhabib, J. Butler, D. Cornell and N. Fraser (eds), *Feminist Contentions: a Philosophical Exchange*. London: Routledge, 145–56.

Couture, P.D. and Hunter, R.J. (eds) (1995) *Pastoral Care and Social Conflict*. Nashville: Abingdon.

Crawford, J. and Kinnamon, M. (eds) (1983) *In God's Image: Reflections on Identity, Human Wholeness and the Authority of Scripture*, Geneva: World Council of Churches.

Critchley, S. and Mooney, T. (1994) Deconstruction and Derrida. In R. Kearney (ed.), *Continental Philosophy in the 20th Century*. London: Routledge, History of Philosophy Volume VIII, 441–73.

Cupitt, D. (1989) *Radicals and the Future of the Church*. London: SCM Press.

Cupitt, D. (1994) *After All: Religion without Alienation*. London: SCM Press.

Davie, G. (1994) *Religion in Britain since 1945: Believing without Belonging*. Oxford: Blackwell.

Davies, M. (1991) *Industrial Mission: the Anatomy of a Crisis*. Manchester: William Temple Foundation.

Davis, C. (1994) *Religion and the Making of Society.* Cambridge: Cambridge University Press.

Dawe, A. (1979) Theories of Social Action. In T. Bottomore and R. Nisbet (eds), *A History of Sociological Analysis.* London: Heinemann, 362–417.

Day Williams, D. (1961) *The Minister and the Cure of Souls.* New York: Harper.

Denham, P.L. (1991) Life-Styles: A Culture in Transition. In M. Glaz and J.S. Moessner (eds), *Women in Travail and Transition.* Minneapolis: Fortress, 162–83.

Dewar, L. and Hudson, C.E. (1932) *A Manual of Pastoral Psychology.* London: Philip Allen.

Dews, P. (1987) *Logics of Disintegration: Post-Structuralist Thought and the Claims of Critical Theory.* London: Verso.

Dicks, R.L. (1944) *Pastoral Work and Personal Counseling.* New York: Macmillan.

Dicks, R.L. and Cabot, R. (1936) *The Art of Ministering to the Sick.* New York: Macmillan.

Doherty, T. (1994) Postmodernist Theory: Lyotard, Baudrillard and others. In R. Kearney (ed.), *Continental Philosophy in the 20th Century.* London: Routledge, History of Philosophy Volume VIII, 474–505.

Dudley, C.S. (ed.) (1983) *Building Effective Ministry,* San Francisco: Harper and Row.

Duffy, R.A. (1983) *A Roman Catholic Theology of Pastoral Care.* Philadelphia: Fortress Press.

Duffy, R.A. (1990) Roman Catholic Pastoral Care. In R.J. Hunter (ed.), *Dictionary of Pastoral Care and Counseling.* Nashville: Abingdon, 1093–95.

Durber, S. and Walton, H. (eds) (1994) *Silence in Heaven: a book of women's preaching.* London: SCM Press.

Dyson, A.O. (1983) Pastoral Theology: Toward a New Discipline. *Contact: The Interdisciplinary Journal of Pastoral Studies* 78, 2–8.

Edwards, O.C. (1985) Preaching and Pastoral Care. In J.E. Griffis (ed.), *Anglican Theology and Pastoral Care.* Wilton, CT: Morehouse-Barlow, 133–58.

Evans, E. (1961) *Pastoral Care in a Changing World.* London: Epworth.

Evans, J. (1995) *Feminist Theory Today: An Introduction to Second-Wave Feminism.* London: Sage.

Fabella, V.M.M. and Oduyoye, M.A. (eds) (1988) *With Passion and Compassion: Third World Women doing Theology.* Maryknoll, NY: Orbis.

Fageol, S. (1991) Celebrating Experience. In St. Hilda Community, *Women Included: A Book of Services and Prayers.* London: SPCK, 16–26.

Farley, E. (1983) Theology and Practice Outside the Clerical Paradigm. In D.S. Browning (ed.), *Practical Theology: the emerging field in theology, church, and world.* San Francisco: Harper and Row, 21–41.

Farley, E. (1983) *Theologia: The Fragmentation and Unity of Theological Education.* Philadelphia: Fortress Press.

Farley, E. (1987) Interpreting Situations: An Inquiry into the Nature of Practical Theology. In L.S. Mudge and J.N. Poling (eds), *Formation and Reflection: The Promise of Practical Theology.* Philadelphia: Fortress Press, 1–26.

Farley, E. (1990) *Good and Evil: Interpreting a Human Condition.* Minneapolis: Fortress Press.

Finn, G. (1992) The Politics of Spirituality: the Spirituality of Politics. In P. Berry and A. Wernick (eds), *Shadow of Spirit: Postmodernism and Religion.* London: Routledge, 111–22.

Fiorenza, E.S. (1983) *In Memory of Her: A Feminist Theological Reconstruction of Christian Origins.* London: SCM Press.

Fischer, K. (1989) *Women at the Well: Feminist Perspectives on Spiritual Direction.* London: SPCK.

Flax, J. (1990) *Thinking Fragments: Psychoanalysis, Feminism, and Postmodernism in the Contemporary West.* Berkeley, CA: University of California Press.

Flax, J. (1993) *Disputed Subjects: Essays on Psychoanalysis, Politics and Philosophy.* London: Routledge.

Forder, C.R. (1947) *The Parish Priest at Work.* London: SPCK.

Forrester, D.B. (1990) Divinity in Use and Practice. In D.B. Forrester (ed.), *Theology and Practice.* London: Epworth, 3–9.

Forrester, D.B. (1994) Can Liberation Theology Survive 1989? *Scottish Journal of Theology.* Vol. 47, 245–53.

Foucault, M. (1979) *Discipline and Punish.* New York: Vintage Books.

Foucault, M. (1980) *History of Sexuality Volume I.* New York: Pantheon Books.

Fraser, N. (1987) What's Critical About Critical Theory? In S. Benhabib and D. Cornell (eds), *Feminism as Critique: Essays on the Politics of Gender in Late Capitalist Societies.* Cambridge: Polity Press, 30–56.

Fraser, N. (1989) *Unruly Practices: Power, Discourse and Gender in Contemporary Social Theory.* Cambridge: Polity Press.

Fraser, N. (1995) Pragmatism, Feminism and the Linguistic Turn. In S. Benhabib, J. Butler, D. Cornell and N. Fraser (eds), *Feminist Contentions: a Philosophical Exchange.* London: Routledge, 157–71.

Fraser, N. and Nicholson, L. (1988) Social Criticism without Philosophy: an encounter between feminism and postmodernism. *Theory, Culture and Society.* 5, No. 2–3, 373–94.

Fuller, R.C. (1986) *Americans and the Unconscious*, Oxford: Oxford University Press.

Gay, P. (1973) *The Enlightenment: an interpretation. Volume I: The Rise of Modern Paganism.* London: Wildwood House.

Gebara, I. (1989) Women Doing Theology in Latin America. In E. Tamez (ed.), *Through Her Eyes : Women's Theology in Latin America.* Maryknoll, NY: Orbis Press, 37–48.

Gerkin, C.V. (1984) *The Living Human Document: Re-visioning Pastoral Counseling in a Hermeneutical Mode.* Nashville: Abingdon.

Gerkin, C.V. (1986) *Widening the Horizons: Pastoral Responses to a Fragmented Society.* Philadelphia: Westminster.

Gerkin, C.V. (1990) Interpretation and Hermeneutics, Pastoral. In R.J. Hunter (ed.), *Dictionary of Pastoral Care and Counseling.* Nashville: Abingdon, 592–3

Gerrish, B.A. (1984) *A Prince of the Church: Schleiermacher and the Beginnings of Modern Theology.* London: SCM Press.

Gerstein, B. (1991) Rape: Violence against women. In A.L. Milhaven (ed.), *Sermons Seldom Heard.* New York: Crossroad, 40–51.

Gibbs, M. and Morton, R. (1964) *God's Frozen People.* London: Collins.

Giddens, A. (1984) *The Constitution of Society.* Cambridge: Polity Press.

Gladden, W. (1898) *The Christian Pastor and the Working Church.* Edinburgh: T & T Clark.

Glaz, M. (1991) Debates in the Psychology of Women and Pastoral Care. In M. Glaz and J.S. Moessner (eds), *Women in Travail and Transition: A New Pastoral Care.* Minneapolis: Fortress, 42–60.

Graham, E.L. (1990) Pastoral Theology, Feminism and the Future. *Contact: the Interdisciplinary Journal of Pastoral Studies.* 103, 2–9.

Graham, E.L. (1993) The Sexual Politics of Pastoral Care. In E.L. Graham and M. Halsey (eds), *Life-Cycles: Women and Pastoral Care.* London: SPCK, 210–24.

Graham, E.L. (1995) *Making the Difference: Gender, Personhood and Theology.* London: Mowbray.

Graham, E.L. and Halsey, M. (1993) *Life-Cycles: Women and Pastoral Care.* London: SPCK.

Graham, L.K. (1992) *Care of Persons, Care of Worlds: a Psychosystems Approach to Pastoral Care and Counseling.* Nashville: Abingdon.

Graham, L.K. (1995) From Relational Humanness to Relational Justice: Reconceiving Pastoral Care and Counseling. In P.D. Couture and R.J. Hunter (eds), *Pastoral Care and Social Conflict.* Nashville: Abingdon, 220–34.

Greeves, F. (1960) *Theology and the Cure of Souls.* London: Epworth. 1960.

Gregory the Great (1950) *The Book of Pastoral Rule*. Trans. H. Davis, Ancient Christian Writers Series, No. 11, Westminster, MD: Newman Press.

Grosz, E. (1990) A Note on Essentialism and Difference. In S. Gunew (ed.), *Feminist Knowledge: Critique and Construct*. London: Routledge, 332–44.

Gutiérrez, G. (1988) *A Theology of Liberation*. Second Edition. Maryknoll, NY: Orbis.

Haber, H.F. (1994) *Beyond Postmodern Politics: Lyotard, Rorty, Foucault*. London: Routledge.

Habermas, J. (1970) *Toward a Rational Society*. Boston: Beacon Press.

Habermas, J. (1971) *Knowledge and Human Interests*. Boston: Beacon Press.

Habermas, J. (1984) *The Theory of Communicative Action, Vol. 1: Rationality and Rationalization*. Trans. T. McCarthy, Boston: Beacon Press.

Habermas, J. (1989) *The Theory of Communicative Action, Vol. 2: Lifeworld and System: The Critique of Functionalist Reason*. Trans. T. McCarthy, Boston: Beacon Press.

Halberg, M. (1989) Feminist Epistemology: An Impossible Project? *Radical Philosophy* 53, 3–7.

Hall, C.E. (1969) Some contributions of Anton T. Boisen to Understanding Psychiatry and Religion. *Pastoral Psychology*, 1, 40–8.

Hall, S. (1992) The Question of Cultural Identity. In S. Hall, D. Held and T. McGrew (eds), *Modernity and its Futures*. Cambridge: Polity Press, 273–316.

Halmos, P. (1965) *The Faith of the Counsellors*. London: Constable.

Hamilton, P. (1992) The Enlightenment and the Birth of Social Science. In S. Hall and B. Gieben (eds), *Formations of Modernity*. Cambridge: Polity Press, 17–58.

Haraway, D. (1991) *Cyborgs, Simians and Women*. London: Polity Press.

Harding, S. (1986) *The Science Question in Feminism*. Milton Keynes: Open University Press.

Harding, S. (1989) Feminist justificatory strategies. In A. Garry and M. Pearsall (eds), *Women, Knowledge and Reality: Explorations in Feminist Philosophy*. Boston: Unwin Hyman, 189–201.

Harding, S. (1991) *Whose Science? Whose Knowledge? Thinking from Women's Lives*. Milton Keynes: Open University Press.

Harris, J.H. (1991) *Pastoral Theology: A Black-Church Perspective*. Minneapolis: Fortress Press.

Hart, D.A. (1994) On Not Quite Taking Leave of Don. *Modern Believing*, New Series, Vol. XXXV, No. 4, 6–9.

Hauerwas, S. (1974) *Vision and Virtue: Essays in Christian Ethical Reflection*. Notre Dame, IN: Fides Publishers.

Hauerwas, S. (1981) *A Community of Character*. Notre Dame, IN: University of Notre Dame Press.

Hauerwas, S. (1983) *The Peaceable Kingdom: A Primer in Christian Ethics*. Notre Dame, IN: University of Notre Dame Press.

Hauerwas, S. (1985) *Against the Nations*. Minneapolis: Fortress Press.

Hauerwas, S. (1988) *Suffering Presence: Theological Reflections on Medicine, the Mentally Handicapped, and the Church*. Edinburgh, T & T Clark.

Hauerwas, S. (1994) *Dispatches from the Front: Theological Engagements with the Secular*. Durham, NC: Duke University Press.

Hauerwas, S. and Willimon, W.H. (1989) *Resident Aliens: Life in the Christian Colony*. Nashville: Abingdon.

Hawkesworth, M. (1989) Knowers, Knowing, Known: Feminist Theory and Claims of Truth. *Signs: Journal of Women in Culture and Society*, 14, No. 3, 533–57.

Hekman, S.J. (1986) *Hermeneutics and the Sociology of Knowledge*, Cambridge: Polity Press.

Hekman, S.J. (1990) *Gender and Knowledge: Elements of a Postmodern Feminism*. Cambridge: Polity Press.

Held, D. (1992) The Development of the Modern State. In S. Hall and B. Gieben (eds), *Formations of Modernity*, Cambridge: Polity Press, 71–119.

Hilkert, M.C. (1987) Women Preaching the Gospel. In M. Kolbenschlag (ed.), *Women in the Church*. Washington D.C.: Pastoral Press, 65–91.

Hiltner, S. (1943) *Religion and Health*. London: Macmillan.

Hiltner, S. (1949) *Pastoral Counseling*. Nashville: Abingdon.

Hiltner, S. (1958) *Preface to Pastoral Theology*. Nashville: Abingdon.

Hiltner, S. (1972) *Theological Dynamics*. Nashville: Abingdon.

Hodgson, P.C. (1994) *Winds of the Spirit: A Constructive Christian Theology*. London: SCM Press.

Holifield, E.B. (1983) *A History of Pastoral Care in America: from Salvation to Self-Realisation*. Nashville: Abingdon.

Holifield, E.B. (1990) Psychology in American Religion. In R.J. Hunter (ed.), *Dictionary of Pastoral Care and Counseling*. Nashville: Abingdon, 1001–5.

Holub, R.C. (1991) *Jürgen Habermas: Critic in the Public Sphere*. London: Routledge.

hooks, bell (1991) *Yearning: Race, Gender, and Cultural Politics*. London: Turnaround.

Hopewell, J.F. (1987) *Congregation: Stories and Structures*. London: SCM Press.

Howe, L.T. (1984) Pastoral Care in Today's Church and World. *Modern Churchman*, New Series, XXVI, No. 4, 31–41.

Hunt, M. (1991) Overcoming the Fear of Love. In A.L. Milhaven (ed.), *Sermons Seldom Heard*. New York: Crossroad, 157–67.

Hunter, R.J. (1995) The Therapeutic Tradition of Pastoral Care and Counseling. In P.D. Couture and R.J. Hunter (eds), *Pastoral Care and Social Conflict*. Nashville: Abingdon, 17–31.

Hunter, R.J. and Patton, J. (1995) The Therapeutic Tradition's Theological and Ethical Commitments Viewed Through its Pedagogical Practices. In P.D. Couture and R.J. Hunter (eds), *Pastoral Care and Social Conflict*. Nashville: Abingdon, 32–43.

Imbelli, R.P. and Groome, T.H. (1992) Signposts Towards a Pastoral Theology. *Theological Studies* Vol. 53, No. 1, 127–37.

Jameson, F. (1991) *Postmodernism: or the cultural logic of late capitalism*. London: Verso.

Jones, R. (1983) On Dispensing with Shepherds? *Modern Churchman*, New Series, XXV, No. 2, 16–26.

Justes, E.J. (1978) Theological Reflections on the Role of Women in Church and Society. *Journal of Pastoral Care* 32, 42–54.

Justes, E.J. (1985) Women. In R.J. Wicks, R.D. Parsons and D. Capps (eds), *Handbook of Pastoral Counseling*. Mahwah, NJ: Integration/ Paulist Press, 279–99.

Kamionkowski, S.T. (1991) Anti-Semitism: Looking Beyond Hostility. In A.L. Milhaven (ed.), *Sermons Seldom Heard*. New York: Crossroad, 252–64.

Kanyoro, M.R.A. (ed.) (1991) *Our Advent: African women's experiences in the Lutheran tradition*. Geneva: Lutheran World Federation.

Kearney, R. (1994) *Modern Movements in European Philosophy: Phenomenology, Critical Theory, Structuralism*. 2nd edn. Manchester: Manchester University Press.

Kelsey, D.H. (1989) Paul Tillich. In D.F. Ford (ed.), *The Modern Theologians*. Vol. I, Oxford: Blackwell, 134–51.

Kent, S. (1995) Old job, new job – no job? *Guardian 2*. 4 March, 2–3.

Kim, Hyo-Jung (1991) Review: *Struggle to be the Sun Again. Boston Women's Theological Center Quarterly Newsletter*. Boston, MA, Vol. 9, No. 3, 7–8.

Kinast, R.L. (1990) Pastoral Theology, Roman Catholic. In R.J. Hunter (ed.), *Dictionary of Pastoral Care and Counseling*, Nashville: Abingdon, 873–4.

King, U. (ed.) (1994) *Feminist Theology from the Third World: A Reader*. London: SPCK.

Küng, H. and Tracy, D.(eds) (1991) *Paradigm Change in Theology*. New York: Crossroad.

Lake, F. (1966) *Clinical Theology.* Abridged by M. Yeomans (1986). London: Darton, Longman and Todd.

Lake, F. (1978) The Newer Therapies: Transactional analysis, Gestalt therapy, Bioenergetics and Encounter groups. *Contact: The Interdisciplinary Journal of Pastoral Studies.* 58, 2–27.

Lake, F. (1981) *Tight Corners in Pastoral Counselling.* London: Darton, Longman and Todd.

Lakeland, P. (1993) (En)countering the (post)modern. *The Month,* February, 63–70.

Lambourne, R.H. (1983) Essays. In M. Wilson (ed.), *Explorations in Health and Salvation.* University of Birmingham: Institute for the Study of Worship and Religious Architecture.

Lapsley, J.H. (1969) Pastoral Theology Past and Present. In W.B. Oglesby Jr. (ed.) *The New Shape of Pastoral Theology,* Nashville, Abingdon, 31–48.

Lapsley, J.H. (1983) Practical Theology and Pastoral Care: an Essay in Pastoral Theology. In D.S. Browning (ed.) *Practical Theology: The Emerging Field in Theology, Church, and World.* San Francisco: Harper and Row, 167–86.

Lartey, E.Y. (1993) African Perspectives on Pastoral Theology. *Contact: The Interdisciplinary Journal of Pastoral Studies.* 112, 3–11.

Lindbeck, G.A. (1984) *The Nature of Doctrine: Religion and Theology in a Post-Liberal Age.* London: SPCK.

Lindbeck, G.A. (1989) The Church's Mission to a Postmodern Culture. In F.C. Burnham (ed.), *Postmodern Theology: Christian Faith in a Pluralist World.* San Francisco: Harper and Row, 37–55.

Lovibond, S. (1989) Feminism and Postmodernism. *New Left Review* 178, 5–28.

Lukes, S. (1974) *Power: A Radical View.* London: Macmillan.

Lyall, D. (1995) *Counselling in the Pastoral and Spiritual Context.* Buckingham: Open University Press.

Lyon, K.B. (1995) Aging and the Conflict of Generations. In P.D. Couture and R.J. Hunter (eds), *Pastoral Care and Social Conflict.* Nashville: Abingdon, 86–98.

Lyotard, J.-F. (1984) *The Postmodern Condition: a Report on Knowledge.* Translated by G. Bennington and B. Massumi. Manchester: Manchester University Press.

Ma Mpolo, M. (1990) African Pastoral Care Movement. In R.J. Hunter (ed.), *Dictionary of Pastoral Care and Counseling.* Nashville: Abingdon, 11–12.

McCarthy, M. (1990) Vatican II and Pastoral Care. In R.J. Hunter (ed.), *Dictionary of Pastoral Care and Counseling.* Nashville: Abingdon, 1298–300.

McGovern, A.F. (1989) *Liberation Theology and Its Critics.* Maryknoll, NY: Orbis.

MacIntyre, A. (1987) *After Virtue: A Study in Moral Theory.* 2nd edn, London: Duckworth.

McLennan, G. (1992) The Enlightenment Project Revisited. In S. Hall, D. Held and T. McGrew (eds), *Modernity and its Futures.* Cambridge: Polity Press, 327–55.

McNeill, J.T. (1951) *The History of the Cure of Souls.* New York: Harper and Row.

Maddox, R.L. (1990) The Recovery of Theology as a Practical Discipline. *Theological Studies* Vol. 51, No. 4, 650–72.

Mahoney, J. (1987) *The Making of Moral Theology.* Oxford: Oxford University Press.

Marshall, J.L. (1995) Pastoral Care with Congregations in Social Stress. In P.D. Couture and R.J. Hunter (eds), *Pastoral Care and Social Conflict.* Nashville: Abingdon, 167–79.

Milbank, A.J. (1993) *Theology and Social Theory: Beyond Secular Reason.* 2nd edn, Oxford: Blackwell.

Milhaven, A.L. (ed.) (1991) *Sermons Seldom Heard: Women Proclaim Their Lives.* New York: Crossroad.

Miller-McLemore, B.J. (1991) Women who Work and Love: Caught between Cultures. In M. Glaz and J.S. Moessner (eds), *Women in Travail and Transition.* Minneapolis: Fortress Press, 63–85.

Miller-McLemore, B.J. and Anderson, H. (1995) Gender and Pastoral Care. In P.D. Couture and R.J. Hunter (eds), *Pastoral Care and Social Conflict.* Nashville: Abingdon, 99–113.

Mitchell, K.R. (1990) Review of *Pastoral Counsel. Journal of Pastoral Care,* Volume XLIV, No. 3, 290–92.

Moseley, R.M. (1990) Liberation Theology and Pastoral Care. In R.J. Hunter (ed.), *Dictionary of Pastoral Care and Counseling.* Nashville: Abingdon, 645–6.

Murphy, N. and McClendon, J.W. (1989) Distinguishing Modern and Postmodern Theologies. *Modern Theology,* vol. 5, 3, 191–214.

Neuger, C.C. (1995) The Challenge of Abortion. In P.D. Couture and R.J. Hunter (eds), *Pastoral Care and Social Conflict.* Nashville: Abingdon, 125–40.

Nicholson, L.J. (1980) Why Habermas? *Radical Philosophy* 25, 21–26.

Nouwen, H.J.M. (1969) Anton T. Boisen and Theology through Living Human Documents. *Pastoral Psychology,* 49–63.

Oates, W. (1953) *The Bible in Pastoral Care.* Philadelphia: Westminster Press.

Oates, W. (1962) *Protestant Pastoral Counseling.* Philadelphia: Westminster Press.

Oates, W. (1974) *Pastoral Counseling.* Philadelphia: Westminster Press.

Oden, T.C. (1966) *Kerygma and Counseling*. Philadelphia: Westminster Press.

Oden, T.C. (1972) *The Intensive Group Experience: the New Pietism*. Philadelphia: Westminster Press.

Oden, T.C. (1979) *Agenda for Theology: Recovering Christian Roots*. San Francisco: Harper and Row.

Oden, T.C. (1980) Recovering Lost Identity. *Journal of Pastoral Care*, Volume XXXIV, No. 1, 4–19.

Oden, T.C. (1983) *Pastoral Theology; essentials of ministry*. San Francisco: Harper and Row.

Oden, T.C. (1984) *The Care of Souls in the Classical Tradition*. Philadelphia: Fortress Press.

Oden, T.C. (1986) *Crisis Ministries*. New York: Crossroad.

Oden, T.C. (1987) *Becoming a Minister*. New York: Crossroad.

Oden, T.C. (1989a) *Ministry Through Word and Sacrament*. New York: Crossroad.

Oden, T.C. (1989b) *Pastoral Counsel*. New York: Crossroad.

Oduyoye, M.A. (1986) *Hearing and Knowing: Theological Reflections on Christianity in Africa*. Maryknoll, NY: Orbis.

Oglesby, W.B. Jr. (ed.) (1969) *The New Shape of Pastoral Theology: Essays in Honor of Seward Hiltner*. Nashville: Abingdon.

Oliver, G. (1991) Counselling, Anarchy and the Kingdom of God. *Lingdale Papers*, 16. Oxford: Clinical Theology Association.

O'Neill, M.A. (1975) Toward a Renewed Anthropology. *Theological Studies*, 36, No. 4, 725–36.

Outram, D. (1995) *The Enlightenment*. Cambridge: Cambridge University Press.

Parsons, S. (1993) Women and Ministerial Training. In E.L. Graham and M. Halsey (eds), *Life-Cycles: Women and Pastoral Care*. London: SPCK, 200–9.

Pattison, S. (1989) *Alive and Kicking: Towards a Practical Theology of Illness and Healing*. London: SCM Press.

Pattison, S. (1993) *A Critique of Pastoral Care*. 2nd edn., London: SCM Press.

Pattison, S. (1994a) *A Vision of Pastoral Theology*. Edinburgh: Contact Pastoral Monograph No. 4.

Pattison, S. (1994b) *Pastoral Care and Liberation Theology*. Cambridge: Cambridge University Press.

Patton, J. (1990) *From Ministry to Theology: Pastoral Action and Reflection*. Nashville: Abingdon.

Patton, J. (1993) *Pastoral Care in Context*. Louisville, KY: Westminster/ John Knox.

Peters, J. (1986) *Frank Lake: the man and his work*. London: Darton, Longman and Todd.

Poling, J.N. (1991) *The Abuse of Power: a theological problem*. Nashville: Abingdon.

Poling, J.N. (1995) Sexuality: a Crisis for the Churches. In P.D. Couture and R.J. Hunter (eds), *Pastoral Care and Social Conflict*. Nashville: Abingdon, 114–24.

Porter, R. (1990) *The Enlightenment*. London: Macmillan.

Poster, M. (ed.) (1988) *Baudrillard: Selected Writings*. Cambridge: Polity.

Rabinow, P. (ed.) (1984) *The Foucault Reader*. New York: Pantheon.

Rahner, K. (1968) *Theology of Pastoral Action*. New York: Herder and Herder.

Rahner, K. (ed.) (1969) *Sacramentum Mundi*. New York: Herder and Herder.

Rahner, K. (1971) The New Claims Which Pastoral Theology makes upon Theology as a Whole. *Theological Investigations*. Volume XI, trans. D. Bourke. New York: Herder and Herder.

Ramsay, N. (1991) Sexual Abuse and Shame: The Travail of Recovery. In M. Glaz and J.S. Moessner (eds), *Women in Travail and Transition*. Minneapolis: Fortress Press, 109–45.

Rasmussen, D. (1994) Critical Theory: Horkheimer, Adorno, Habermas. In R. Kearney (ed.), *Continental Philosophy in the 20th Century*. London: Routledge, History of Philosophy Volume VIII, 254–89.

Reader, J. (1994) *Local Theology: Church and Community in Dialogue*. London: SPCK.

Roderick, R. (1986) *Habermas and the Foundations of Critical Theory*. London: Macmillan.

Rogers, Carl R. (1942) *Counseling and Psychotherapy*. Boston MA: Houghton Miffin.

Rogers, Carl R. (1951) *Client-Centred Therapy*. Boston MA: Houghton Miffin.

Rogers, Carl R. (1961) *On Becoming A Person*. London: Constable.

Rogers, Clement W. (1912) *An Introduction to the Study of Pastoral Theology*. Oxford: Clarendon Press.

Rorty, R. (1980) *Consequences of Pragmatism*. Minneapolis: University of Minnesota Press.

Rorty, R. (1989) *Contingency, Irony and Solidarity*. Cambridge: Cambridge University Press.

Rosa, R.S. (1990) Latin American Pastoral Care Movement. In R.J. Hunter (ed.), *Dictionary of Pastoral Care and Counseling*. Nashville: Abingdon, 631–2.

Rouse, R. and Neill, S.C. (eds) (1967) *A History of the Ecumenical Movement 1517–1948*. 2nd edn, London: SPCK.

Ruether, R.R. (1985) *Women-Church: Theology and Practice*. San Francisco: Harper and Row.

Ruether, R.R. (1992) *Sexism and God-Talk: Toward a Feminist Theology.* 2nd edn., London: SCM Press.

Russell, L.M., Kwok, Pui-Lan, Isasi-Diaz, A.M. and Cannon, K.G. (eds) (1988) *Inheriting Our Mothers' Gardens: Feminist Theology in Third World Perspective.* Philadelphia: Westminster.

Sacks, O. (1986) A Question of Identity. In *The Man Who Mistook His Wife For A Hat.* London: Picador, 103–10.

St. Hilda Community (1991) *Women Included: A Book of Services and Prayers.* London: SPCK.

Saiving, V. (1979) The Human Situation: A Feminine View. In C. Christ and J. Plaskow (eds), *Womanspirit Rising.* San Francisco: Harper and Row, 25–42.

Schleiermacher, E.F. (1966) *Brief Outline on the Study of Theology.* Trans. T.N. Tice, Richmond, VI: John Knox Press.

Schuster, H. (1967) Pastoral Theology. In K. Rahner (ed.) *Sacramentum Mundi.* New York, Herder and Herder, 365–8.

Segundo, J.L. (1982) *The Liberation of Theology.* 3rd Impression, Maryknoll, NY: Orbis.

Selby, P. (1983) *Liberating God: Private Care and Public Struggle.* London: SPCK.

Seller, A. (1988) Realism versus Relativism: Towards a Politically Adequate Epistemology. In M. Griffiths and M. Whitford (eds), *Feminist Perspectives in Philosophy.* London: Macmillan, 169–86.

Smith, C.M. (1989) *Weaving the Sermon: Preaching in a Feminist Perspective.* Louisville, KT: Westminster/John Knox Press.

Smith, C.T. (1991) Wonderfully Made: Preaching Physical Self-Affirmation. In A.L. Milhaven (ed.), *Sermons Seldom Heard.* New York: Crossroad, 243–51.

Snyder, R. (1968) The Boisen Heritage in Theological Education. *Pastoral Psychology,* 9–14.

Soper, K. (1989) Feminism as Critique. *New Left Review* 176, 91–112.

Soper, K. (1990) Feminism, Humanism and Postmodernism. *Radical Philosophy* 55, 11–17.

Soper, K. (1991) Postmodernism, Subjectivity and the Question of Value. *New Left Review* 186, 120–8.

Stokes, A. (1985) *Ministry after Freud.* New York: Pilgrim Press.

Stroup, G. (1981) *The Promise of Narrative Theology.* London: SCM Press.

Stuart, E. (1992) *Daring to Speak Love's Name: a Gay and Lesbian Prayer Book.* London: Hamish Hamilton.

Sunderland, R.H. (1990) Lay Pastoral Care and Counselling. In R.J. Hunter (ed.), *Dictionary of Pastoral Care and Counseling.* Nashville: Abingdon, 632–4.

Tamez, E. (1987) *Against Machismo*. Oak Park, IL: Meyer-Stone Books.

Tamez, E. (ed.) (1989) *Through her Eyes: Women's Theology from Latin America*. Maryknoll, NY: Orbis.

Taylor, M.C. (1984) *Erring: a postmodern a/theology*. London: University of Chicago Press.

Taylor, M.C. (1992) Reframing postmodernisms. In P. Berry and A. Wernick (eds), *Shadow of Spirit: Postmodernism and Religion*. London: Routledge, 11–29.

Thistlethwaite, S.B. (1990) *Sex, Race, and God: Christian Feminism in Black and White*. London: Geoffrey Chapman.

Thompson, K. (1992) Social Pluralism and Post-Modernity. In S. Hall, D. Held and T. McGrew (eds), *Modernity and its Futures*. Cambridge: Polity Press, 221–55.

Thornton, M. (1958) *Pastoral Theology: A Reorientation*. London: SPCK.

Thurneysen, E. (1962) *A Theology of Pastoral Care*. London: John Knox Press.

Tillich, P. (1948) *The Shaking of the Foundations*. New York: Scribner.

Tillich, P. (1951, 1957, 1963) *Systematic Theology*, 3 Vols, London: Nisbet.

Tillich, P. (1952) *The Courage to Be*. New Haven: Yale University Press.

Tillich, P. (1959) The Theological Significance of Existentialism and Psychoanalysis. In R.C. Kimball (ed.), *Theory of Culture*. New York: Oxford University Press.

Tinsley, E.J. (ed.) (1973) *Paul Tillich*. Modern Theology: Selections from Twentieth-Century Theologians, Volume 3. London: Epworth.

Tracy, D. (1971) *Blessed Rage for Order: The New Pluralism in Theology*. New York: Seabury.

Tracy, D. (1981) *The Analogical Imagination: Christian Theology and the Culture of Pluralism*. London: SCM Press.

Tracy, D. (1983) The Foundations of Practical Theology. In D.S. Browning (ed.), *Practical Theology*. San Francisco: Harper and Row, 61–82.

Tracy, D. (1987) *Plurality and Ambiguity: Hermeneutics, Religion, Hope*. San Francisco: Harper and Row.

Tracy, D. (1994) Theology and the Many Faces of Postmodernity. *Theology Today*, Vol. 51, No. 1, 104–14.

Trible, P. (1984) *Texts of Terror: Literary-Feminist Readings of Biblical Narratives*. Philadelphia: Fortress Press.

van Gennep, A. (1977) *The Rites of Passage*. London: RKP.

van Oosterzee, J.J. (1878) *Practical Theology: A Manual for Theological Students*. Translated by M.J. Evans. New York: Scribner.

Vinet, A. (1855) *Pastoral Theology: the Theory of a Gospel Ministry*. Edinburgh: T & T Clark.

Ward, K. (1991) *A Vision to Pursue: Beyond the Crisis in Christianity*. London: SCM Press.

Waterhouse, E.S. (1939) *Psychology and Pastoral Work*. London: Hodder and Stoughton.

Weatherhead, L.D. (1929) *Psychology in Service of the Soul*. London: Epworth.

Weatherhead, L.D. (1951) *Psychology, Religion and Healing*. London: Epworth.

Weber, H.R. and Neill, S.C. (1963) *The Layman in Christian History*. London: SCM Press.

Weber, M. (1978) *Max Weber: Selections in Translation*. Edited by W.G. Runciman and translated by E. Matthews. Cambridge: Cambridge University Press.

Weedon, C. (1987) *Feminist Practice and Poststructuralist Theory*. Oxford: Blackwell.

Weil, L. (1985) Worship and Pastoral Care. In J.E. Griffis (ed.), *Anglican Theology and Pastoral Care*. Wilton, CT: Morehouse-Barlow, 115–31.

Welch, S.D. (1985) *Communities of Resistance and Solidarity: A Feminist Theology of Liberation*. Maryknoll, NY: Orbis.

Welch, S.D. (1990) *A Feminist Ethic of Risk*. Minneapolis: Fortress Press.

Wheeler, B.G. and Farley, E. (eds) (1991) *Shifting Boundaries: Contextual Approaches to the Structure of Theological Education*. Louisville, KY: Westminster/John Knox Press.

Whitehead, J.D. and Whitehead, E.E. (1980) *Method in Ministry: Theological Reflection and Christian Ministry*. San Francisco: Harper and Row.

Wickham, E.R. (1957) *Church and People in an Industrial City*. London: Lutterworth.

Wickham, E.R. (1964) *Encounter with Modern Society*. London: Lutterworth.

Williams, R. (1989) Postmodern Theology and the Judgement of the World. In F.C. Burnham (ed.), *Postmodern Theology: Christian Faith in a Pluralist World*. San Francisco: Harper and Row, 92–112.

Williams, R. (1992) Hegel and the gods of postmodernity. In P. Berry and A. Wernick (eds), *Shadow of Spirit: Postmodernism and Religion*. London: Routledge, 72–80.

Wilson, B.R. (1966) *Religion in Secular Society*. London: C.A. Watts.

Wilson, B.R. (1976) *Contemporary Transformations of Religion*. Oxford: Clarendon Press.

Wise, C. (1966) *The Meaning of Pastoral Care*. New York: Harper and Row.

Yearley, S. (1992) Environmental Challenges. In S. Hall, D. Held, and T. McGrew (eds), *Modernity and its Futures*. Cambridge: Polity Press, 117–53.

Young, P.D. (1990) *Feminist Theology/Christian Theology: In Search of Method*. Minneapolis: Fortress Press.

Index of Names

Index of Subjects

231